NEW GENDER MAINSTREAMING SERIES ON DEVELOPMENT ISSUES

Gender Mainstreaming in Poverty Eradication and the Millennium Development Goals

A handbook for policy-makers and other stakeholders

Naila Kabeer

Commonwealth Secretariat

International Development Research Centre
Ottawa · Cairo · Dakar · Montevideo · Nairobi · New Delhi · Singapore

 Canadian International   Agence canadienne de
Development Agency   développement international

Gender Section
Commonwealth Secretariat
Marlborough House
Pall Mall, London SW1Y 5HX
United Kingdom

Email: gad@commonwealth.int
http://www.thecommonwealth.org/
gender
http://www.gender-budgets.org

Layout design: Wayzgoose
Cover design: Pen and Ink
Cover photo: Shehzad Noorani/
Still Pictures
Printed by Ashford Colour Press

Copublished by the
Commonwealth Secretariat,
the International Development
Research Centre and the
Canadian International
Development Agency

International Development
Research Centre
PO Box 8500, Ottawa, ON
Canada K1G 3H9
ISBN: 1-55250-067-5 (Canada)
This book may be browsed online:
www.idrc.ca/pub@idrc.ca

Canadian International
Development Agency
200 Promenade du Portage, Hull
Quebec, Canada K1A 0G4

Copies of this publication can
be ordered direct from:
The Publications Manager
Communications and Public
Affairs Division
Commonwealth Secretariat
Marlborough House
Pall Mall, London SW1Y 5HX
United Kingdom
Tel: +44 (0)20 7747 6342
Fax: +44 (0)20 7839 9081
E-mail:
r.jones-parry@commonwealth.int

ISBN: 0-85092-752-8

Price: £12.99

Produced by Bookchase
Printed in E.U.
L.D. SE-6280-2004

About the author

Naila Kabeer is Professorial Fellow at the Institute of Development Studies, University of Sussex. She is a social economist and has been involved in teaching, research and advisory work in the field of gender, poverty, population and social policy. She is the author of *Reversed Realities: Gender Hierarchies in Development Thought* (1994) and *The Power to Choose: Bangladeshi Women and Labour Market Decisions in London and Dhaka* (2000).

Publication team

GMS Series Coordinator: Rawwida Baksh-Soodeen
Editor: Tina Johnson
Picture research: Tina Johnson
Production: Rupert Jones-Parry
Production support: Linda Etchart
IDRC team: Randy Spence, Bill Carman, Anyck Dauphin

*We hereby acknowledge the invaluable contribution of the members
of the Commonwealth Expert Panel who met at Marlborough House on
3 December 2001 to review the first draft of this publication:*

Rudo Chitiga, Commonwealth Foundation
Francesca Cook, DAC-Secretariat, OECD
Malcolm Ehrenpreis, World Bank, UK
Lucia Hanmer, Department for International Development (DfID), UK
Gerd Johnsson-Latham, Ministry of Foreign Affairs, Sweden
Shireen Lateef, Asian Development Bank (ADB)
Lin Lean Lim, International Labour Organization (ILO)
Rachel Masika, Oxfam UK
Donna St Hill, Women's Budget Group, UK
John Sender, School of Oriental and African Studies (SOAS), University
    of London
Randy Spence, International Development Research Centre (IDRC)
Howard White, Institute of Development Studies, University of Sussex
Anne Whitehead, Faculty of Arts, University of Sussex
Sushila Zeitlyn, Department for International Development (DfID), UK
Tim Shaw, Institute of Commonwealth Studies, University of London

Staff members of Commonwealth Secretariat Divisions:

Economic Affairs Division: Indrajit Coomaraswamy
Governance and Institutional Development Division: Michael Gillibrand,
    Jasim Jasimuddin
Political Affairs Division: Chuks Ihekaibeya
Social Transformation Programmes Division: Rawwida Baksh-Soodeen,
    Lucia Kiwala, Valencia Mogegeh, Maryse Roberts, Nancy Spence
Special Advisory Services Division: Kamala Bhoolai, Rosemary Minto
Strategic Planning and Evaluation Division: Richard Longhurst
Youth Affairs Unit: Jane Foster, Andrew Simmons

Contents

Abbreviations

AIDS	Acquired Immunodeficiency Syndrome
ACC/SCN	Subcommittee on Nutrition of the UN Administrative Committee on Coordination
BMI	Body mass index
CGE	Computable general equilibrium
CYSD	Centre for Youth and Social Development
DAWN	Development Alternatives with Women for a New Era
DfID	Department for International Development
DHS	Demographic and Health Survey
GDI	Gender Development Index
GDP	Gross Domestic Product
GEM	Gender Empowerment Measure
GMS	Gender Management System
GNP	Gross National Product
GRB	Gender-responsive budget
HDI	Human Development Index
HDR	Human Development Report
HIPC	Highly Indebted Poor Countries
HIV	Human Immunodeficiency Virus
IDRC	International Development Research Centre
IDTs	International Development Targets
IFAD	International Fund for Agricultural Development
ILO	International Labour Organization
IMF	International Monetary Fund
I-PRSP	Interim Poverty Reduction Strategy Paper
JSRs	Juvenile sex ratios
LDCs	Least Developed Countries
MDB	Multilateral development bank
MDGs	Millennium Development Goals
MFIs	Micro-finance institutions
NGO	Non-governmental organisation
NIUA	National Institute of Urban Affairs
NSS	National Sample Survey
NTAEs	Non-traditional agricultural exports
NUDE	National Union of Domestic Employees

ODA	Official development assistance
OECD	Organisation for Economic Cooperation and Development
PPA	Participatory Poverty Assessment
PR	Proportional representation
PRA	Participatory Rural Appraisal
PRSP	Poverty Reduction Strategy Paper
RSW	Relative Status of Women
SAPs	Structural adjustment policies
SEWA	Self-Employed Women's Association
SNA	System of National Accounts
STI	Sexually transmitted infection
UN	United Nations
UNDP	United Nations Development Programme
UNICEF	United Nations Children's Fund
UNIFEM	United Nations Development Fund for Women
UNRISD	United Nations Research Institute for Social Development
WBI	Women's Budget Initiative
WDR	World Development Report
WHO	World Health Organization
WIEGO	Women in Informal Employment Globalizing and Organizing
WILPF	Women's International League for Peace and Freedom

Foreword

Gender Mainstreaming in Poverty Eradication and the Millennium Development Goals: A Handbook for Policy-makers and Other Stakeholders forms a timely inclusion into the Commonwealth Secretariat series on gender mainstreaming in critical multi-sectoral development issues. It is hoped that it will be used by development policy-makers, planners and others, in conjunction with other publications relating to particular national contexts.

In 1996, the Commonwealth Ministers Responsible for Women's/Gender Affairs mandated the Commonwealth Secretariat to develop the concept and methodology of the Gender Management System (GMS), a holistic system-wide approach to bringing a gender perspective to bear in the main-stream of all government policies, plans and programmes.

The success of the GMS depends on a broad-based partnership in society in which government consults and acts co-operatively with other key stakeholders, who include civil society and the private sector. The task of gender mainstreaming has both technical and managerial dimensions, as well as the political, economic and socio-cultural aspects of creating equality and equity between women and men as partners in the quest for social justice.

At the Sixth Meeting of Commonwealth Ministers Responsible for Women's/Gender Affairs (6WAMM), held in April 2000 in New Delhi, India, Ministers commended the GMS series. They encouraged the Gender Section of the Commonwealth Secretariat to continue the development of user-friendly publications adaptable to the different needs of member countries. This handbook is designed to fulfil that request.

The Millennium Development Goals (MDGs), adopted by the world's Heads of Governments/States at a special United Nations summit in 2000, include quantified and monitorable goals for development and poverty eradication by 2015. One of these goals is the empowerment of women. In the Coolum Declaration of March 2002, Commonwealth Heads of Government endorsed the Millennium Development Goals, and announced their determination to work to eliminate poverty and to promote people-centred sustainable development. They also declared that "in too many societies women continue to face discrimination" (Coolum Declaration, 5 March 2002).

We in the Commonwealth feel that gender equality is essential to eradicating poverty. The MDs can only be achieved by addressing the disproportionate burden of poverty, lack of access to education and health services and lack of productive opportunities borne by women. Women's empowerment matters for poverty eradication. Evidence shows that empowering and investing in women brings a huge development dividend.

We trust that the publication of this handbook and its implementation by policy-makers and other stakeholders will make a contribution to eradicating poverty by highlighting the need for a gender perspective of greater reach than that envisioned in the MDGs.

The development of this book has been a collective effort of the Commonwealth Secretariat's Social Transformation Programmes Division and many individuals and groups. Their contributions are most gratefully acknowledged.

The publication of this book was possible thanks to contributions from the International Development Research Centre (IDRC) and the Canadian International Development Agency (CIDA).

I would also like to thank our colleagues from the multilateral and bilateral agencies, academic institutions and NGOs, who participated in the Expert Panel at the Commonwealth Secretariat in December 2001, to review the first draft. Thanks are due to Randy Spence of IDRC, who participated in the Expert Panel in December 2001 to review the first draft, and Bill Carman of IDRC for his editorial advice. We are also grateful to Diana Rivington of CIDA, and to Beatrice Mann of the International Labour Organization (ILO) who supplied us with many of the photographs.

This handbook is an adaptation of an extended book by Naila Kabeer provisionally entitled *Gender Equality, Poverty Eradication and the Millennium Development Goals: Maximising Synergies and Minimising Trade-offs*, to be published jointly by the Commonwealth Secretariat and Routledge in autumn 2003. Readers may wish to refer to the full text contained within the Routledge publication for greater depth and elaboration of some of the more complex arguments developed in this hand-book.

Our special thanks to Tina Johnson who has worked won-ders in adapting the manuscript for use as a handbook, and to Rawwida Baksh-Soodeen who initiated the project, co-ordi-nated the team and resources, and worked closely with Naila Kabeer to bring the project to fruition. We would also like to thank Rahul Malhotra who assisted Naila in the compilation of statistics used in this book.

And last but not least, to the author, Dr Naila Kabeer, who continues to inspire us by her conceptual thinking that garners real results, her compassion towards women's economic and social realities as she sees them on the ground, and her ability to harness rigorous economic analysis and devote it to making the lives of women better.

This handbook is being launched at the UN during the 47th meeting of the Commission on the Status of Women (CSW), in celebration of International Women's Day (8 March 2003) and Commonwealth Day (10 March 2003). We do hope that it will contribute to better understanding of the critical linkages between women's empowerment, poverty eradication and the Millennium Development Goals (MDGs). And import-antly, to greater co-ordination and synergy in all our efforts to promote gender equality in poverty eradication programmes and the MDGs.

Nancy Spence
Director, Social Transformation Programmes Division
Commonwealth Secretariat
March 2003

Executive Summary

In September 2000, at the United Nations Millennium Summit, 189 governments across the world made a commitment to take collective responsibility for halving world poverty by 2015. The Millennium Declaration laid out a number of key development goals framed to reflect its fundamental values. Along with the reduction of poverty and hunger, these included commitments to the promotion of human development, environmental sustainability and development partnership. In addition, they included an explicit commitment to gender equality as an end in itself: "No individual and no nation must be denied the opportunity to benefit from development. The equality rights and opportunities of women and men must be assured."

This book brings together arguments, findings and lessons from the development literature that are relevant to the achievement of the Millennium Development Goals (MDGs) from the standpoint of gender equality. This is because, firstly, while there may be other forms of socio-economic disparity in a society that are far wider than gender – e.g. race in apartheid South Africa, caste in India or class in Brazil – gender inequality is more pervasive than other forms of inequality. It is a feature of social relations in most societies, although it may take different forms. Consequently, understanding the causes and consequences of gender inequality should be of concern to all societies in the world, rich as well as poor.

Secondly, gender inequality is also pervasive across different groups *within* societies. It cuts across other forms of inequality so that it is a feature of rich as well as poor groups, racially dominant as well as racially subordinate groups, privileged as well as 'untouchable' castes. Within a society, the forms taken by gender inequality may vary across different strata. They are often, though not invariably, more severe among the poor. Consequently, gender inequality intersects with economic deprivation to produce more intensified forms of poverty for women than men. Gender inequality is part and parcel of the processes of causing and deepening poverty in a society and must therefore constitute part and parcel of measures to eradicate poverty.

And finally, gender inequality structures the relations of production and reproduction in different societies. Men play a critical role in earning household livelihoods in much of the world but generally play a negligible role in the unpaid work of reproduction in the domestic arena. Women, on the other hand, play a critical role in the unpaid work of caring for the family. While their role in the productive sphere varies, it is generally highest among poorer households. However, there is a marked inequality in the resources that men and women are able to mobilise to carry out their responsibilities, in the value and recognition given to their contributions and in their capacity to exercise agency on their own behalf.

As the evidence marshalled in this handbook demonstrates, despite decades of gender research and advocacy, policy-makers continue to operate with the notion of the 'male breadwinner'. Efforts to promote the productivity of the poor are largely targeted to men while women are expected to carry on contributing to household livelihoods and caring for the family with little or no recognition or support for their efforts. If households had been the egalitarian institutions portrayed in conventional economics and in the imagination of many policy-makers, the preoccupation with 'the male breadwinner' would have mattered less. A redistribution of resources and responsi-bilities among family members would have prevented the emergence, or exacerbation, of inequalities in the household.

However, households are not necessarily egalitarian. Rather, they operate as sites of co-operative conflict in which men as a group have been able to use their privileged access to resources both in the household and in the wider public domain to defend and promote their own interests, often at the expense of women and girls. In other words, inequalities in the domestic domain intersect with inequalities in purportedly gender-neutral institutions of markets, state and community to make gender inequality a society-wide phenomenon. This means that women and men experience poverty differently and unequally and become poor through different, though related, processes. Poverty – and gender inequalities – there-fore have to be tackled at the societal level as well as through explicit interventions tailored to addressing specific forms of disadvantage.

Chapter 1 provides a brief history of the changing policy

discourse and the processes that led to the greater visibility of both poverty reduction and gender equality. It argues that this visibility reflects the increased attention to human agency, human capital and human capabilities as factors in the achievement of pro-poor growth, combined with evidence that gender is one of the critical variables mediating economic growth and human development. However, it notes that because women continue to be perceived primarily in terms of their reproductive roles, there is no explicit mention of gender inequality in relation to the Millennium Development Goal (MDG) on poverty eradication. Indeed, gender equality largely appears in the MDGs in relation to health and education. Women's economic agency as a force for poverty reduction continues to be overlooked in the policy discourse. However, enhancing women's access to various resources and ensuring that greater social value is given to their contributions lies within the domain of policy-makers and its pay-offs are likely to be enormous.

Chapter 2 charts the gradual evolution of macroeconomic analysis from its earlier gender-blindness to current attempts to make it more gender aware. In some cases, conventional models are disaggregated where possible by gender; in others, gender inequality is introduced as a variable; and in still others, attempts are made to re-conceptualise the economy in terms of the interacting gender relations of production and reproduction. Within this literature, there is a greater appreciation of women's economic agency as well as their role in reproduction. The chapter also reports on attempts to explore these relationships empirically, particularly in the context of globalisation. These findings necessarily take the form of broad generalisations since they deal with national and international data. However, they help to generate some important hypotheses and propositions about the interactions between gender and poverty that help frame the more detailed, micro-level and contextual analysis in the rest of the book. While a number of studies suggest that there is indeed a relationship between gender equality and economic growth, there are conflicting findings as to whether the relationship is a synergy (greater equality translates into greater growth) or trade-off (greater inequality fuels higher levels of growth). This debate forms the starting point of the analysis in the rest of the book and is returned to in the final chapter.

Chapter 3 sketches out an 'institutional framework' for the analysis of gender inequality within the economy and explores its variation across the world. In the context of economic analysis, attention to institutions helps to reveal that a great deal of human behaviour is governed by social norms and that such norms have powerful material ramifications in people's lives. The discussion shows that while gender inequalities may be near universal, they are not uniform, either across space or over time. There is now a body of work testifying to the existence of a 'geography of gender' – regional differences in the forms and magnitude of gender inequality. While family and kinship ideologies and relations play an important role in the construction of these inequalities, they are also reinforced, modified or transformed by the interaction between family, kinship and wider social processes, including state legislation, public action and macroeconomic change. What seems to emerge out of the empirical findings is that gender inequality in such dimensions as education, wages and legal infrastructure is only partly related to per capita GNP. It is also related to broad regional variations in patriarchal regimes, particularly among the poorer countries of the world.

This chapter goes on to consider the extent to which the geographical distribution of inequality has changed in recent times, particularly given the accelerating forces of globalisation and the internationalisation of production. It concludes that there has been some reduction in gender inequality in important aspects of women's lives, but to a greater extent in some regions than others, and to a greater extent in some dimensions of inequality than others. However, while there has been an undoubted 'feminisation of labour' in recent years, the terms on which women have entered the labour market, and the accompanying implications for men, mean that this has had contradictory implications for gender equality.

Chapter 4 turns to a more detailed examination of the relationship between gender inequality and poverty at regional and national levels, drawing on findings from three different approaches to poverty analysis: the poverty line approach; the capabilities approach (using human development indicators); and participatory poverty assessments. The rationale for this focus is that these are the main approaches through which policy-makers in a range of development agencies obtain their insights into poverty. The discussion confirms the overall conclusion of the previous chapter that institutional norms and practices play an important role in shaping gender inequality. Consequently, the relationship between poverty and inequality varies in different parts of the world. In some regions, it take the form of inequality at the level of life expectancy and survival chances; in others, it takes the forms of heavier work burdens and greater time poverty.

A number of important implications can be drawn from this chapter. First of all, it presents a challenge to conventional models of the household, which perceive it as a site of co-operation and which have led in the past to the neglect of critical forms of gender inequality. Secondly, it reinforces the message that gender inequality takes different forms in different societies and hence cannot be addressed through any kind of blue-print approach. And finally, given that gender inequality is not just a product of scarcity, it suggests that economic growth alone may not be adequate to address gender inequality.

Women's role as economic actors – and its critical importance to the livelihoods of the poor across the world – is considered in Chapter 5. However, different regional constraints on women's economic agency differentiate the relationship between women's work and household poverty. In those regions of the world where these constraints are particularly severe, the relationship takes the form of one between women's paid work and household poverty. In other regions, there are higher levels of paid work by women generally and the relationship between household poverty and women's work relates to the kinds of economic activity women engage in. It is clear, however, that women's work is critical to the survival and security of poor households and an important route through which they are able escape out of poverty. Greater importance should therefore be given to women's economic contributions in the design of policy. The chapter argues that economic growth must be accompanied by a genuine effort to address the constraints that undermine returns to women's labour if women from low-income households are to be able to take advantage of the opportunities generated. This means dismantling various forms of discrimination in the public domain and paying greater attention to women's workloads in the domestic domain.

Chapter 6 focuses on the human development concerns of the MDGs. The first part of the chapter examines the distribution of gender inequalities in a number of key human development outcomes and links them to gender inequalities in forms of agency permitted to women and girls in different parts of the world and to the successes and failures of different governments in addressing these inequalities. It considers factors such as child survival rates, women's nutritional levels and hazardous livelihoods, and also discusses the HIV/AIDS epidemic. It suggests that improving women's access to resources is one route through which the MDGs on human development – including those relating in gender inequalities – can be achieved. The second part of the chapter explores how, as well as an end goal of development, gender equality can also be seen as a route through which other human development goals can be achieved. There are a number of links between women's well-being, agency and resources, on the one hand, and a variety of demographic and welfare outcomes on the other. These include the link between mothers' education and child mortality and the positive connection between increased income in the hands of women and improved family well-being.

Chapter 7 reinforces the critical importance of certain resources to women's capacity to exercise agency, but this time focuses on forms of agency that are in the interests of women themselves – in other words, those that serve the goals of women's empowerment and gender justice. Using the three indicators used to track the goal of women's empowerment in the MDGs, the chapter considers the transformatory potential of women's access to education and literacy; to paid work, particularly waged employment; and to political representation. The discussion considers the arguments and evidence supporting access to these different resources as preconditions for women's empowerment. It also looks at some of the qualifications that have been put forward to suggest that, although necessary, these resources are not always sufficient. Such reservations provide some insights into the kinds of policies needed to realise the potential of these resources to transform the life chances of poor women. The chapter also notes that not all forms of public action have to be undertaken by the state or international development agencies but that political pressure also has to come from below. Arguing that collective action is central to social transformation, it offers a number of examples that have given a voice to women, as well as men, from poorer sections of the population.

The final chapter (Chapter 8) attempts to draw out the implications of the relationship between gender equality and pro-poor growth for policy efforts to achieve the MDGs. It first returns to the question that has framed the discussion throughout the book of whether the relationship is one of synergy or a trade-off. Examining the evidence, it concludes that there does appear to be a trade-off between gender inequality and economic growth in the present era of intensified global competition. Women's lower costs and lesser bargaining power in the market place have been the basis of export-oriented growth based on labour-intensive manufacturing. However, if attention is turned to countries that had high levels of gender equality but grew more slowly during this period, the trade-off appears to be less stark. These tend to be countries that prioritised investment in the human capabilities of their population so that the fruits of growth were distributed more evenly across the population in the course of growth rather than in its later phase. There is, in other words, no trade-off between gender equality and economic growth once the focus moves from short-rate gains to long-term, sustainable and pro-poor growth.

Chapter 8 also provides a gender audit of Poverty Reduction Strategy Papers (PRSPs), since many current efforts to centralise poverty concerns in national development policies are organised around these papers. It offers some lessons learned and stresses the importance of participatory approaches and of wide-ranging stakeholder consultations, which both governments and international development agencies have committed themselves to building and strengthening. Finally, it suggests that there is a need for active and organised constituencies at the grassroots level to exercise pressure for gender equality goals and to hold governments, donors and international agencies accountable for their action or inaction.

1. Gender, Poverty and Development Policy

A gender perspective means recognising that women stand at the crossroads between production and reproduction, between economic activity and the care of human beings, and therefore between economic growth and human development. They are workers in both spheres – those most responsible and therefore with most at stake, those who suffer most when the two spheres meet at cross-purposes, and those most sensitive to the need for better integration between the two.
Gita Sen

Introduction

The main focus of this book is the gender dimensions of poverty and their implications for public policy. Poverty is 'gendered' because women and men experience poverty differently – and unequally – and become poor through different, though related, processes. This book brings together concepts, arguments and findings to show: (a) what these gender dimensions are; and (b) how they affect poverty reduction strategies. In particular, it shows that such strategies need to take gender into account if they are to be effective (*see box 1.1*).

The problems of gender inequality and poverty are not the same and have different causes and consequences. For example, a change in the price of a country's staple food may be an issue of life and death for poor families, but it is unlikely to affect women (or men) in wealthier households. Equally, the existence of a 'glass ceiling' in senior management discriminates against professional women but has little direct relevance to the lives of the poor, men or women.

Nevertheless, there is overwhelming evidence that women and girls are more disadvantaged than men and boys, both across societies and among the poor. Promoting gender equality in the wider society – or reinforcing inequality – can therefore have effects that cut across class and social status. For example, government departments that work with the poor need to challenge gender inequality in their own ranks if they are to provide equitable services. This handbook, however,

Poverty is 'gendered' because women and men experience poverty differently – and unequally – and become poor through different, though related, processes.

The argument for addressing gender inequality, therefore, is not simply that it exists in all societies but that it exists at all levels of society. It makes the effects of poverty worse for women and biases the form taken by economic growth.

only discusses the wider gender inequalities in society when they relate to the gender dimensions of poverty.

Box 1.1 Gender, Gender Equality and Gender Inequality

'Gender' refers to the rules, norms, customs and practices by which *biological* differences between males and females are translated into *socially constructed* differences between men and women and boys and girls. This results in the two genders being valued differently and in their having unequal opportunities and life chances.

In the context of this book, 'gender equality' means both equality of treatment under the law and equality of opportunity. In addition, since these do not take structural inequality into account, it also includes substantive equality and equality of agency. Substantive equality means that the different circumstances and characteristics of men and women have to be considered to avoid unfair gender-related outcomes. For example, in a case where a man and a woman both have the qualifications for a particular occupation, the latter may be unable to take it up if there is no childcare available. Equality of agency means ensuring that both women and men can make strategic life choices for themselves (and help determine the conditions under which these choices are made).

Gender inequality is constructed both through society's formal laws and statutes and through unwritten norms and shared understandings. It is not only pervasive across all societies but also the most prevalent form of social disadvantage *within* societies. It cuts across all other forms of inequality, such as class, caste and race. And because gender is key to the organisation of production and reproduction, women are also "at the crossroads between . . . . economic growth and human development". The argument for addressing gender inequality, therefore, is not simply that it exists in all societies but that it exists at all levels of society. It makes the effects of poverty worse for women and biases the form taken by economic growth.

While the analysis focuses mainly on female disadvantage, the situation of men and boys will also be included for several reasons:

* Women's poverty relative to men and absolute levels of poverty among women may have different implications for public policy;

* The needs and priorities expressed by poor households, as well as their ability to meet them, are influenced by prevailing social models of masculinity as well as femininity. Both of these can prevent household members escaping from poverty; and

* In certain contexts, or in relation to certain aspects of poverty, men have been found to be at a greater disadvantage than women.

There are two main ways in which national policy can try to reduce absolute levels of poverty: forms of economic growth that benefit the poor along with the rest of society; and redistribution of national income to pull people out of poverty.

Box 1.2 Poverty and National Policy

A nation's poverty is measured by the number of households that are unable to meet certain minimum basic needs. It is determined by two central variables:

i. the Gross National Product (GNP), which measures the total amount of goods and services available at a particular point in time; and

ii. the distribution of GNP, which determines the extent to which different households have access to the goods and services necessary to meet their basic needs.

There are two main ways in which national policy can try to reduce absolute levels of poverty:

* forms of economic growth that benefit the poor along with the rest of society; and

* redistribution of national income to pull people out of poverty.

... both the economic crisis and the structural adjustment policies had tremendous social costs.

A Brief History of Poverty Reduction Policies

Up to the 1960s: Early strategies for growth

In the early post-war years, development policy emphasised economic growth. In fact, development was equated with economic growth, economic growth with industrialisation and industrialisation with investment in physical capital formation. 'Import-substituting' industrialisation (replacing imported goods with domestic production) was recommended as the way for countries to become more self-reliant. The benefits of this were expected to gradually 'trickle down' through society to its poorer members. The role of labour and human capital was seen almost entirely in terms of 'manpower' needs. However, by the end of the 1960s, it was obvious that such strategies had failed to bring about the expected reductions in poverty and inequality.

1970s and 1980s: Economic crises and structural adjustment

In the 1970s, there was a greater concern with the productivity of small farmers, with meeting basic needs and with income-generation for the landless poor. These approaches, however, tended to be project-based and piecemeal. Also, they were soon overtaken by the accumulated effects of the oil crisis, the slow-down in growth rates in the advanced industrialised countries and the increasing debt burden of the less developed countries. This led to poverty reduction being seen in the 1980s as less important than the problems of unsustainable budget deficits and balance of payments.

Structural adjustment policies (SAPs) were then imposed by the World Bank and the International Monetary Fund (IMF). These: (a) let market forces set relative prices; (b) cut back state expenditure and intervention; and (c) liberalised economies and opened them up to international trade and foreign investment. However, both the economic crisis and the SAPs had tremendous social costs. An influential study by UNICEF argued that, while these policies might be necessary, their human costs had to be an integral part of the package rather than an additional welfare component. Such arguments helped bring about a return to a more direct concern with poverty reduction.

1990s: Reports from the World Bank and UNDP

The 1990 *World Development Report* (WDR) from the World Bank moved away from the preoccupation with 'getting prices right' that had dominated the Bank's policies in the 1980s. Its new poverty agenda put forward two ways of promoting pro-poor growth:

* broad-based, labour-intensive strategies to generate income-earning opportunities for the poor by using their most abundant asset – their labour power; and

* social investment in basic health and education to improve the productivity of labour.

These were to be supplemented by transfers and safety nets to assist the most vulnerable and least accessible sections of the poor, such as those in remote areas, the elderly and the disabled. Key influences on the Bank's thinking were the East Asian 'miracle' and the new theory of 'endogenous' growth (*see box 2.1, page 25*). The report attributed the former primarily to: (a) open economies; (b) labour-intensive and export-oriented production (particularly in the manufacturing sector); and (c) state investment in basic education. The latter stressed the interaction between human and other forms of capital in generating economic growth.

The 1990 *Human Development Report* (HDR) from the

A woman garment cutter at a ready-to-wear clothing factory in Japan
INTERNATIONAL LABOUR ORGANIZATION

Amartya Sen's idea of human 'capabilities' ... put human agency at the heart of development.

United Nations Development Programme (UNDP) owed a great deal to the work of Amartya Sen. It drew on his idea of human 'capabilities' – the resources and abilities that enable people to achieve the range of valued ways of being and doing possible in a particular society. This put human agency at the heart of development. Poverty was seen to refer not only to the impoverished state in which the poor lived but also to their lack of opportunities – for both social and personal reasons – to choose other ways to live. UNDP recommended a 'judicious' mix of institutions to promote 'human-centred' growth.

The HDR created the Human Development Index (HDI), based on a composite of life expectancy, infant mortality and educational attainment. This offered an alternative measure of development progress to GNP. Although there was a broadly positive relationship between per capita GNP and levels of human development, the extent to which increased per capita GNP had led to improvements in human development varied considerably among countries. It appeared that the more equal the conditions from which a country started out, the more likely it was that subsequent growth would lead to poverty reduction.

2000: World Development Report (WDR)

The 2000 WDR provided a deeper understanding of the relationship between poverty and growth than the 1990 Report. It was organised around the three themes of 'opportunity', 'security' and 'voice'.

Opportunity was still discussed in the context of market-led, labour-intensive growth. However, the idea of the 'assets' of the poor was expanded to include not only labour and human capital but also natural, financial, social and physical assets. This reflected the influence of the growing literature on poor people's livelihoods (*see Chapter 4*). The report noted that lack of assets was both a cause and an effect of poverty. It suggested that simultaneous action was needed on several fronts, with priority given to what poor people lacked most relative to the opportunities available to them. The idea of 'synergies' was emphasised as a guiding principle for promoting livelihood strategies. These synergies included, for example, that between a mother's education and her children's nutritional levels and those between the causes of poverty.

Security was much more prominent than in the 1990 report. This was because of the growing globalisation of production and trade and the financial crisis caused by short-term fluctuations in international capital flow (e.g. in the 'miracle' economies of East Asia).

Voice was related in particular to the inability of the poor to influence policies that directly affected their lives. The question of 'voice' had recently been given increasing attention in policy discussions about national strategies. Participatory methodologies intended to include the voices of the poor were part of country poverty assessments carried out by the Bank and other donors throughout the 1990s. Worldwide consultations with the poor contributed to the analysis in this report.

The United Nations Millennium Development Goals (MDGs)

In the course of the 1990s, poverty reduction was adopted as an overarching goal by almost every major international and bilateral development agency and as the basis of development co-operation. In 1996, the Organisation for Economic Cooperation and Development (OECD) countries laid out their strategy for the twenty-first century in terms of a number of International Development Targets (IDTs). These were based on agreements that had been reached in various meetings during the 1990s. The first target was halving world poverty by 2015. The IDTs were subsequently revised to become the basis of the Millennium Development Goals (MDGs), agreed to at the United Nations Millennium Summit in 2000 and subscribed to by both developed and developing countries. The main goals concern income poverty, human development, gender equality, environmental sustainability and global partnership. Targets and indicators were set to assess progress in achieving them (*see Table 1.1*).

The main goals [of the MDGs] concern income poverty, human development, gender equality, environmental sustainability and global partnership.

Table 1.1: The Millennium Development Goals

Goals and Targets	Indicators
Goal 1: Eradicate extreme poverty and hunger	
Target 1: Halve, between 1990 and 2015, the proportion of people whose income is less than one dollar a day	1. Proportion of population below $1 per day 2. Poverty gap ratio (incidence x depth of poverty) 3. Share of poorest quintile in national consumption
Target 2: Halve, between 1990 and 2015, the proportion of people who suffer from hunger	4. Prevalence of underweight children (under five years of age) 5. Proportion of population below minimum level of dietary energy consumption
Goal 2: Achieve universal primary education	
Target 3: Ensure that, by 2015, children everywhere, boys and girls alike, will be able to complete a full course of primary schooling	6. Net enrolment ratio in primary education 7. Proportion of pupils starting grade 1 who reach grade 5 8. Literacy rate of 15–24-year-olds
Goal 3: Promote gender equality and empower women	
Target 4: Eliminate gender disparity in primary and secondary education, preferably by 2005, and to all levels of education no later than 2015	9. Ratio of girls to boys in primary, secondary and tertiary education 10. Ratio of literate females to males of 15–24-year-olds 11. Share of women in wage employment in the non-agricultural sector 12. Proportion of seats held by women in national parliament
Goal 4: Reduce child mortality	
Target 5: Reduce by two-thirds, between 1990 and 2015, the under-five mortality rate	13. Under-five mortality rate 14. Infant mortality rate 15. Proportion of 1-year-old children immunised against measles
Goal 5: Improve maternal health	
Target 6: Reduce by three-quarters, between 1990 and 2015, the maternal mortality ratio	16. Maternal mortality ratio 17. Proportion of births attended by skilled health personnel

Table 1.1: The Millennium Development Goals (continued)

Goals and Targets	Indicators
Goal 6: Combat HIV/AIDS, malaria and other diseases	
Target 7: Have halted by 2015, and begun to reverse, the spread of HIV/AIDS	18. HIV prevalence among 15–24-year-old pregnant women 19. Contraceptive prevalence rate 20. Number of children orphaned by HIV/AIDS
Target 8: Have halted by 2015, and begun to reverse, the incidence of malaria and other major diseases	21. Prevalence and death rates associated with malaria 22. Proportion of population in malaria risk areas using effective malaria prevention and treatment measures 23. Prevalence and death rates associated with tuberculosis 24. Proportion of TB cases detected and cured under DOTS (Directly Observed Treatment Short Course)
Goal 7: Ensure environmental sustainability*	
Target 9: Integrate the principles of sustainable development into country policies and programmes and reverse the loss of environmental resources	25. Proportion of land area covered by forest 26. Land area protected to maintain biological diversity 27. GDP per unit of energy use (as proxy for energy efficiency) 28. Carbon dioxide emissions (per capita) plus two figures of global atmospheric pollution: ozone depletion and the accumulation of global warming gases
Target 10: Halve, by 2015, the proportion of people without sustainable access to safe drinking water	29. Proportion of population with sustainable access to an improved water source
Target 11: By 2020, to have achieved a significant improvement in the lives of at least 100 million slum dwellers	30. Proportion of people with access to improved sanitation 31. Proportion of people with access to secure tenure. (Urban/rural disaggregation of several of the above indicators may be relevant for monitoring improvement in the lives of slum dwellers)

* The selection of indicators for Goals 7 and 8 is subject to further refinement.

Table 1.1: The Millennium Development Goals (continued)

Goals and Targets	Indicators

Goal 8: Develop a Global Partnership for Development*

Target 12: Develop further an open, rule-based, predictable, non-discriminatory trading and financial system. Includes a commitment to good governance, development, and poverty reduction – both nationally and internationally

Target 13: Address the Special Needs of the Least Developed Countries. Includes: tariff and quota free access for LDC exports; enhanced programme of debt relief for HIPC and cancellation of official bilateral debt; and more generous ODA for countries committed to poverty reduction

Target 14: Address the Special Needs of landlocked countries and small island developing states (through Barbados Programme and 22nd General Assembly provisions)

Target 15: Deal comprehensively with the debt problems of developing countries through national and international measures in order to make debt sustainable in the long term

Target 16: In cooperation with developing countries, develop and implement strategies for decent and productive work for youth

Target 17: In cooperation with pharmaceutical companies, provide access to affordable, essential drugs in developing countries

Target 18: In cooperation with the private sector, make available the benefits of new technologies, especially information and communications

Some of the indicators listed below will be monitored separately for the Least Developed Countries (LDCs), Africa, landlocked countries and small island developing states.

Official Development Assistance
32. Net ODA as percentage of DAC donors' GNI (targets of 0.7% in total and 0.15% for LDCs)
33. Proportion of ODA to basic social services (basic education, primary health care, nutrition, safe water and sanitation)
34. Proportion of ODA that is untied
35. Proportion of ODA for environment in small island developing states
36. Proportion of ODA for transport sector in land-locked countries

Market Access
37. Proportion of exports (by value and excluding arms) admitted free of duties and quotas
38. Average tariffs and quotas on agricultural products and textiles and clothing
39. Domestic and export agricultural subsidies in OECD countries
40. Proportion of ODA provided to help build trade capacity

Debt Sustainability
41. Proportion of official bilateral HIPC debt cancelled
42. Debt service as a percentage of exports of goods and services
43. Proportion of ODA provided as debt relief
44. Number of countries reaching HIPC decision and completion points
45. Unemployment rate of 15-24-year-olds
46. Proportion of population with access to affordable essential drugs on a sustainable basis
47. Telephone lines per 1000 people
48. Personal computers per 1000 people

* The selection of indicators for Goals 7 and 8 is subject to further refinement.

Putting Gender on the Policy Agenda

1970s and 1980s: Making the links between gender and development

It is not surprising that gender concerns were missing from early growth-oriented strategies since these generally did not consider the 'human factor' in development. In the 1970s, however, when greater attention began to be paid to basic needs, rural productivity and informal sector activity, there was growing advocacy on the issue of women in development. This took two distinct forms: an argument for economic equity and depiction of women as the poorest of the poor. Both started from the premise that women were important economic actors. However, they emphasised different aspects of women's performance and used different analytical approaches.

Conventional measures of economic activity ... significantly underestimated the level of women's economic contributions.

The economic equity argument

This argument focused on the effects of development planning on women's economic status. An influential example is a 1970 publication by Boserup (*see box 1.3*). It basically maintained that national governments and international development agencies had not understood that women had productive, as well as reproductive, roles. Conventional measures of economic activity, based on Western market-based economies, significantly underestimated the level of women's economic contributions. They both

* failed to acknowledge the magnitude and value of women's unpaid work; and

* undercounted women's paid work outside the 'modern' sector.

The 'household' was assumed to follow the model of an idealised 'Western nuclear family' with a male breadwinner and dependent women and children. This led planners to focus mainstream development interventions on men. At the same time, they directed various welfare programmes – such as maternal and child health, family planning and nutrition – to women. The result was the emergence and widening of a gender-based productivity gap and negative impacts on women's status in the economy.

playing into stereotype

> **Box 1.3** The Geography of Gender Roles in Farming
>
> Boserup pointed out that gender roles in farming had a distinct geographical pattern. In areas of agriculture based on shifting cultivation, women played the major role in food production, with some help from men. Sub-Saharan Africa was described as a prime example of these 'female farming systems'. Similar patterns, however, were also found among 'Indian and Negro' communities in parts of Latin America and among many tribal groups in north-eastern India and South-East Asia. Female labour force participation tended to be extremely high in these areas. Women also played an active role in trading activities in some of them (namely, South-East Asia, southern India and western Africa).
>
> In 'male farming systems', on the other hand, agriculture was largely the responsibility of men, with women confined to a limited number of tasks. These were mainly found in regions of settled farming with plough-based cultivation and private ownership of land. Due to the practice of female seclusion, women did very little work in the fields and concentrated mainly on tasks that could be undertaken in the domestic domain. Instead, cultivating families relied on hired labour from landless families. Male farming systems characterised the Middle East, India and Pakistan. These were also regions with very low female participation in trading activities. In addition, a number of countries in Latin America also followed this pattern of low participation by women in agriculture and high percentages of wage labour.

Boserup's equity-based argument saw women as economic actors rather than welfare clients and focused on the need to improve their productivity. It had limited success in the 1970s, however. The type of programmes needed to improve women's economic opportunities implied a change in gender relations that would have affected the cultural fabric of society. Moreover, the call for gender equality at all levels also included

within development agencies — hence an understandable reluctance by largely male-staffed agencies to implement such programmes.

Woman planting rice, Indonesia
INTERNATIONAL LABOUR ORGANIZATION

Women as the poorest of the poor

What made greater headway in development circles in the 1970s was the argument that there was a link between women and poverty. Attention was drawn to the disproportionate number of female-headed households among the poor and the fact that women in poor households were largely responsible for meeting families' basic needs. This led to the spread of income-generating projects for women intended to help them meet these needs, but which had little effect on their marginalised status in the development process. Genuine anti-poverty strategies, which justified assistance to poor women on the grounds of poverty reduction rather than family welfare, would have meant significant disbursements for women. They therefore ran into the same problems as 'equity-based' programmes. Early initiatives on women in development thus did little to

Gender analysis of adjustment policies by the Commonwealth Secretariat showed how cutbacks in public social services were forcing women to increase their own efforts in the reproductive arena.

change gender biases in poverty alleviation efforts and left them intact in macroeconomic policies.

SAPs and the 'invisible adjustments' made by women

The SAPs that dominated development policy in the 1980s emphasised market-oriented growth strategies, with a stress on 'getting prices right'. This was also a period when attempts were made to link gender concerns with macroeconomic policy. UNICEF, for example, drew attention to the 'invisible adjustments' being made by women in poor households in their attempts to cope with the economic crisis. It called for adjustment 'with a human face'. Gender analysis of adjustment policies by the Commonwealth Secretariat combined welfare and efficiency arguments. It showed how cutbacks in public social services were forcing women to increase their own efforts in the reproductive arena (e.g. by caring for sick family members who might previously have been hospitalised). The increased burden of reproductive work: (a) meant that women were less able to respond to economic incentives; (b) slowed the reallocation of resources into the traded sector; and (c) made economic reform less effective.

Gender and the 1990 WDR

The World Bank's 1990 WDR had little to say about the gender dimensions of poverty in its analysis. It did point out that figures on health, nutrition, education and labour force participation showed that women were often severely disadvantaged compared to men and faced "all manner of cultural, social, legal and economic obstacles that men – even poor men do not. They typically work longer hours and, when they are paid at all, for lower wages." It noted the large number of single-mother households, and that "raising women's incomes directly is a good way to reach children as well as to strengthen women's status and bargaining power within the household". In addition, it referred to the gender bias of agricultural extension services even where many, if not most, farmers were women. However, although its discussion of economic opportunities for the poor covered a range of issues – including infrastructure, land rights, credit, non-farm linkages, rural-urban migration, the informal sector and technological change – gender analysis was confined to a couple of boxes and to a brief mention of women's higher rates of loan repayment compared to men's.

More attention was given to gender issues in the section on social services for the poor. These included: (a) gender inequalities in education and literacy; (b) high levels of maternal mortality; and (c) the negative effects of high fertility on mothers' health. In policy terms, family planning services together with female education and employment were seen as important for reducing fertility rates. It also suggested that primary health care targeted at mothers could help to reduce maternal mortality. Girls' education was given special attention. Scholarships for girls and an increase in the number of female teachers in countries with strong gender discrimination were recommended as ways to overcome gender bias, as well as longer-term policies to increase women's participation in the labour market.

The 1995 HDR ... stated that "poverty has a woman's face – of 1.3 billion people in poverty, 70 per cent are women".

Gender and the Human Development Report (HDR)

The first HDR in 1990 also barely touched on gender issues. It did note, however, that the increasing number of female-headed households has led to a 'feminisation of poverty' and that problems of gender inequality were relevant in both the North and South. It also pointed out that women "are typically less qualified than men [and] tend to get into lower paying jobs, having fewer opportunities to be upwardly mobile, leaving them less able than men to provide a decent living to their families".

The 1995 Report, on the other hand, focused on gender inequality to tie in with the UN Fourth World Conference on Women in Beijing. It therefore offered a much more elaborate analysis of gender issues. It stated that the purpose of development was "to enlarge all human choices, not just income". It also suggested that removing gender inequality had very little to do with the level of national income and stated that "poverty has a woman's face – of 1.3 billion people in poverty, 70 per cent are women". It noted that the causes behind the 'feminisation of poverty' differed in the South and North. For the former it was "the tragic consequence of women's unequal access to economic opportunities". However, in the latter, it

The HDR concluded that ... governments ... needed to ... introduce affirmative actions to promote equality and ensure that women had access to productive resources.

was linked to "the unequal situation in the labour market, [women's] treatment under social welfare system and status power in the families". Attempts to estimate women's unpaid work helped draw attention to the size of the contribution that they made to the economic growth of their countries.

The HDR concluded that, because of inequities in the structures of power, gender equality would not come about through the free workings of economic and political processes. Governments therefore needed to reform their policies and introduce affirmative actions to promote equality and ensure that women had access to productive resources (*see box 1.4*).

Box 1.4 UNDP's Five Steps to Gender Equality

Concluding that government intervention was necessary to bring about gender equality, the 1995 *Human Development Report* offered a five-point agenda for accelerating progress towards that goal:

1. Mobilisation of national and international efforts to bring about legal equality in an agreed period of time;

2. Altering economic and institutional arrangements to promote more choices for women and men in the work place (e.g. paternity as well as maternity leave, flexible work schedules, family-friendly taxes and social security incentives);

3. At least 30% of decision-making positions to be held by women;

4. Programmes to ensure universal female education, improved reproductive health and increased credit for women; and

5. National and international programmes to provide people, especially women, with more access to economic and political opportunities (e.g. basic social services for all, reproductive health care, credit for the poor, poverty reduction and capacity building and empowerment).

Gender and the 2000 World Development Report

The 2000 WDR focused on poverty and offered a more complex view of gender than the 1990 report. Gender featured at various points in its discussion of the key themes of opportunity, empowerment and security, but particularly under empowerment. Here the Report recognised the institutional nature of gender inequality, tracing women's disadvantage to kinship rules, community norms, legal systems and public provision. Critical kinship rules that help determine the extent of gender equality were identified as:

* the rules of inheritance, which determine women's ownership of resources; and

* the rules of marriage, which determine women's domestic autonomy.

The 2000 WDR argued for a gender approach to understanding poverty, noting that greater gender equity is not only desirable in its own right but also for "its instrumental social and economic benefits for poverty reduction". There was no analysis, however, of gender biases in labour and other markets. This suggests that the Bank continued to see the market as impersonal, and hence 'gender-neutral'. In addition, the 2000 WDR failed to note that gender inequality is central to both how poverty is caused and the form it takes.

The World Bank's most comprehensive treatment of gender to date is the 2001 Policy Research Report, Engendering Development: Through Gender Equality in Rights, Resources, and Voice.

The World Bank's 2001 report

The World Bank's most comprehensive treatment of gender to date is the 2001 Policy Research Report, *Engendering Development: Through Gender Equality in Rights, Resources, and Voice.* This documented different aspects of gender inequality using evidence from both the developed and developing world. Like the 2000 WDR, *Engendering Development* noted how important kinship systems are in constructing gender inequality. It drew on the new thinking on 'household economics' to explore the structure of power, incentives and resources in the household (*see Chapter 3*). It also looked at the ways in which the beliefs and values of households and communities interact with wider

Female earnings are around 70–80 per cent of male earnings in both developed and developing countries. Only 20 per cent of this difference can be explained by conventional economic variables ... Rather ... these inequalities are perpetuated by 'taboos and prejudices' in the labour market.

legal frameworks to reproduce gender bias in key institutions. These include those of the state as well as those of the market.

The report noted that labour markets around the world have a hierarchical structure in which sectors, occupations and activities are segregated by gender. Women tend to be under-represented in better-paid formal sector jobs and over-represented in the unpaid and informal sectors (particularly in subcontracting, temporary, casual or home-based work). As a result, female earnings are around 70–80 per cent of male earnings in both developed and developing countries. Only 20 per cent of this difference can be explained by conventional economic variables, such as educational attainment, work experience and job characteristics. Rather, the report makes clear that these inequalities are perpetuated by 'taboos and prejudices' in the labour market.

The report also documented how globalisation is opening and expanding national markets, and pointed to the potential gains and costs associated with this. Gains include some signs that the gender gap in wages is decreasing in industries in both North and South. Costs include the failure of legislation to prevent continued discrimination against women workers, as well as the exposure of those in the 'traded' industries to fluctuations in the global economy. As a result, the report concluded that, "competitive markets may not be the best way to eliminate gender discrimination, so government has a role to play in regulating markets and in providing critical economic infrastructure" (*see box 1.5*).

The overall analysis of *Engendering Development* suggests a combination of the sort of broad-based pro-poor economic growth strategies being promoted by the World Bank and IMF and the kind of rights-based approach to human development adopted by a number of UN and bilateral donor agencies. However:

* It is much stronger on growth-based policies than rights-based ones. It understands rights in terms of regulation rather than redistribution, i.e. getting rid of discriminatory laws and introducing more equitable ones. It stresses civil and political rights (and their negative 'freedom from') rather than economic and social rights (and their positive 'freedom to').

> **Box 1.5 How the State can Address Gender Inequality**
>
> *Engendering Development* suggests some positive actions that a state can take to reduce the gender discrimination that causes harm to society as a whole. It can "tax and subsidise, persuade and regulate, prohibit and punish, or provide services ... It can directly prohibit prejudicial behaviour – such as when it requires enterprises to hire workers on the basis of skills rather than on the basis of sex, and sanctions or fines violations".
>
> The report also proposes a three-part strategy to promote gender equality in the development process:
>
> 1. Reforming institutions to establish equal rights and opportunities for women and men;
>
> 2. Fostering a rights-based approach to development and growth as the most effective way to reduce gender disparity; and
>
> 3. Taking active measures to redress persistent inequalities in political voice.

- It is concerned with gender inequality in a wide sense, and does not pay much specific attention to its links with poverty.

- It comes from the Bank's research division, so it is not clear that it commits the institution to adopting the recommendations in its own work.

Gender and the Millennium Development Goals

Although international organisations approached poverty and human development in different ways during the 1990s, their treatment of gender was similar. They mainly looked at it in terms of the social sectors, focusing on inequalities in access to education, particularly primary education. However, gender has had a very limited place in economic policies and production-related strategies.

*Mother with a baby tending
a market stall in Senegal*

INTERNATIONAL LABOUR ORGANIZATION

The International Development Targets (IDTs) – on which the MDGs were based – also addressed gender issues only in relation to human development goals, with "progress towards gender equality and the empowerment of women" shown by the elimination of gender disparity in primary and secondary education. There was also a commitment to reproductive health services and to the reduction of maternal mortality – a major cause of female deaths in poorer countries – by three-fourths by 2015. While these are important goals, closing the gender gap in indicators of health and education not only requires better service delivery. It also means increasing women's economic agency and the value they give themselves and are given by their community.

The MDGs are only a partial improvement on the IDTs as women are still not part of the poverty reduction goal. Instead women continue to be identified with human development goals – in relation to education, maternal mortality and the incidence of HIV/AIDS. There are, however, a number of important new features:

* Gender equality is treated as an explicit goal.

* Indicators of progress to reduce gender disparities in primary and secondary education include:

  – the ratio of boys and girls at all levels of education;

  – gender disparities in adult literacy;

  – the percentage of women in waged employment in the non-agricultural sector; and

  – the percentage of women holding seats in national parliament.

Unless macro-economic thinking is better informed by gender analysis, macroeconomic policy will remain gender blind.

Conclusion

It has taken nearly half a century for the goals of poverty reduction and gender equality to achieve this prominence in mainstream policy concerns. In the process, the understanding of poverty has been transformed from the early equation with income poverty to a more multi-dimensional understanding. This includes its human dimensions as well as its structural causes (*see Chapter 4*). The understanding of gender issues has also grown, but more slowly and unevenly. This is partly political, since gender equity may be threatening to the power and privilege of policy-makers themselves rather than being confined to a constituency 'out there'. However, it is also partly conceptual and lies in the nature of mainstream macro-economic analysis, models and methodologies.

The work of gender advocates and feminist academics has helped to keep gender issues alive in the development agenda in some form or other since the 1970s. Moreover, the clear links that have been identified between poverty and gender inequality, particularly where SAPs have been imposed, have shown that unless macroeconomic *thinking* is better informed by gender analysis, macroeconomic *policy* will remain gender blind.

2. Integrating Gender into Macroeconomic Analysis

Introduction

This chapter discusses attempts to integrate gender into macroeconomic analysis. It looks at both: (a) mainstream economists working within a conventional neo-classical framework; and (b) other economists working within political economy frameworks. It starts by exploring some of the theory and then looks at a number of empirical findings. These findings offer some important insights into the relationship between gender and poverty.

Gender Bias in Macroeconomic Analysis

Neo-classical economics is mainly concerned with the factors influencing the supply of, and demand for, goods and services by a variety of individual economic agents (producers, consumers, workers, entrepreneurs, etc.). The activities of these agents together give rise to the aggregated forces of supply and demand in an economy.

Economists have conventionally viewed markets simply as places where individuals meet to engage in economic transactions, guided by the pursuit of private gain. However, it is increasingly recognised that certain conditions have to be in place for markets to work effectively. These include open entry, competitive rather than monopolistic prices, enforceable contracts, respect for property and the absence of coercion or interference with individual choice. Economic analysis has therefore had to consider not only individual behaviour but also institutional factors.

Analysis at the macro-level looks at the economy in terms of total marketed output (domestic, private sector and public sector production plus imports) and expenditure (consumption, private investment, government expenditure plus exports). It is concerned with the broad stocks and flows of goods and

It has been extremely difficult to have gender included as a variable in macroeconomic analysis – or even to get macro-economists to acknowledge that its omission might be a problem.

services in an economy that influence national income (economic growth) as well the rate of returns to different factors of production (distribution). Its categories of analysis are the measures of these stocks and flows: Gross National Product (GNP), investment, savings, balance of payments, etc.

Economic policy instruments try to influence economic behaviour by intervening either: (a) at the broad macro level (e.g. exchange rates, public revenues and expenditures, interest rates, imposing or removing barriers to trade); or (b) at the meso level (e.g. changes in the provision of social services, such as health or transport, or investments in economic infrastructure, such as roads and bridges).

It has been extremely difficult to have gender included as a variable in macroeconomic analysis – or even to get macro-economists to acknowledge that its omission might be a problem. This can be seen by looking at some of the models of economic growth contributed by macroeconomic theorists to the field of development studies.

Early models of economic growth

Models of economic growth in the post-war decades barely recognised the role of the 'human factor' in development. Many of them assumed that the rate of growth of the labour force was given by the rate of population growth and hence exogenous to (i.e. outside) the model. The influential Harrod-Domar model, for example, emphasised the attainment of a full-employment, steady growth path. It centred on two variable rates of growth:

* the 'warranted' rate, i.e. the rate of growth of output that would generate a level of savings equal to the level of investment undertaken; and

* the 'natural' rate, i.e. the maximum rate of growth possible given the rate of growth of the labour force and in labour-saving technological processes.

In the model itself, a balanced rate of economic growth in the long run in conditions of full-employment depended on the 'natural' and 'warranted' rates being in line with each other. Since there was no mechanism to link them, only chance would bring this about. There was thus a 'knife-edge' balance between cumulative deflation when the warranted rate of growth exceeded the natural and cumulative inflation when it fell short. A great deal of subsequent work on this model explored this instability problem and whether there were adjustment mechanisms in the economy that could help achieve a balance.

Neo-classical economists focused on shifts in technology that would reflect labour scarcity or labour surplus in the economy. Neo-Keynesians focused on adjustments through the distribution of income between capital and labour, the former being associated with higher propensity to save than the latter. Variations in the distribution of income when the full employment barrier was reached or when there was growing unemployment would lead to variations in savings and help bring about an adjustment between natural and warranted rates of growth.

An important modification to neo-classical models was made by 'endogenous growth' theories (*see box 2.1*). These saw labour as an endogenous variable (i.e. to be explained by the model rather than taken as a given). As will be seen below, they opened up a space for the introduction of gender concerns into theories of growth.

Box 2.1 Endogenous Growth Theories

Early models of economic growth saw the rate of growth of the labour force as determined by rate of population growth and no attention was paid to factors that determine the efficiency of labour. Endogenous growth theories introduced the idea of 'labour-augmenting' technological change as something that could be brought about by decisions taken within the economy. Investment in human capital was seen as a key means by which a given stock of labour could be make more productive at any point of time. Economic growth thus became a function of investments in education, something that could be undertaken by government or by other actors in the economy.

Elson argued that the gender-neutrality of macroeconomic analysis was an illusion. It was not only the impact of policies but also the view of the economy on which they were based that was gender-biased.

Economic models that looked at developing countries paid more attention to the role of labour. Of these the best known is the two-sector model. It suggested that most developing countries had both: (a) a traditional subsistence sector dominated by family farming, with an 'unlimited' supply of unskilled labour; and (b) a modern industrial sector that used reproducible capital and produced for profit. The labour surplus would allow wages to be set initially at subsistence levels rather than being competitively determined through market forces. Reinvestment of profit and constant wages would lead to economic growth. Then, once the surplus was absorbed, competition would set in between the sectors to retain or attract labour. The rise in real wages in the agricultural sector would lead in due course to the emergence of competitive, commercialised agriculture where productivity would be equal to that in industry.

The gender bias in macroeconomic analysis

This kind of macroeconomic analysis did not consider the human dimensions of economic growth except at a very general and abstract level. It is therefore not surprising that it had almost no concern with gender. There has been some debate about what this absence of gender concerns means in conceptual and practical terms. Some writers made a distinction between policy 'intent' and policy 'impact'. They saw macroeconomic models as gender-neutral in themselves, and suggested that the policies led to gender-biased outcomes because they were implemented in a world of gender inequality.

However, Elson argued that the gender-neutrality of macroeconomic analysis was an illusion. It was not only the impact of policies but also the view of the economy on which they were based that was gender-biased. Human resources were treated as 'non-produced factors of production' like natural resources. The implication was that they could be transferred between activities without cost in the same way that land could be used for growing different crops at different times. Yet this is clearly not the case. Alongside the stream of activities that are labelled 'production' by economists, there is a parallel stream of activities that constitute 'reproduction' (*see box 2.2*).

Box 2.2 Production and Reproduction

'Production' traditionally refers to all the activities that contribute to a country's GNP – in other words, that are bought and sold in the market place. 'Reproduction', on the other hand, refers to those activities that add to, and take care of, society's human resources. These include bearing and rearing of children, reproduction of people on a daily basis and caring for the old, the sick, the disabled and others who find it difficult to take care of themselves. Human beings have to be born, brought up, cared for and taught a variety of norms, values and skills before they become the 'factors of production' that are taken for granted in macroeconomic models.

Some aspects of reproductive work may become part of the public arena of state and market during industrialisation (e.g. health care, socialisation of children, family planning services, child care). In poorer countries, however, much of it is carried out on an unpaid basis in the household in response to the combination of social norms, habit, custom, affection and obligation that make up family life. In most cultures, women have the main responsibility for the reproduction of 'labour' on a daily and generational basis.

Reproductive work has typically been excluded from economic analysis. There is a tendency to view it as a 'natural' aspect of women's roles and as not being 'work' because it is unpaid.

Reproductive work has typically been excluded from economic analysis. There is a tendency to view it as a 'natural' aspect of women's roles and as not being 'work' because it is unpaid. By using male economic activity as its standpoint, economic analysis has become skewed and failed to appreciate what is distinctive about women's work patterns. It has thus had an 'iceberg' view of the economy, seeing only the tip of what actually goes on by way of productive work. The activities that entered the System of National Accounts (SNA) and help to calculate the GNP are only those that represent market transactions (*see Fig. 2.1*).

Strategies for economic growth aimed to increase the volume and value of marketed activities in an economy, with different strategies prioritising different sectors. While early growth strategies focused on the internationally 'traded' sector,

Figure 2.1: The 'Iceberg' View of the Economy

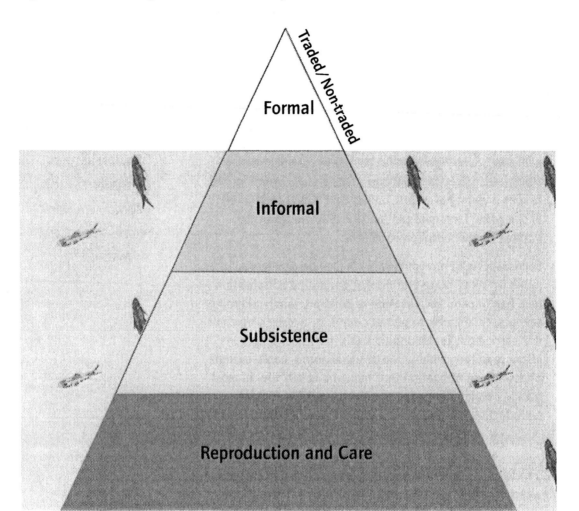

it was largely to produce goods domestically that would reduce their reliance on imports. Recent liberalisation policies have also been concerned with the traded sector, but the emphasis has shifted to the production of goods for export. Regardless of their specific focus, however, both sets of strategies focus on market-oriented activity at the expense of non-market work.

Beyond the visible economy, however, there is a less visible, informal economy. Here goods and services are still marketed but go undocumented by official statistics. This is the informal economy. Beyond that is the subsistence economy, where goods and services are produced for own consumption. All these activities, in turn, rest on the unpaid work of reproduction and care in the household that ensures the production and productivity of the labour power that keeps the entire economy working. Although the 1993 SNA was revised to assign a market value to some subsistence activities, where goods were produced and consumed in the household, the bias against this unpaid work remains. Yet it is critical to the reproduction, care and maintenance of labour as well as to the accumulation of human capital. These are both seen as increasingly important in the 'new growth theories' as well as in current policy agendas.

The relative size of these sub-economies varies considerably across the world. In general, however, the visible economy is smaller and the less visible economy larger, the poorer the country and, within poor countries, the poorer the household. Production and reproduction in poor countries are far more 'socially embedded' in family, kinship and community than has been recognised by conventional economic analysis. The gender dimensions of this can be seen by comparing the gender distribution of labour between SNA and non-SNA activities in different parts of the world (*see box 2.3*).

[T]he reproduction, care and maintenance of labour as well as to the accumulation of human capital ... are both seen as increasingly important ... in current policy agendas.

Box 2.3 Women's and Men's Work Time

A comparison of nine developing and 13 industrialised countries by the United Nations Development Programme (UNDP) showed that women and men generally worked longer hours a day in the former than in the latter. The average working day was 419 minutes in industrialised countries, 471 minutes in urban developing countries and 566 in rural developing countries. The study also noted that women accounted for 51% of the total work burden in industrialised countries and 53% in developing countries. However, while women in both contexts spent about a third of their time in SNA activities, and the rest in unpaid work, men spent 66% of their time in SNA activities in industrialised countries and 76% in developing countries.

The continued tendency to record only primary activity often leads to women being classified as 'housewives' despite the variety of different ways in which they contribute economically.

Activities outside the formal economy are often overlooked in official data-gathering exercises because they tend to be irregular, part-time, subsistence-oriented or else carried out as unpaid family labour. By extension, data on women's labour force participation are most likely to be incomplete, unreliable and underestimates. This is because: (a) more economically active women are likely to be found in the informal economy and in subsistence production; and (b) many more are likely to be classified as unpaid family labour than paid workers.

To overcome this problem, the International Labour Organization (ILO) has adopted two definitions of economic activity: (a) a conventional one that includes only activities done for pay or profit; and (b) an 'extended' one that also includes productive work done for own consumption. The difference made by these different definitions can be illustrated by a number of examples (*see box 2.4*). Estimates of female labour force participation based on the first definition provide information on women's contributions in the 'visible' economy. Estimates based on the second definition give a more accurate idea of the extent of their productive contribution across the economy. However, neither provides information on women's contribution to the care and maintenance of the family, and hence of the labour efforts that underpin survival, subsistence and accumulation. In addition, the continued tendency to record only primary activity often leads to women being classified as 'housewives' despite the variety of different ways in which they contribute economically.

To make macroeconomic analysis more gender-aware, therefore, it is necessary to:

* reveal the connection between production and reproduction in different parts of the world through an analysis of institutional sites and social relationships; and

* identify gender inequalities in these different institutions and relationships and explore their implications for macroeconomic policy.

*Women in Mali collect
firewood for cooking*
UN/DPI

Box 2.4 Women's Workload Depends on how it is Defined

According to the Dominican Republic's 1981 census, the rural female labour force participation rate was 21%. However, a study that included activities such as homestead cultivation and livestock care gave an estimate of 84%. In India, narrow and extended definitions of work gave estimates of women's participation rates of 13% and 88% respectively. Narrow estimates of female labour force participation in rural areas in Pakistan were 13.9% compared to an estimate of 45.9% by the 1991–92 Labour Force Survey. The extended definition included post-harvest processing of crops; rearing livestock; construction work; collecting firewood and fetching water; making clothes, weaving and embroidery; and undertaking domestic work on a paid basis.

A wide range of labour-related variables can ... be seen to play a role in economic growth, including care, fertility, health, nutrition and education. All of these have gender implications.

Making models less gender-blind

A major source of gender blindness in early models of economic growth was their lack of interest in how the labour supply is produced (and hence in the reproductive sector). More attention to this, however, makes it clear that the family is the key institution in the reproductive economy. It also becomes apparent that influences other than population growth can contribute to, or reduce, the effectiveness and availability of labour. A wide range of labour-related variables can then be seen to play a role in economic growth, including care, fertility, health, nutrition and education. All of these have gender implications.

In fact, there is long-standing evidence that rates of population are not 'given', as suggested by Malthusian theories. Instead, they respond to levels of income, both in society as a whole and in family-based households where reproductive decisions are made. There is emerging evidence that the costs and incentives associated with bearing and caring for children are unevenly distributed across gender and generation due to the way households are organised. Women and men may have different stakes in both the quantity and 'quality' of children they have. The 'quality' of children refers to the resource investments per child. This is generally taken by economists to refer to education, but it could equally refer to health, nutrition and even time investments. Economists suggest that there is a trade-off between quantity and quality since both more children and higher quality children cost more. The 'quantity-quality trade-off' is one route by which economies move from reliance on unlimited supplies of 'basic labour' to relying on a more skilled, healthy and educated labour force.

When 'endogenous' growth theories showed that the labour supply could be improved through investments in human capital, it became possible to see labour itself as something that is 'produced' and that thus requires prior commitments of other labour and goods. This provides another promising opening for integrating gender perspectives in macroeconomic theory. In particular, if women and men have different attitudes to investing in their children, then the gender distribution of income should be recognised as a significant determinant of economic growth.

A re-interpretation of the two-sector model from the per-spective of the reproductive economy would also enrich macroeconomic understanding of the limits to growth. This would mean considering women's actual activities instead of treating them as part of the pool of 'surplus labour' in the trad-itional sector. Efforts to improve the productivity of labour in the unpaid 'care' economy would have important implications for the growth process – and for women themselves.

Gender and micro-economic responses

Other studies that show the relevance of gender to macro-economic analysis started by looking at micro-economic responses. Much of this analysis focused on the economic recession and structural adjustment policies (SAPs) of the 1980s. The 'gender-efficiency' approach looked at how gender inequalities limited effective adjustment through market liber-alisation, while 'the vulnerable group' approach examined the costs of adjustment to women. However, many studies went beyond specific policy initiatives to make broader generalisa-tions about the economy.

Collier, for example, argued that in order to understand the economic environment in which SAPs were to be imple-mented – and hence their likely impact – it was necessary to understand that men and women were located in different sectors and faced different incentives and constraints. He identified four different factors that might account for the differences:

* discrimination outside the household (e.g. in labour and credit markets);

* gender-specific role models that channel boys/men and girls/women into different activities, preventing them from moving easily between sectors;

* unequal rights and obligations between husband and wife, giving wives little incentive to contribute more to activities controlled by husbands; and

* women's reproductive role, which pre-commits their time to bearing and caring for children during the middle phase

Efforts to improve the productivity of labour in the unpaid 'care' economy ... have important implications for the growth process – and for women themselves.

Women's reproductive work is a 'tax' on their labour that they have to pay before undertaking income-generating or expenditure-saving activities.

of their lives. This restricts their economic choices as they are limited to work where interruptions in labour force participation are not a major disadvantage.

Other writers have pointed to gender differences in the ability to cope with the changing costs of reproduction (e.g. the cutbacks in public expenditure associated with adjustment) and to respond to changing incentives for production. Such differences reflect constraints caused by gender discrimination, the multiple demands on women's time, etc.

Collier suggested that it was necessary to disaggregate market and non-market sectors, capital and consumption goods, tradable and non-tradable goods, and protected and non-protected industries. In order to understand the constraints that women were likely to face, he also suggested disaggregation by institutional location (waged work, enterprise work, home-based work, etc.) and by nature of the contract (waged labour; family-based work, etc.).

Palmer, looking at sub-Saharan Africa, suggested that relations in the household should be at the centre of macroeconomic policy. This was where responses to market signals took place that determined rates of economic growth in areas of smallholder farming. Gender inequalities: (a) in the household meant that market prices failed to assign the correct value to labour; and (b) in market and state provision led to resources in the economy not necessarily going to those who could make the best use of them. These gender inequalities are found in:

* The domestic division of labour. Women's reproductive work is a 'tax' on their labour that they have to pay before undertaking income-generating or expenditure-saving activities. Since men do not have to trade off their economic activities against domestic responsibilities, the reproductive tax distorts how labour is allocated in the household.

* The terms of exchange in households. Members are involved in separate economic activities and may maintain separate accounts. This leads to inefficient household resource allocation since men can make demands on women's labour that they only partly reciprocate (if at all).

* The disposition of income and other proceeds to household

labour. This distorts incentives and how proceeds are allocated. Women as well as men are likely to prefer to put their efforts into forms of production whose proceeds they can control, regardless of whether this is best for the household as a whole.

Institutions and actors in a gendered economy

Elson has integrated the insights from these various theories into her analysis of what she calls the 'gendered economy'. She argues that economies are organised through institutions that determine what is 'appropriate' male and female behaviour. These institutions include not only family and kinship structures but also private firms and the state. They are all governed by social relationships that structure the way activities, resources, power and authority are divided between women and men. Thus although economic institutions may be seen as gender-neutral, they are not.

Whether economic analysis is conducted at the macro-, meso- or micro-level, it therefore needs to ask questions about the gender division of labour, resources, power and decision-making:

1. Macro-level analysis involves examining the gender division of the labour force between the different productive sectors (agriculture, industry and services) and in the unpaid reproductive sector. In principle, national accounts can be produced that give monetary value to activities in the reproductive economy. UNDP, for example, has estimated that women's 'invisible' non-SNA output amounts to around US$11,000 billion a year worldwide. This is equivalent to an extra 48 per cent of the world's GDP.

2. Meso-level analysis looks at the institutions – firms, community-based organisations, local government offices, etc. – that help structure the distribution of resources and activities at micro-level. It involves examining gender inequalities in public provision as well as gender biases in the rules of operation of different markets. It also explores the structure of decision-making at this level – for example, in different ministries and in corporations and financial

Whether economic analysis is conducted at the macro-, meso- or micro-level, it ... needs to ask questions about the gender division of labour, resources, power and decision-making.

[Under SAPs] women's unpaid labour increased to compensate for cutbacks in public services or to substitute for food or clothing that the household could no longer afford.

institutions. For policy purposes, Elson draws attention in particular to the activities of the state in the provision of physical and social infrastructure and to the operation of labour, commodity and other markets.

3. Micro-level analysis explores in greater detail the gender division of labour, resources, responsibility and decision-making in different sectors in terms of paid and unpaid work. It also examines the structure of decision-making, particularly in the household. Such analysis is central to understanding: (a) how macroeconomic forces, filtered through the various institutions of society, impact on, and are responded to by, individual women and men in households, firms and other organisations; and (b) how their responses in turn feed into the wider economy.

Empirical Findings

Along with these various theoretical attempts to integrate gender into macroeconomic analysis, a number of studies have explored the empirical links between gender and the macro-economy. This section looks at two approaches to this research.

The impact of macro-level policy

The imposition of SAPs gave rise to a large body of research on its gender implications, and those of economic recession, at the micro-level and how these affected macro-level outcomes. Some studies used small-scale, often qualitative data and documented a 'scissors-effect' on women's time:

* women's unpaid labour increased to compensate for cutbacks in public services or to substitute for food or clothing that the household could no longer afford; and

* women tried to increase their paid work to compensate for rising male unemployment and increases in the cost of living.

The long hours that women – particularly poorer women – worked in and outside the home was at the expense either of their own sleep, leisure and, in the long-run, health or their daughters' education or leisure. Women's time emerged as a crucial variable of adjustment, as it was allocated to numerous different responsibilities in the home, market and community. At the same time, preconceptions about the primacy of the male breadwinner led in several countries to women being excluded from social fund programmes put in place to protect the poor in the course of structural adjustment (e.g. Honduras, Mexico and Nicaragua). This was because it was assumed that a reduction of men's poverty would automatically help women.

Other studies used large-scale data to look at the micro-level impacts of macro-level change. One example is research on the negative supply response to market liberalisation in Zambian agriculture (*see box 2.5*).

Women's time emerged as a crucial variable of adjustment, as it was allocated to numerous different responsibilities in the home, market and community.

Box 2.5 Gender Constraints in Agriculture in Zambia

A study of supply response in Zambia found that the lower the price of maize fell, the higher the volume of maize produced. This 'negative supply response' was stronger in the case of women. While some male farmers switched to relatively better-paid crops, women responded more weakly to price changes. The study suggested that this reflected the gender division of roles in the household and women's responsibility for growing traditional food crops. However, other analysis has pointed out that the research showed that male and female farmers faced very different institutional and resource constraints. For example, the most important factors affecting the increased production of maize were the ownership of a plough, non-farm sources of income, use of fertiliser and access to different kind of marketing channels, all of which men were more likely to have than women. Rather than explaining women's supply response purely in terms of the division of responsibilities in the household, this latter explanation indicates the need for policies that give women equitable access to resources.

Examining interactions ... among different sectors of the market economy and between market and non-market spheres makes it possible to understand or predict the effects of changes in policies or other economic circumstances on women.

Gender and 'computable general equilibrium' (CGE) models

Studies exploring micro-level responses to macroeconomic change are necessarily 'partial' in their analysis since they look at particular sub-sets of the population or particular sectors of the economy. They cannot capture how SAPs – or any other form of macroeconomic policy – affect the economy as a whole. Recent attempts to incorporate gender-related variables into computable general equilibrium (CGE) models offer a promising way around this problem.

CGE models are simulation models. Their major advantage lies in the way they can track how changes in one sector of the economy affect other sectors. For example, partial forms of analysis have concentrated on women's increasing share of employment in a number of countries as a result of the switch to export-oriented manufacturing. However, they have largely ignored the simultaneous loss of employment opportunities due to industries having to compete with increasing imports. CGE analysis can show how macroeconomic changes affect women and men in different sectors of the economy and reveal whether the net overall effect is beneficial, adverse or biased. However, such studies are still few and far between because the data requirements of these models are extremely demanding.

A CGE model was used to simulate the gendered effects of changes in trade policies and capital flows in Bangladesh (see box 2.6). It tracks how the effects in specific sectors affect the rest of the market economy. Unusually for CGE models, it also considers how these influence, and are influenced by, behaviour in the unpaid household economy where women are the main workers. Examining interactions both among different sectors of the market economy and between market and non-market spheres makes it possible to understand or predict the effects of changes in policies or other economic circumstances on women.

Box 2.6 **A Simulation Exercise Looking at Bangladesh**

A simulation exercise explored the effects of various trade-related policy changes in Bangladesh, paying particular attention to the following gender-related impacts:

- how labour, particularly female labour, was allocated between leisure, reproduction and employment in the market economy (and between its different sectors);

- the average female wage in the economy, both absolute and relative to male wages; and

- the female wage bill in manufacturing and services, as an indicator of women's cash income from employment. This affects their bargaining power in the household and hence their well-being (and that of their children).

The simulation also explored the effects in the country of a decline in the export garment sector. This – as elsewhere – uses predominantly female labour (83% compared to an economy wide average of 24%). Asked what would happen if there was a 30% decline in world prices of garments, it suggested that the volume of garment exports would go down by more than half because of reduced profitability. This would lead to a decline in women's wages, particularly affecting women with low or medium levels of education who make up the majority of the garment work force.

Gender Equality and Economic Growth: Competing Hypotheses

A final set of studies, which take a macro-level approach to gender analysis, are based on cross-country and, in some cases, time series comparisons. Their findings have been somewhat varied and often conflicting. Some suggest a positive relationship between gender inequality and economic growth. Seguino, for example, found that gender inequality in wages led to higher levels of economic growth while another study

A study using data from 99 countries for 1960 and 1990 found that gender inequalities had a significant negative impact on economic growth.

found that high levels of gender inequality in secondary education had a similar effect. On the other hand, Dollar and Gatti found that: (a) gender equality in education and legal rights led to an increase in per capita economic growth; and (b) increases in per capita GNP led to increases in equality for women. Similarly, a study found that gender inequalities had a significant negative impact on economic growth (*see box 2.7*).

Box 2.7 Negative Impacts of Gender Inequalities on Economic Growth

A study using data from 99 countries for 1960 and 1990 found that gender inequalities had a significant negative impact on economic growth. This was particularly so in South Asia and sub-Saharan Africa, the two poorest regions in the world. Drawing on these findings, the 1998 Status of Poverty in Africa report – which focused on gender, growth and poverty reduction – concluded that sub-Saharan Africa could have added several percentage points to its annual per capita growth rates if it had increased female education relative to male (0.5%), and increased women's employment in the formal sector (0.3%) to the levels prevailing in East Asia.

There are various reasons for these apparently contradictory findings. Firstly, there is a differential use of cross-sectional versus time-series data and different time periods. Country-based cross-sectionals tend to average out important country level differences and may lead to false 'similarities' between different countries. Secondly, the studies use somewhat different measures of gender inequality. For example, most focus on gender equalities in education while Dollar and Gatti also look at life expectancy and 'rules and conventions' relating to gender equality. Seguino, on the other hand, focuses on wage inequality. There is also a difference in country coverage. Dollar and Gatti focus on rich developed countries and poor developing countries while Seguino focuses on middle-income, semi-industrialised countries with a high reliance on export-led growth. Bearing these caveats in mind, a more detailed account is given below of Dollar and Gatti, who suggest a (qualified) synergy, and of Seguino as an example of a study that suggests a trade-off between gender equality and economic growth.

a. The 'positive synergy' hypothesis

The study by Dollar and Gatti is one of the few of its kind that explores both the effects of gender inequality on economic growth and, conversely, the effects of economic growth on gender inequality. It also includes a measure of gender equality of rights and looks at social as well as economic variables. It found that:

* Economic growth only affected gender inequality when countries moved from lower middle income to higher income levels;

* Muslim and Hindu majority populations had higher levels of gender inequality for most of the measures used; and

* Japan had higher levels of gender inequality than other countries at similar levels of per capita GNP, except in relation to secondary education.

A second set of findings found that female educational attainment – mainly measured by secondary education – had a positive effect on economic growth. The effects of both male and female education on per capita income were low for less developed countries where female secondary attainment covered less than 10 per cent of the population. Once countries had achieved a certain level of female education, however, an increase of 1 per cent in the share of women with secondary school education implied a 0.3 per cent increase in per capita income. The authors suggest that the absence of a relationship between gender equality in education and economic growth in poor, primarily agrarian economies is due to the limited returns that female secondary education brings. There is little reason to invest in it if men have preferred access to types of employment for which secondary education is a qualification.

Certain aspects of the study will be returned to in the course of the discussion in the rest of this book:

1. Gender equality has a positive effect on per capita economic

Once countries had achieved a certain level of female education ... an increase of 1 per cent in the share of women with secondary school education implied a 0.3 per cent increase in per capita income.

The range of rights adopted and implemented by a society will reflect the value it gives to the 'human' dimension of development, and the translation of these rights from formal to 'real' will require social and economic rights and political will as much as economic growth.

growth once a certain stage of development has been reached. Thus the growth-based rationale for reducing the gender gap in education in poorer countries is in terms of long-run rather than immediate returns.

2. Regional as well as religious differences are important sources of variation in the relationships between gender equality and economic growth.

3. While the focus on education as a measure of inequality reflects the increasing importance given to 'human capital' in the international development agenda, 'capital' can also include material and financial resources and social relationships and networks. Gender inequalities in access to credit, land, wages, capital equipment and trade networks may be more relevant for economic growth in poorer countries than inequalities in education or even formal rights.

4. It is crucial to distinguish between intrinsic and instrumental arguments for policies relating to gender inequality (*see box 2.8*).

> **Box 2.8 The Intrinsic Case for Rights**
>
> The recent emergence of a 'rights-based' approach to development may explain why measures of women's political and civil rights are found in Dollar and Gatti's analysis and why this is being linked to economic growth. Economic growth may, as it suggests, be facilitated by the growth of civil and political rights. However, the case for rights that promote gender equality rests on intrinsic, rather than instrumental, grounds. The range of rights adopted and implemented by a society will reflect the value it gives to the 'human' dimension of development, and the translation of these rights from formal to 'real' will require social and economic rights and political will as much as economic growth.

b. The trade-off hypothesis

Seguino's study focused on the relationship between gender inequality and economic growth in the context of export-

oriented industrialisation. It looked at the relationship between economic growth and gender inequality in wages. Her sample was drawn from lower and middle-income countries (as defined by the 1995 *World Development Report*).

Women on a cosmetic industry assembly line in Seoul, Republic of Korea
INTERNATIONAL LABOUR ORGANIZATION

The findings from the cross-country analysis suggested that, along with levels of human capital and investment, inequality in male and female wages was positively associated with economic growth. A 10-point increase in the gap between male and female returns per year of secondary education was seen to raise GDP growth by .10 per cent. Or to put it another way, 4 percentage points of the gap between the rate of GDP growth in the Republic of Korea (9.2%) and Costa Rica (3.9%) between 1985 and 1989 could be explained by the gender wage gap. The results from the time-varying country specific analysis confirm the significance of investment as well as human capital, but suggest that female educational attainment has a more significant effect than male. The wage gap variables remain significant. Gender disparities in wages were found to increase levels of investment. The study concludes that gender inequality in returns to labour have led to higher rates of growth in countries that have relied on export-oriented industrialisation.

Seguino notes that the gender disparities in earnings are only partly related to a country's GNP. Other factors that play a role include policy regimes as well as the 'gender regimes' prevailing in different countries. It is striking that of the Asian countries for which she provides data, three of the four fast-growing 'miracle' economies, all East Asian, report the largest gender disparities in earnings (Republic of Korea, Singapore and Taiwan). However, it also suggests that economic growth is likely to be higher in this set of countries if investments in female education co-exist with greater gender disparities in wages.

Overall, Dollar and Gatti's findings provide support for gender equality on 'efficiency' grounds and for greater economic growth on equity grounds. Seguino's findings suggest that there may be a trade-off between gender equality and economic growth due to the intensified competition unleashed by globalisation. However, the findings clearly need to be explored further through more detailed analysis at the country level.

Conclusion

This chapter has touched on some theoretical and empirical attempts to explore the relevance of gender to macroeconomic analysis and policy. A number of the studies have drawn attention to 'institutions' as a concept for understanding gender inequality. Certain recurring themes include:

1. the role of norms and customs in shaping relationships in the household and the behaviour of its members;

2. unequal roles, responsibilities and resources in the household, leading to different constraints on men's and women's responses and behaviour;

3. the significance of women's unpaid work for their capacity to respond to market signals; and

4. the existence of gender discrimination in markets as well as in systems of public provision and hence the relevance of factors outside the household in shaping gender inequality.

Most of these studies give a central place to the household and family in understanding gender inequality. However, while many note discriminatory provisions in the legal system and state provision, they vary in the degree of attention paid to discrimination in the market place. Orthodox economists, particularly neo-liberals, tend to see market forces as impersonal aggregations of numerous individual activities. At the other end of the spectrum, feminist political economists insist that markets be recognised as social institutions in which social networks and norms have as important a role to play as economic agency and incentives.

An institutional focus suggests a very different approach to the analysis of gender inequality than an individualistic one. This can be illustrated by comparing the explanations that the authors of the two studies discussed in the last section give for their findings on gender inequality. Dollar and Gatti interpret the fact that religion features as statistically significant in explaining variations in gender inequality across countries as showing the importance of different 'cultural preferences'. They conclude that "those who control resources in the society have a preference for gender inequality that they are willing to pay for". However, this does not take account of either the extent to which individuals who do not share these 'cultural preferences' can challenge them or of the division between those who have the power to express and enforce their preferences socially and those who pay the price.

Seguino, on the other hand, concludes that the systemic nature of gender inequalities reflect how institutions are structured in different countries. She suggests that gender disparity in wages is likely to have more positive effects on growth in countries with patriarchal gender systems because their institutions "reinforce the internalisation of social norms that favour men, reducing political resistance and therefore the costliness of gender inequality".

It is clear from the studies in this chapter that gender inequality is relevant in a range of contexts and that it varies across them. These variations reflect a number of different factors, including strategies for achieving growth, levels of per capita GNP, various forms of public policy (particularly those directly related to gender equality) and investments in human capital. In addition, the analysis suggests that institutions – and more specifically their patriarchal construction – are a particularly important factor. This is explored in the next chapter.

[F]eminist political economists insist that markets be recognised as social institutions in which social networks and norms have as important a role to play as economic agency and incentives.

3. The Geography of Gender Inequality

Introduction

A great deal of human behaviour is not the result of individual preferences. Rather, it is governed by institutional rules, norms and conventions that have powerful material effects on people's lives. Institutions have been defined as the 'rules of the game' in a society. These rules may be written or unwritten, explicit or implicit, codified in law, mandated by policy, sanctified by religion, upheld by convention or embodied in the standards of family, community and society. They play a powerful role in shaping human behaviour, in terms of both what is permitted and what is prohibited. In the economy, they:

a) influence the gender division of labour between production and reproduction in different parts of the world; and

b) give rise to distinctive regional patterns in labour force participation and economic activity by women and men.

While institutions themselves are abstract concepts, they take concrete form in organisations – the 'teams' that play the game. There are four key categories of institutions, each with a particular domain (or area of influence) in society and each associated with a different set of organisations and groups. These are states, markets, civil society/community, and kinship/family (*see box 3.1*).

These institutions govern the processes of production, reproduction and distribution in a society. The way they are set up varies by level of economic development, structure of economy and extent of commodification (i.e. the extent to which a market value has been given to previously non-commercial goods and services). In terms of the productive pyramid shown in Fig. 2.1, there are likely to be differences across the world in the extent both of formal markets and state regulation and of subsistence production.

A great deal of human behaviour is not the result of individual preferences. Rather, it is governed by institutional rules, norms and conventions ...

Four key categories of institutions in society are: states, markets, civil society/ community and kinship/family.

Box 3.1 Key Categories of Institutions in Society

States: The state is responsible for the overall governance of society. It enforces the rules and procedures that regulate how the different institutional domains interact. Access to state resources, including employment, is through its legislation, policies and regulations. Examples of state organisations include those associated with the bureaucracy, the police, the legislature, the judiciary and local government.

Markets: Markets are organised around a commercial logic – the maximisation of profit – and resources are exchanged on the basis of contract-based entitlements. Market-based organisations include firms, commercial farms, micro-enterprises, trade networks and multinational corporations.

Civil society/community: Civil society refers to a range of associations whose members pursue a variety of interests. The membership and goals are usually 'chosen', and members determine how resources and responsibilities will be distributed on the basis of some agreed set of principles. Such organisations include trade unions, non-governmental organisations (NGOs) and professional associations. Community is used here to refer to associations and groups based on what sociologists call 'primordial' ties. Membership of these groups is ascribed rather than chosen. Individuals' access to their resources depends on how they are positioned in the group by these ascribed identities. Examples of community include caste, tribe and patron-client relationships.

Kinship/family: Kinship and family refer to forms of social organisation, including lineages and clans, that are based on descent, marriage and various forms of adoption or fostering. One of the key organisations associated with kinship and family is 'the household', usually based on shared residence and/or shared budgets. Elson calls households the site par excellence of 'provisioning', that is, "the activity of supplying people with what they need to thrive, including care and concern as well as material goods".

Institutions provide a structure, and hence a degree of stability, to everyday life. They reduce uncertainty, make certain forms of behaviour more predictable and allow individuals to co-operate with others to produce results that they would not be able to achieve on their own. At the same time, however – and whatever their official ideologies – institutions rarely operate in egalitarian ways. Rather, they tend to support hierarchical relationships organised around:

a) inequalities of ownership or access to the means of production (land, capital, finance, equipment);

b) achieved or acquired attributes (education, skills, contacts); and

c) various socially-ascribed attributes (gender, age, caste, etc.).

A variety of explanations and justifications are given for these hierarchies, including merit, capacity, aptitude, biology, nature or divine will. Institutions' rules of access – and exclusion – also intersect and overlap (*see box 3.2*).

Society's institutional framework – its rules, norms, beliefs and practices – means that individuals and social groups not only start from different places, but also have different opportunities to improve their situation in the course of their lives.

Box 3.2 Intersecting Inequalities and the State

Institutional inequalities in one area can be offset or worsened by access or exclusion in another. For example, inequalities in a community on the basis of caste, race or gender can be countered by anti-discrimination laws in employment or by the ability of subordinate groups to take advantage of new opportunities in the market place. On the other hand, prejudice by employers or exclusionary practices by trade unions and professional associations can make these inequalities worse. Society's institutional framework – its rules, norms, beliefs and practices – means that individuals and social groups not only start from different places, but also have different opportunities to improve their situation in the course of their lives. Given its importance in the overall governance of society, the state can play a critical role in maintaining, reinforcing or countering inequalities in other domains.

Gender inequality ... is one of the most pervasive forms of inequality ... not just because it is present in most societies, but also because it cuts across other forms of inequality.

Institutions and Gender Inequality

Gender inequality, the main focus of this book, is one of the most pervasive forms of inequality. This is not just because it is present in most societies, but also because it cuts across other forms of inequality (*see introduction to Chapter 1*). It is constructed through both:

* the formal laws and statutes that make up the official ideologies of a society and its institutions; and

* the unwritten norms and shared understandings that help shape everyday behaviour in the real world.

Although gender inequality is thus found throughout society, institutional analyses of it generally start by looking at kinship and family. This is because these are the primary forms of organisation that are inherently gendered. Women's and men's roles and responsibilities in the domestic domain also reveal how the wider society views their natures and capabilities and hence constructs gender difference and inequality. In addition, a great deal of productive, as well as reproductive, activity is organised through kinship and family. This is particularly the case among the poor in poorer parts of the world. Consequently, even when women and men participate in the wider economy, their participation is partly structured by relations in the household.

Families and kinship are different from other institutions because of the nature of the relationships within them. These are usually based on intimate ties of blood, marriage and adoption (in contrast to the more impersonal relationships of contract and statute found in the market and state). They are also generally 'gender-ascriptive'. In other words, to be a husband, wife, brother or daughter is to be a male or a female. In most societies, women are associated with the functions of care and maintenance. These include bearing and rearing children and the wider range of activities necessary to the survival and well-being of family members on a daily basis. While men may participate in some of these activities, particularly in training boys 'how to be men' or sharing in certain household chores, they tend to have far less involvement than women.

Women thus play a key role in unpaid processes of social

reproduction (i.e. reproducing society's human resources on a daily and intergenerational basis). They may also predominate when these activities are shifted into the market, for example, nursing, teaching and social work. However, the part they play in production and accumulation – and the form that their involvement takes – varies considerably across cultures. Different rules, norms and values govern the gender division of labour and the gender distribution of resources, responsibilities, agency and power. These are critical elements for understanding the nature of gender inequality in different societies. Ideas and beliefs about gender in the domestic sphere often get reproduced in other social relations, either consciously as gender discrimination or unconsciously as gender bias. Rather than being impersonal, state or market institutions thus become 'bearers of gender'. They position women and men unequally in access to resources and assign them unequal value in the public domain.

Regional Perspectives on Gender Inequality

Gender inequality varies at the regional level, suggesting a 'geography' of gender. This geography reflects systematic regional differences in:

a) the institutions of kinship and family;

b) the household patterns they have given rise to; and

c) the associated gender division of resources and responsibilities.

These have in turn given rise to regional differences in the gender division of labour between production and reproduction, paid and unpaid work, and the domestic and public domains.

Regional differences mean not only that women and men participate in their national economies differently from each other, but also that these differences are not uniform across the world. Two factors are particularly important for the extent to which women play a role in the wider economy, the scope of their agency and their access to socially valued resources:

1. how corporate the unit is around which the household economy is organised (i.e. the extent to which resources and efforts are managed and allocated on a joint basis); and

[The] different rules, norms and values [that] govern the gender division of labour and the gender distribution of resources, responsibilities, agency and power ... are critical elements for understanding the nature of gender inequality in different societies.

There are a range of household types associated with distinct 'regional patriarchies'. These have particular patterns of land inheritance, marital practices, economic activity and welfare outcomes.

2. how rigid the 'public-private' divide is, and hence women's degree of public mobility and opportunities for direct economic participation.

Research from a variety of social science disciplines suggests that there are a range of household types associated with distinct 'regional patriarchies'. These have particular patterns of land inheritance, marital practices, economic activity and welfare outcomes.

Asia

Despite variations in women's public mobility and labour force participation across the region, 'Asian' households are generally organised along corporate lines, usually centred on the conjugal relationship.

Western Asia, South Asia and East Asia

The most marked forms of gender inequality in the region are associated with regimes of extreme forms of patriarchy. These include the belt stretching from North Africa and western Asia across the northern plains of South Asia, including Bangladesh and Pakistan. They also take in the countries of East Asia – China, Japan, Republic of Korea and Taiwan. These countries clearly have widely differing economies, histories, cultures and religions. However, they have certain historical similarities in how family, kinship and gender relations are organised and in patterns of female economic activity.

Kinship structures in these regions are predominantly patrilineal: descent is traced and property transmitted through the male members. Marriage tends to be exogamous and patrilocal: women marry outside their kin and often outside their village community, leaving their own homes at marriage to join their husband's family. Households are organised along highly corporate lines, with strong conjugal bonds and cultural rules that emphasise male responsibility for protecting and provisioning women and children. Household resources and income are pooled under the management and control of the male patriarch. The payment of dowry by the bride's family to the groom is the norm in the northern plains of India, though not necessarily elsewhere in East or western Asia.

Female chastity is emphasised (with severe penalties for any transgression). This is considered essential to ensure that property is transmitted based on biological fatherhood. Female sexuality is controlled through a strong public-private divide, with women secluded in the private domain. While the practice of 'purdah' is usually associated with Muslim societies, female seclusion based on norms of honour and shame is also practiced by Hindus, particularly the upper castes. Restrictions on female mobility, patrilineal inheritance and patrilocal marital practices have meant the economic devaluation of women and their overall dependence on men in much of this region. 'Son preference' is also marked.

Boserup pointed to the extremely low percentages of women in agriculture and trade in western Asia, North Africa and Pakistan, which she called 'male farming systems'. Female family labour did not exceed 15 per cent of the total agricultural labour force (with the exception of Algeria, Tunisia and Turkey). Women made up less than 10 per cent of the labour force in trade in South and western Asia, and less than one-

Women in agriculture, Jordan

INTERNATIONAL LABOUR ORGANIZATION

Somewhat less rigid gender relations are found in the way kinship and family are organised in South-East Asia ... and, to some extent, the southern states of India and Sri Lanka.

third in East Asia and areas of Chinese influence (Hong Kong, Singapore, Republic of Korea and Taiwan). In China, too, prior to the revolution, only 7 per cent of the Chinese labour force in trade were women. However, Boserup also noted variations to the pattern within the region. In South Asia, for example, women's participation in trade varied from 2–6 per cent in Bangladesh, the northern plains of India and Pakistan to around 17 per cent in the southern states of India.

South-East Asia

Somewhat less rigid gender relations are found in the way kinship and family are organised in South-East Asia (Burma, Cambodia, Indonesia, Lao PDR, Malaysia, the Philippines, Thailand and Vietnam) and, to some extent, the southern states of India and Sri Lanka. The structure of households is still along corporate lines, but with important differences. For example, a child is considered equally related to both its parents and a person's most important social grouping comprises relatives from both sides. Son preference is moderate or non-existent.

There are more cases of women as well as men being able to inherit property, and a greater incidence of matrilineal kinship, where property and descent are traced through women. While income is likely to be pooled in these households, women are often responsible for managing the household budget. A greater number of newly married couples set up their own households and more wives retain links with their natal families. The exchange of wealth at marriage tends to be reciprocal between the families of bride and groom, or else greater on the part of the latter in the form of 'bride-wealth'. Most South-East Asian countries have traditionally been more tolerant of sexual freedom for both women and men, although colonialism brought in more restrictions, particularly for women.

Boserup noted that female family labour made up around 50 per cent of the total agricultural force in Thailand and 75 per cent in Cambodia, both areas of female farming. Women also made up around half of the labour force engaged in trade and commerce in Burma, Cambodia, Lao PDR, the Philippines, Thailand and Vietnam (*see box 3.3*).

> ### Box 3.3 Gender Relations in Vietnam
>
> Despite the strong influence of Confucianism among the ruling elite in pre-revolutionary Vietnam, most rural women worked daily in the fields and were largely responsible for trade. Vietnamese women were not only involved in managing the household budget, but also in direct production such as transplanting rice and, importantly, in marketing the produce. Husbands could not dispose of harvested rice without their wives' consent. Although there was patrilocal-patrilineal marriage and some evidence of son preference, women were not regarded as 'helpers to men' but as their equals.

However, the absence of any marked restrictions on women's mobility, and some degree of symmetry in the division of labour in the household, should not be taken to imply an absence of gender inequality in general in these societies. For example, even though Filipino women may have high status relative to women in some other countries, this needs to be assessed in relation to Filipino men to be meaningful. It should also be noted that it is in the relatively more egalitarian regimes of South-East Asia – Thailand and the Philippines – that sex tourism has emerged as a key source of income for women. Clearly, labour markets continue to reproduce gender disadvantage. Bearing this in mind, it is still clear that gender regimes in this part of the world do not result in the very marked gender inequalities in survival and well-being which, as shown in the next chapter, continue to characterise regions marked by 'extreme' patriarchy.

Sub-Saharan Africa

Research on household arrangements in sub-Saharan Africa point to the wide prevalence of highly complex, lineage-based homesteads with considerable gender segmentation. Women and men from the same homestead may work in separate groups, in different economic crops or on separate fields, and spouses may maintain individual accounting units. This presents a different challenge to mainstream economic portrayals

Along with [some] similarities there are important differences in the social organisation of kinship and gender relations across the African sub-continent, and even in the same country.

of the household (as a unified entity whose members pool and share their resources in order to maximise their joint welfare) to that posed elsewhere. Where households are organised on a corporate basis, as described earlier, the challenge has consisted of noting the existence of gender and other inequalities in the distribution of household welfare. There, certain members are systematically discriminated against in the distribution of the gains to household production. Here, however, household goods and incomes are generally not even meant to be held in common. Instead, cultural ideas and practices require that male and female income and resources belong to different spheres and are intended for different uses. Hence the need for a complex set of transactions in the household through which labour and incomes are used and needs met.

Much of sub-Saharan Africa is patrilineal. Women's access to land is usually through usufructuary rights (i.e. rights to farm the land and profit from the produce but not to ownership) through their husband's lineage group. Since women's obligations to the family include food provisioning and caring for their children, they are granted this access to enable them to carry out these responsibilities. Female seclusion is uncommon, although it does occur among some communities such as the Muslim Hausa in Nigeria. However, such seclusion occurs in segmented households and Hausa women retain considerable economic autonomy. They manage their own enterprises and engage in 'internal market' transactions with their husbands. Marriage in the region usually involves the contractual payment of bride-wealth to the lineage of the woman by the husband's family.

As might be expected, along with these similarities there are important differences in the social organisation of kinship and gender relations across the African sub-continent, and even in the same country. The organisation of gender relations in Uganda varies from region to region, but is generally strongly patrilineal and patriarchal structures predominate, with women's economic autonomy and independent access to land being relatively more constrained than elsewhere in East Africa. Under customary law and practice in Uganda, women were minors without adult legal status or rights. In general, in much of eastern and southern Africa, women's labour contribution tends to be subsumed in the cultivation of 'household fields' over which men have ultimate control. However, studies from Zambia report evidence of jointly managed fields as well as fields individually managed by both sexes.

In parts of West Africa on the other hand (e.g. Burkina Faso, the Gambia, Ghana and Nigeria), women generally have usufruct rights to separate holdings through their husband's lineage. Both women and junior men also provide labour on household fields that are controlled by the compound head. These domestic groups are characterised by strong lineage ties and weak conjugal ties. Moreover, women enjoy direct access to land in matrilineal areas, many of which are also in West Africa (including Côte d'Ivoire, southern Ghana, Malawi and Zambia), as well as in areas of Muslim influence. Matrilineality means married women are able to retain links with their families of origin and gain access to land as members of their own lineage groups. As a result, their obligations are not limited to the conjugal unit but extend to natal family networks.

In addition, there are more polygamous marriages in West and central Africa (with over 40 per cent of currently married women in such unions). The equivalent figures are 20–30 per cent in East Africa and 20 per cent or less in southern Africa. Polygamy contributes to a pattern of separate (rather than pooled) spousal budgets, assets and income flows and may include separate living arrangements. Women exercise considerable economic agency in the family structure and are not dependent on their husbands in the way that they are in much of South Asia.

Latin America and the Caribbean

Countries in Latin America and the Caribbean have experienced very different histories and patterns of economic development within three broad cultural traditions: indigenous, Hispanic and Afro-Caribbean. This has led to considerable diversity in their household arrangements. Nevertheless, many of the countries share certain features in common, including the intersection of colonialism and slavery, and large urban populations (around 70 per cent).

The region belongs to the weaker corporate end of the spectrum. The Spanish and Portuguese colonisers introduced their own version of the public-private divide into Latin America,

Women enjoy direct access to land in matrilineal areas, many of which are also in West Africa ..., as well as in areas of Muslim influence.

57

Boserup noted that women's economic activity in the public domain varied across the [Latin American and Caribbean] region. There were higher rates in populations with a strong African or Asian presence than in countries on the Atlantic coast where the Spanish influence is stronger.

associating men with the *calle* (street) and women with the *casa* (home). However, this division is far stronger among the upper classes in areas with Hispanic, and hence Roman Catholic, influence. It is far less often found among the black and indigenous populations. While legal marriage may be the social ideal, as well as the norm in many parts of the region, there is a high incidence of consensual or visiting unions. In some areas of Latin America, this appears to reflect partly indigenous antecedents and partly the precariousness of marriage when male mobility is an integral part of economic strategies. In the Caribbean, it reflects the impact of slavery, which weakened ties between children and their fathers as slave children became the property of their mother's owner. One result of this is a high number of female-headed households, as well as complex extended households made up of children from different unions.

Boserup noted that women's economic activity in the public domain varied across the region. There were higher rates in populations with a strong African or Asian presence than in countries on the Atlantic coast where the Spanish influence is stronger. The region as a whole is characterised by low levels of female economic activity in rural areas and higher levels in urban areas. Women tend to be more active in agriculture in the Caribbean region, where there are more smallholder farms, than in Latin America. Large-scale plantation agriculture, and the fact that commoditisation and mechanisation have gone further in Latin American agriculture than elsewhere in the Third World, explain why it is less significant as a source of overall as well as of female employment. However, women are active in trade throughout the region and also dominate in the flows of migration into urban areas. This is an indication of the lack of strict restrictions on women's mobility.

Updating the Geography of Gender

There have been significant changes since the period that informed Boserup's analysis, including:

* the oil shocks of the 1970s and subsequent debt crisis and recession;

* the structural adjustment programmes (SAPs) of the 1980s;

* the collapse of some socialist societies and the managed transition to the market economy of others; and

* the acceleration of the forces of economic deregulation, liberalisation and globalisation.

Most economies today are far more oriented to the market, far more open to international competition and far more integrated on a global basis than they were in the 1960s. The rest of this chapter looks at the extent to which changes in the wider economic environment have influenced the gender division of labour in different regions and modified the geography of gender described above.

Most economies today are far more oriented to the market, far more open to international competition and far more integrated on a global basis than they were in the 1960s.

Globalisation and the rise of flexible labour markets

Two factors have been particularly significant in driving the pace of globalisation:

* the changing technology of transport and telecommunications, which served to compress time and space across the world; and

* the dismantling of the regulatory frameworks that had provided some degree of national stability in markets for labour and capital in the post-war decades.

There has been a massive increase in world trade flows. Trade now accounts for 45 per cent of world Gross National Product (GNP) compared to 25 per cent in 1970. Much of this increase is in manufacturing, which accounts for 74 per cent of world merchandise exports (compared to 59 per cent in 1984). Developing countries have performed well in this sector. The share of manufactured goods in developing country exports tripled between 1970 and 1990 from 20 to 60 per cent. Exports in labour-intensive manufacturing have grown particularly rapidly, the most important and fastest growing being electronic components and garments. These accounted respectively for 10 and 6 per cent of total developing country exports in 1990–91.

There has also been a dramatic increase in the inter-

Different forms of labour, such as outworking, contract work, casual labour, part-time work and home-based work have been replacing regular, full-time wage labour.

national mobility of capital. Capital flows in the industrial countries rose from around 5 per cent of Gross Domestic Product (GDP) in the early 1970s to around 10 per cent in the early 1990s. The equivalent figures for transitional and developing countries were 7 and 9 per cent. Previously, transactions between countries occurred mainly in the form of trade in goods. Today, however, it is possible for individuals and firms to invest freely in foreign exchange and financial markets. This increased movement of capital between countries is often motivated by short-term opportunities to gain from more favourable interest or exchange rates. As recent crises in East Asia and Latin America have demonstrated, economies are extremely vulnerable to the ups and downs of this global market.

However, the movement of labour has not been deregulated to the same degree. On the contrary, there have been increasing restrictions on the mobility of unskilled labour, particularly by the developed countries. Migration per 1,000 of population declined during this period from around 6.5 to 4.5 in the industrialised countries and remained static at around one elsewhere (though this does not take account of illegal labour movements, particularly increasing trafficking in women).

At the same time, within national economies, labour markets have become increasingly 'informalised' and social protection has been eroded. Different forms of labour, such as outworking, contract work, casual labour, part-time work and home-based work have been replacing regular, full-time wage labour. These changes have largely affected the organised labour force in industrialised countries and the small minority in formal labour in poorer countries. The overwhelming majority of the working population in these poorer countries is still engaged in livelihood strategies outside the formal, protected economy. These strategies include a diverse set of activities, contractual arrangements and working conditions. There is consequently a social hierarchy to the labour market, depicted in Fig. 3.1, that loosely overlaps with the economic pyramid depicted in Fig. 2.1.

The occupational hierarchy in the formal labour market consists of:

* An elite group of wealthy industrialists, financiers, entrepreneurs, etc. at the pinnacle. They make the 'rules of the

Figure 3.1: Social Hierarchy of Livelihoods

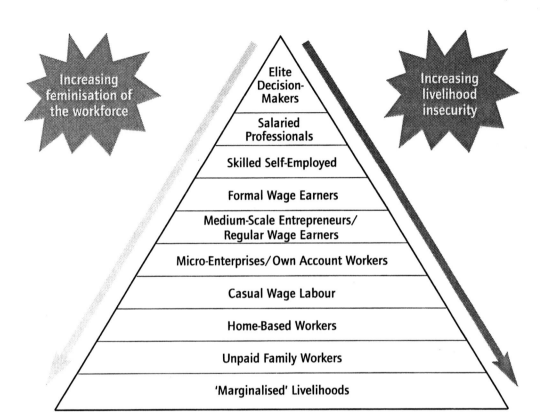

game' in their society, are wealthy enough to ensure their own security and often take advantage of the growing global market in savings, pensions and insurance.

- Salaried and professional classes. They generally enjoy a considerable degree of job security and social status in the labour market.

- 'Core workers'. They are in full-time employment, often unionised and protected by state provision. Some may be unemployed but they may still have some security in the form of state unemployment assistance.

The elite is likely to be smaller and much less wealthy in the poorer countries than in the richer countries. The second and third groups also represent a far smaller proportion of the total

Comparing women's labour force participation around the globe is problematic, and the difficulty of capturing often irregular, casual forms of work in the informal economy is compounded by the different definitions used in measurement.

work force in developing countries than in Organisation for Economic Cooperation and Development (OECD) countries. They are likely to have shrunk even further with the downsizing of the public sector in the wake of SAPs.

Meanwhile, the informalised workforce – which has little stability of work, social security provision or state regulation – has expanded. It makes up more than 80 per cent in low-income countries and around 40 per cent in middle-income countries. The informal economy has its own hierarchy, distinguishing those with some degree of security in their lives from those without any:

* Owners of some land or capital. They are in a position to hire labour on their farms or in their enterprises.

* Waged workers in some form of regular employment. They often work in medium-sized enterprises, or on plantations or commercial farms.

* Own-account workers, with little or no capital. They rely on their own or family labour.

* Casual labourers and home-based workers. They are either unpaid family workers or disguised wage workers who earn a fraction of their directly employed counterparts.

* A category of 'detached' labour. They eke out a living from various stigmatised occupations: prostitution, pimping, recycling trash, picking pockets, begging and so on. They not only lack any formal ties to the state, pension and insurance markets, but may also have lost their place in kin or community structures.

Gender and labour force participation in the 1980s and 1990s

Comparing women's labour force participation around the globe is problematic, and the difficulty of capturing often irregular, casual forms of work in the informal economy is compounded by the different definitions used in measurement. The discussion here uses the conventional definition (i.e. activities done for pay or profit). While this does not fully capture women's contribution to the economy, nor show what is happening in the unpaid economy, it reveals the restrictions

Table 3.1: Estimated Economic Activity Rate of Women and Female Percentage of the Labour Force

	Estimated economic activity rate of women aged 15 years and over (%)		Female % of labour force	
	1970	1990	1980	1999
MIDDLE EAST/ NORTH AFRICA				
Morocco	12	19	33.5	34.7
Egypt	6	9	26.5	30.1
Algeria	4	8	21.4	27
Kuwait	11	24	13.1	31.3
Oman	6	9	6.2	16.4
Saudi Arabia	5	9	7.6	15.5
UAE	9	18	5.1	14.5
Yemen, Rep. of	6	10	32.5	28
SOUTH ASIA				
India	38	29	33.7	32.2
Bangladesh	5	7	42.3	42.3
Pakistan	9	13	22.7	28.1
Nepal	47	43	38.8	40.5
Sri Lanka	31	29	26.9	36.4
EAST ASIA				
Taiwan				
Rep. of Korea	38	40	38.7	41.2
Dem. People's Rep. of Korea	65	64	44.8	43.3
China	67	70	43.2	45.2
Japan	51	46	37.9	41.3
SOUTH EAST ASIA				
Thailand	75	68	47.4	46.3
Malaysia	37	44	33.7	37.7
Indonesia	36	37	35.2	40.6
Lao People's Dem. Rep.	80	71		
Vietnam	71	70	48.1	49
Philippines	42	36	35	37.7
Cambodia	59	52	55.4	51.8
WEST AFRICA				
Ghana	59	51	51	50.5
Cameroon	51	41	36.8	37.9
Burkina Faso	85	77	47.6	46.5
Côte d'Ivoire	64	48	32.2	33.3
Mali	17	16	46.7	46.2
Gambia	65	58	44.8	45
Senegal	60	53	42.2	42.6

Table 3.1: Estimated Economic Activity Rate of Women and Female Percentage of the Labour Force (continued)

	Estimated economic activity rate of women aged 15 years and over (%)		Female % of labour force	
	1970	1990	1980	1999
EAST AFRICA				
Tanzania	89	77	49.8	49.2
Kenya	65	58	46	46.1
Uganda	68	62	47.9	47.6
CARIBBEAN				
Jamaica	58	68	46.3	46.2
Barbados	43	61		
Trinidad and Tobago	33	34	31.4	34
Guyana	22	28		
LATIN AMERICA				
Brazil	23	30	28.4	35.4
Mexico	18	30	26.9	32.9
Argentina	27	28	27.6	32.7
Chile	22	29	26.3	33.2
Peru	20	25	23.9	31
COMMONWEALTH (OTHER)				
UK	41	46	38.9	43.9
Australia	37	46	36.8	43.5
New Zealand	33	40	34.3	44.8
Canada	37	49	39.5	45.6
EAST ASIA & PACIFIC			42.5	44.4
EUROPE & CENTRAL ASIA			46.7	46.2
LATIN AMERICA & CARIBBEAN			27.8	34.6
MIDDLE EAST & N.AFRICA			23.8	27.3
SOUTH ASIA			33.8	33.3
SUB SAHARAN AFRICA			42.3	42.2
EUROPE EMU			36.7	41.2

Source: *The World's Women 1970–1990: Trends and Statistics*   Source: *2001 World Development Indicators*

that women face in terms of paid work relative to men and how these vary across the world. It also has something important to say about the pattern of women's work in recent decades and the extent to which the geography of gender difference in labour market participation has changed from that observed by Boserup.

The most striking features of labour force participation patterns in the last few decades are: (a) the rise in the percentage of women in the labour force; and (b) the accompanying increase in their share of overall employment. In almost every region, there are now many more women involved in the visible sectors of the economy (*see Table 3.1*). In addition, women's participation has increased faster than men's in almost every region except Africa, where it was already high. With a stagnating or, in some cases, decreasing male labour force, gender differences in labour force participation have shrunk in many regions.

These changes reflect a number of factors:

* Demographic transition (i.e. the change from high to low rates of births and deaths) in most regions and a decline in fertility rates have allowed many more women to go out to work.

* The increasing enrolment of young men in secondary and tertiary education, as well as the growing availability of pensions for older men, partly explain diminishing male participation.

* The changing nature of labour markets has resulted in what can be described as a 'double feminisation' of the labour force internationally. Women have increased their share of employment while employment itself has started to take on some of the 'informalised' characteristics of work conventionally associated with women.

Another major change in patterns of work in recent decades has been in the distribution of the labour force between different sectors of the economy. Only in South Asia and sub-Saharan Africa has female labour remained largely concentrated in the agricultural sector. East and South-East Asian countries, by contrast, are characterised by high levels of female labour force participation and by a more even distribution of female labour across agriculture, industry and services (*see Table 3.2*). Women made up over a third of the labour in each sector during 1970–1990, with their representation increasing in 'services' over this period. There is of course variation across the region (*see box 3.4*).

[W]omen's [labour force] participation has increased faster than men's in almost every region except Africa, where it was already high.

Table 3.2: Employment by Economic Activity

	Agriculture				Industry				Services			
	Percentage of male labour force		Percentage of female labour force		Percentage of male labour force		Percentage of female labour force		Percentage of male labour force		Percentage of female labour force	
	1980	1996-98	1980	1996-98	1980	1996-98	1980	1996-98	1980	1996-98	1980	1996-98
MIDDLE EAST/ NORTH AFRICA												
Morocco	48		72		23		14		29		14	
Egypt	45		10		21		13		33		69	
Algeria	27		69		33		6		40		25	
Kuwait	2		0		36		3		62		97	
Oman	52		24		21		33		27		43	
Saudi Arabia	45		25		17		5		39		70	
UAE	5		0		40		7		55		93	
Yemen, Rep.	60		98		19		1		21		1	
SOUTH ASIA												
India	63		83		15		9		22		8	
Bangladesh	67	54	81	78	5	11	14	8	29	34	5	11
Pakistan		41		66		20		11		39		23
Nepal	91		98		1		0		8		2	
Sri Lanka	44	38	51	49	19	23	18	22	30	37	28	27
EAST ASIA												
Rep. of Korea	31	11	39	14	32	34	24	19	37	55	37	67
Dem. People's Rep. of Korea	39		52		37		20		24		28	
Japan	9	5	13	6	40	39	28	23	51	56	58	71

Table 3.2: Employment by Economic Activity (continued)

	Agriculture				Industry				Services			
	Percentage of male labour force		Percentage of female labour force		Percentage of male labour force		Percentage of female labour force		Percentage of male labour force		Percentage of female labour force	
	1980	1996-98	1980	1996-98	1980	1996-98	1980	1996-98	1980	1996-98	1980	1996-98
SOUTH EAST ASIA												
Morocco	48		72		23		14		29		14	
Thailand	68	52	74	50	13	19	8	16	20	29	18	34
Malaysia	34	21	44	15	26	34	20	28	40	46	36	57
Indonesia	57	41	54	42	13	21	13	16	29	39	33	42
Lao PDR	77		82		7		4		16		13	
Vietnam	71	70	75	71	16	12	10	9	13	18	15	20
Philippines	60	47	37	27	16	18	15	12	25	35	48	61
Cambodia	70		80		7		7		23		14	
WEST AFRICA												
Ghana	66		57		12		14		22		29	
Cameroon	65		87		11		2		24		11	
Burkina Faso	92		93		3		2		5		5	
Cote d' Ivoire	60		75		10		5		30		20	
Mali	86		92		2		1		12		7	
Gambia	78		93		10		3		13		5	
Senegal	74		90		9		2		17		8	
Nigeria	52		57		10		5		38		38	
EAST AFRICA												
Tanzania	80		92		7		2		13		7	
Kenya	23		25		24		9		53		65	
Uganda	84		91		6		2		10		8	
SOUTHERN AFRICA												
Zimbabwe	29		50		31		8		40		42	
Zambia	69		85		13		3		19		13	
Mozambique	72		97		14		1		14		2	
Malawi	78		96		10		1		12		3	

Table 3.2: Employment by Economic Activity (continued)

	Agriculture				Industry				Services			
	Percentage of male labour force		Percentage of female labour force		Percentage of male labour force		Percentage of female labour force		Percentage of male labour force		Percentage of female labour force	
	1980	1996-98	1980	1996-98	1980	1996-98	1980	1996-98	1980	1996-98	1980	1996-98
CARIBBEAN												
Jamaica	47	29	23	10	20	25	8	9	33	46	69	82
Trinidad and Tobago	11	11	9	3	44	37	21	13	45	52	70	83
LATIN AMERICA												
Brazil	34	27	25	20	30	27	13	10	36	46	67	70
Mexico		26		9		27		20		47		71
Argentina	17	2	3	0	40	33	18	12	44	65	79	88
Chile	22	19	3	5	27	31	16	14	51	49	81	82
Peru	45	7	25	3	20	27	14	11	35	66	61	86
COMMONWEALTH												
UK	4	2	1	1	48	38	23	13	49	60	76	86
Australia	8	6	4	4	39	31	16	11	53	64	79	86
New Zealand		11		6		33		13		56		81
Canada	7	5	3	2	37	32	16	11	56	63	81	87
EUROPE & C. ASIA	26	23	27	13	44		31	14	31		42	
LATIN AMERICA & CARIBBEAN			17			27				50		73
MIDDLE EAST & N.AFRICA	39		46		25		13		37		38	
SOUTH ASIA	64		83		14		10		23		8	
SUB-SAHARAN AFRICA	62		74		14		5		24		22	
EUROPE EMU		6		5		41		18		53		77

Source: 2001 World Development Indicators

Box 3.4 Variations in Women's Labour Force Participation in Asia

In Indonesia, there was an overall decline in national labour force participation, partly due to a restrictive time period for measuring economic activity and partly because the working age population was increasing over this period. However, female rural labour force participation continued to increase, outweighing these two factors. In rural areas, women's labour force participation declined slightly in agriculture but increased in manufacturing and trade. In Vietnam, too, rural households rely heavily on off-farm and self-employment to supplement earnings from farming. In the Philippines, female employment is high, with women making up 37 per cent of the total labour force.

According to the UN, industrialisation as part of globalisation is currently as much female-led as it is export-led.

There have not only been changes in the distribution of women's labour between different sectors of the economy. There has also been a change in their participation in the 'traded' sector of the visible economy. In some parts of the world, this has taken the form of higher participation in export manufacturing employment as economies moved from a capital-intensive, import-substituting industrialisation to a labour-intensive export-oriented one. According to the UN, industrialisation as part of globalisation is currently as much female-led as it is export-led.

Women's high rates of participation in export-oriented manufacturing started in the East Asian 'miracle' economies and Mexico and spread to other parts of Asia and Latin America. However, the spread has not been universal. In South Asia, it has mainly taken off in Bangladesh where there has been an astonishing rise in the female labour force in the manufacturing sector since the early 1980s due to the emergence of an export-oriented garment industry. Other countries in Asia that have seen a dramatic increase in both labour-intensive export manufacturing and the share of women in the manufacturing labour force include Indonesia, Malaysia, Mauritius, the Philippines, Sri Lanka and Thailand. On the other hand, as export-production has become more skill- and

*A textile factory in the
Philippines*

INTERNATIONAL LABOUR ORGANIZATION

capital-intensive in a number of middle-income countries, the demand for female labour in manufacturing appears to have weakened (for example, in Puerto Rico, Republic of Korea, Singapore and Taiwan).

Women form at least as high a percentage of the workforce in the 'internationalised' service sector, including data entry and processing, as they do in export-manufacturing. Indeed they make up the entire labour force in this sector in the Caribbean. In a number of countries, such as the Philippines and Thailand, where tourism had become the largest provider of foreign exchange by 1982, a considerable percentage of this income is generated by the sex industry, which largely employs women.

Globalisation and economic liberalisation, often with the imposition of SAPs, have also caused changes in agriculture. There has been a shift from subsistence to cash crops and from weak-performing traditional agricultural products (coffee, tobacco, cotton and cocoa) to higher value non-traditional agricultural exports (NTAEs) such as fresh fruit and nursery products. These require little or no additional processing, and most are produced as part of global supply networks (*see box 3.5*). The need to remain competitive means that production involves flexible and informal work arrangements similar to those seen in manufacturing. These include piecework; temporary, seasonal and casual work; and unregulated labour contracts. Studies suggest that women make up a disproportionate share of the workforce in this sector.

[W]omen make up a disproportionate share of the workforce in the [non-traditional agricultural exports (NTAEs)] sector.

Box 3.5 Women and Non-traditional Agricultural Exports (NTAEs)

In Latin America, particularly Colombia and Mexico where the sector is well established, NTAEs have generated seasonal employment for women. In Mexico in 1990, women made up around 15 per cent of the agricultural labour force but their participation went up to 50 per cent if only the production of fruit and flowers was considered. Women have also found employment in this sector in the Caribbean (leading to a decrease in the availability of the food for the local market that they traditionally produced and sold). In Africa, women make up around 90 per cent of the workforce in the NTAEs produced in large-scale enterprises organised along quasi-industrial lines. They are paid cash in direct exchange for their labour, in contrast to the unpaid labour they provide on family farms. However, many of these products are grown on smallholdings, often on a contract basis. While women provide much of the labour, they do not necessarily receive an equivalent proportion of the proceeds.

Along with these changes, there are still signs of the earlier regional pattern in female activity. Rates of female labour force participation were lowest in the belt of 'extreme' patriarchy, both in 1970 and in 1990, with the smallest increases recorded for the Arab countries of the Middle East.

In countries where there are large numbers of women in the formal economy, they tend to be under-represented at the higher levels and over-represented in those lower down.

Gender and hierarchies in the labour market

The increasing presence of women in paid work, and their greater share of employment, does not mean that gender inequalities have disappeared. It is also important to know where women and men are located in the social hierarchy of the market place. In other words, information on where women are relative to men in the pyramid of production depicted in Fig. 2.1 has to be supplemented by information on where they are in the social pyramid depicted in Fig. 3.2.

The percentages of both women and men in waged and salaried work – those most likely to work outside the home – are high in the industrialised countries of the OECD, in Eastern Europe, in Latin America and the Caribbean and in East Asia. Involvement in unpaid family work is low for both women and men in these regions. The picture is more uneven in South-East Asia, with high involvement in the waged economy in Malaysia, but lower involvement in Indonesia, the Philippines and Thailand. It is generally low in sub-Saharan Africa and South Asia, but with important differences in women's economic activity. Women in South Asia (and in other regions of extreme patriarchy) continue to be concentrated in unpaid family work (over 60 per cent of the female work force) while in sub-Saharan Africa, percentages of women in unpaid family work are generally below 60 per cent. The rest are distributed between self-employment and, in a few countries, in waged employment (*see box 3.6*).

Measuring economic activity in the informal economy is particularly difficult and it varies considerably across the world. In India, for example, formal, protected employment accounts for around 10 per cent of overall employment, but only 4 per cent of female employment. Women's share of formal employment, however, increased from 12 per cent in 1981 to 15 per cent in 1995.

Both formal and informal markets continue to be segmented by gender. In countries where there are large numbers of women in the formal economy, they tend to be under-represented at the higher levels and over-represented in those lower down. In Morocco, for example, 38 per cent of the total labour force is in 'professional and technical' and 'administrative' work, but only 10 per cent of the female labour force is in these categories. In East Asia, South-East Asia and the English-speaking Caribbean, women's participation in clerical, sales and services; production and transport; and agriculture, hunting and forestry is fairly high. However, they are generally under-represented in management and administration. In South Asia, women are concentrated in agriculture/forestry but less well represented in other sectors. There is a generally low representation of women in the labour force in the Middle East and North Africa, with Morocco reporting higher rates than the rest of the region.

Box 3.6 Female Employment in Sub-Saharan Africa and Latin America

In sub-Saharan Africa, women's share of employment in the formal economy between 1970 and 1985 rose from 6 per cent to 25 per cent in Botswana, from 1.5 per cent to 6 per cent in Malawi, from 9 per cent to 20 per cent in Swaziland and from 0.6 per cent to 2 per cent in Tanzania. In Zambia, only 7 per cent of formal wage employment was female. In Guinea-Bissau, women accounted for 3.6 per cent of formal sector employment.

In Latin America, the percentage of the female labour force in formal sector employment was generally high in the 1980s, varying between 32 per cent in Paraguay, 41 per cent in Ecuador, 52 per cent in Chile, 53 per cent in Brazil, 59 per cent in Argentina and 61 per cent in Panama. However, these rates, and the apparent increase they represent over those prevailing in the 1970s, may be somewhat misleading. This is because they are inflated by the inclusion of women working in micro-enterprises, most of which operate in the informal economy.

From 1950 onwards, there has been a systematic rise in female labour force participation in Latin America. One of the most striking features of this has been the increasing share of 'white collar' (professional and technical) employment in almost every major city in the region. In Chile, women made up half this workforce. However, for the majority of poorer women, oppor-

Working hours are on average shorter in industrialised than in developing countries, and shorter in urban areas of developing countries than in rural. Yet women work longer hours than men in every case.

tunities are more limited. In Mexico, women's workforce participation since the early 1990s has increased steadily while that of men has decreased. Gender differences in participation rates have thus declined in both urban and rural areas (particularly in non-agricultural self-employment). Between 1991 and 1995, women made up 68 per cent of the increase in this sector, and 90 per cent in rural areas. However, only women with secondary or higher levels of education were in salaried employment.

Finally, data on gender differences in time allocation show what is occurring in the non-market economy alongside changes in the market economy. They highlight a different, and persisting, dimension of gender inequality. Working hours are on average shorter in industrialised than in developing countries, and shorter in urban areas of developing countries than in rural. Yet women work longer hours than men in every case. The extent of the difference varies considerably. Women work just 10 per cent longer than men in rural Bangladesh, where they spend 35 per cent of their total work time in System of National Accounts (SNA) activities. In Kenya, on the other hand, they work 35 per cent longer and spend 42 per cent of their work time in SNA activities. Women's longer working day – and the extent to which it exceeds that of men – may reflect the difference between situations where seclusion restricts their economic activities and those where they are expected to participate in production. In any case, women continue to put in long hours of unpaid work into the reproductive economy regardless of their role in the productive economy.

Classifying Gender Constraints

This chapter has provided an institutional explanation of gender inequality. It has focused on the organisation of family and kinship, but has also pointed to the relevance of the wider institutions of markets, states and civil society as 'bearers of gender'. This section looks at different categories of gender constraint – those reflecting kinship and family systems and those reflecting the wider institutional environment. These are gender-specific constraints, gender-intensified constraints and imposed forms of gender disadvantage. They provide a background to the analysis of the relationship between gender inequality and poverty that occupies the rest of this book.

Gender-specific constraints

These reflect the rules, norms and values that are part of the social construction of gender. They vary among particular social groups in particular contexts and the way these groups define masculinity and femininity. Ideas about, for example, male and female sexuality, purity and pollution, female seclusion and the 'natural' aptitudes and predisposition of men and women all help to explain differences in what is permitted to men and to women in different cultures.

Gender-intensified constraints

These reflect gender inequalities in resources and opportunities. Class, poverty, ethnicity and physical location may also create inequalities but gender tends to make them more severe. Gender-intensified constraints are found in, for example, workloads, returns to labour efforts, health and education and access to productive assets (*see box 3.7*). They reflect the uneven distribution of resources and opportunities between women and men in the household. Where resources are scarce, women find themselves at a greater disadvantage than male members of the family. Some inequalities may be the result of community norms, such as customary laws governing inheritance. Others arise from decisions in the household, often because females are seen as having less value than males.

Gender-intensified constraints ... reflect the uneven distribution of resources and opportunities between women and men in the household.

Box 3.7 An Example of Gender-intensified Constraints from Uganda

In Uganda, women produce 80 per cent of the food and provide about 70 per cent of total agricultural labour. An assessment of poverty in the country showed how women's gender-specific domestic responsibilities interact with household poverty to increase their disadvantages in farming. Women are mainly found in the unpaid subsistence sector and perform their agricultural tasks without the use of technological innovations, inputs or finance. While it is true that many of these problems also apply to poor male farmers, men are not constrained by competing claims on their labour time.

Gender is a key organising principle in the distribution of labour, property and other valued resources in society.

Imposed forms of gender disadvantage

These reflect the biases, preconceptions and misinformation of those outside the household and community with the power to allocate resources. These institutional actors may actively reproduce and reinforce custom-based gender discrimination. Examples include:

* employers who refuse to recruit women or only recruit them in stereotypically 'female' – and hence usually the most poorly paid – activities;

* trade unions and professional associations that define their membership rules in ways that discourage the membership of women workers and professionals;

* non-governmental organisations (NGOs) that treat women as dependent clients rather than active agents;

* religious associations that define women as somehow lesser than men, refusing to let them become priests or to read the holy texts;

* banks that refuse to lend to women entrepreneurs because they pre-judge them to be credit risks;

* judges who think women get raped through their own fault; and

* states that define women as minors under the guardianship of men or as second-class citizens with fewer rights than men.

These forms of gender disadvantage show how cultural norms and beliefs are also found in the supposedly impersonal domains of markets, states and civil society.

Conclusion

Gender is a key organising principle in the distribution of labour, property and other valued resources in society. Unequal gender relationships are sustained and legitimised through ideas of difference and inequality that express widely held beliefs and values about the 'nature' of masculinity and femininity. Such forms of power do not have to be actively exercised to be effective. They also operate silently and implicitly through compliance with male authority both in the home and outside it. For example, if the senior male in the household or lineage has the main responsibility for members' welfare, he usually also has privileged access to its resources. Women, and junior men, accept his authority partly in recognition of his greater responsibilities and partly because they have less bargaining power.

While institutionalised norms, beliefs, customs and practices help to explain the distribution of gender resources and responsibilities in different social groups, they are clearly not unalterable. This is shown by the significant changes in work patterns that have occurred in the last quarter of the twentieth century. Female labour force participation rates have risen in most countries, while male rates have often stagnated or even declined. Various factors have played a role in different regions, including:

* greater impoverishment in some places and rapid growth in others;

* demographic transition and falling birth rates;

* rising rates of education;

* public policy;

* socialist egalitarianism;

* economic liberalisation; and

* greater integration into the global economy.

Nevertheless, gender inequalities persist. They help explain why regions with extreme forms of patriarchy continue to have lower rates of female labour force participation than can be explained by their levels of per capita income. They may also help to explain some of the regional variations in the relationship between gender equality and economic growth noted in the previous chapter. Indeed, the use of religion as a variable noted in Dollar and Gatti's analysis may simply be picking up regionally clustered institutions of 'extreme patriarchy', of which religion is only one aspect.

These more resilient aspects of patriarchy may also help to explain the positive relationship found by Seguino between gender inequality in wages and rates of economic growth. She suggests that institutions in patriarchal societies reinforce the

While institutionalised norms, beliefs, customs and practices help to explain the distribution of gender resources and responsibilities in different social groups, they are clearly not unalterable.

Gender inequality in areas such as education, wages and legal infrastructure is ... related to broad regional variations in patriarchal regimes ...

internalisation of social norms that favour men. Thus political resistance and therefore the costliness of gender inequality are reduced. For example, the state in the Republic of Korea condoned the marriage ban – the widespread practice by employers to make women quit work on marriage – that limited women's job tenure, organisational ability and potential for wage gains. This explanation is also supported by a study of women's labour market experiences in seven Asian countries (*see box 3.7*).

> **Box 3.7 The Importance of Enforcing Rights to Gender Equality**
>
> A study of women in the labour market in India, Indonesia, Japan, Malaysia, the Philippines, the Republic of Korea and Thailand notes that differences in patriarchal organisation helped explain why Japan and the Republic of Korea, despite their high rates of economic growth, have lower rates of female labour force participation than the Philippines and Thailand. Women had higher relative pay and made greater inroads into higher paying occupations in the latter two countries. Of the five countries where women had lower relative pay, India, Japan and the Republic of Korea had equal pay laws while the latter two had also recently enacted strong equal-opportunity legislation. The institution of formal rights in support of gender equality is an important message about social values. However, legislation is clearly not sufficient on its own to bring this about and makes little difference if not enforced. Public action in the form of strong civil society organisations, including an active women's movement, is necessary to ensure such laws are translated into practice.

The empirical findings show that gender inequality in areas such as education, wages and legal infrastructure is only partly related to per capita GNP. It is also related to broad regional variations in patriarchal regimes, particularly among the poorer countries of the world. The next chapter examines the relationship between gender inequality and poverty revealed by different approaches to poverty analysis.

4. Approaches to Poverty Analysis and its Gender Dimensions

Introduction

Poverty is generally thought of in terms of deprivation, either in relation to some basic minimum needs or in relation to the resources necessary to meet these minimum basic needs. Although there are varying ideas about what this basic level consists of, the three dominant approaches to poverty analysis that have featured in the development literature are:

1. the poverty line approach, which measures the economic 'means' that households and individuals have to meet their basic needs (determined by their income);

2. the capabilities approach, which explores a broader range of means (endowments and entitlements) as well as ends ('functioning achievements'); and

3. participatory poverty assessments (PPA), which explore the causes and outcomes of poverty in more context-specific ways.

Each approach reveals something about the gender dimensions of poverty, the forms these take in different regions and how they might be affected by economic growth.

The Poverty Line Approach
Separating the poor from the non-poor

Poverty line measurements equate well-being with the satisfaction individuals achieve through the consumption of various goods and services. They focus on the ability – shown by income – to 'choose' between different 'bundles' of commodities. This led to:

(a) a focus on growth in national per capita income as the yardstick for measuring development at the macro-level; and

*It has become
clear that
economic growth
does not
necessarily
benefit poorer
sections of
society.*

(b) a focus on increases in per capita household income as the yardstick of prosperity at the micro-level.

Since it has become clear that economic growth does not necessarily benefit poorer sections of society, a concern with poverty reduction has become increasingly important as a measure of development. In order to establish whether or not poverty is being reduced, there has to be some criteria or 'cut-off' point that separates the poor from the non-poor. The poverty line approach became the most widely used way of establishing this (*see box 4.1 and Table 4.1*).

> **Box 4.1 How the Poverty Line was Drawn**
>
> **The cost of purchasing the recommended daily allowance of calories for the average individual was calculated and multiplied by the average household size in a particular context in order to estimate the sum needed to meet the household's daily needs. The annual or monthly equivalent of this daily income was considered to be the minimum level necessary for the survival of household members. The 'poverty line' separates households who earn less than this amount from those earning at least this amount. Data on household income collected routinely through household expenditure surveys is the basis of measuring the incidence of poverty in countries as well as at the international level.**

While the poverty line approach continues to be important, it has been modified in response to the following criticisms, all of which are relevant to the gender dimensions of poverty:

* People meet their survival needs not only through monetary income but through a variety of resources – including subsistence production, access to common property resources and state provision of services;

* People also have 'stocks' of assets, stores and claims;

* The well-being of human beings, and what matters to them, does not only depend on their purchasing power but on other less tangible aspects, such as dignity and self-respect.

The most telling criticism, however, in relation to the gender dimensions of poverty relates to ideas about relations in the household. As noted previously, conventional economics saw the household as organised around the pooling of income and meeting the welfare needs of all members. However, studies from various parts of the world suggest that, on the contrary, there are widespread and systematic inequalities within households. These may be related to age, life cycle status, birth order, relationship to household head and other factors. The most pervasive, however, are those related to gender. Attempts to estimate poverty that overlooked inequalities in the household therefore provided a very incomplete picture. In particular, they had little to say about women's experience of poverty relative to that of men within the same household.

Female-headed households and the 'feminisation of poverty'

Household-level poverty measures did, however, reveal one important aspect of the interaction between gender and poverty: the disproportionate number of female-headed households among the poor. Evidence that the number of female-headed households was increasing in industrialised as well as developing countries led to the claim that there had been a 'feminisation of poverty'. A major report on the state of world rural poverty by the International Fund for Agricultural Development (IFAD) concluded that rural women in developing countries were among the poorest and most vulnerable people in the world, with 564 million living below the poverty line in 1988. This was an increase of 47 per cent over the numbers in 1965–70. In 1995, the United Nations Development Programme (UNDP) suggested that women made up 70 per cent of the poor.

Female headship rapidly became the accepted discourse about gender and poverty among international agencies. However, the relationship between female-headed households and poverty is not consistent. Rather, it seems to have a regional dimension, with female-headed households far more likely to be over-represented among the poor in Latin America and Asia than in Africa. This is because female headship can occur through a variety of processes – custom, widowhood, divorce,

Studies from various parts of the world suggest that ... there are widespread and systematic inequalities within households ... The most pervasive ... are those related to gender.

separation, polygamy, migration by male or female members and so on. Not all of these have the same implications for household poverty. For example, female-headed households set up by wives in polygamous marriages in Africa or in matrilineal societies in Africa and Asia tend to be better off. In Jamaica, female-headed households are widespread and this is not necessarily associated with poverty. Indeed, those where the male partner is present may be worse off.

Recent attempts to take account of size and composition of household membership in calculating income measures have generally strengthened the association between female headship and poverty. An analysis of household poverty in rural Nepal, for example, that took account of the 'economies of scale' associated with larger households found female-headed households to be generally poorer than the rest of the population: they tend to be smaller and have higher dependency ratios. Within the population of female-headed households, *de jure* female

Washing dishes by a pond in Nepal

INTERNATIONAL LABOUR ORGANIZATION

heads (widows) were better off than other categories if they had some source of male earnings, but poorer when only households without male earnings were compared. Clearly the presence and absence of male earnings has to be factored into the analysis.

From a policy perspective, therefore, using female headship as a criterion for targeting anti-poverty programmes is not likely to be effective in all cases. In addition, the gender dimensions of poverty are clearly not confined to the issue of female headship, despite the impression that this is the case conveyed by many policy documents. Inequalities of deprivation in male-headed households also need to be explored. However, this cannot be done on the basis of poverty line measures since these are calculated by looking at household income. Instead, it is necessary to focus on the individual.

From a policy perspective ... using female headship as a criterion for targeting anti-poverty programmes is not likely to be effective in all cases.

The Capabilities Approach

Expanding the concepts of 'means' and 'ends'

The 'basic needs' approach emerged on the development agenda as a response to:

a) the failure of the benefits of economic growth to 'trickle down' to the poor; and

b) the observed success of poor socialist countries, such as China, in improving the nutrition, health and education of large sections of their population.

It expanded the idea of 'means' to include – along with market-generated income – essential services that could help people to meet essential needs (e.g. safe drinking water, sanitation, public health and transportation). It also expanded the idea of 'ends' to include a wider range of needs considered essential for a decent human life (e.g. shelter, health and clothing). Freely chosen employment was included as part of both ends and means – it generated the income or products needed to meet basic needs and gave individuals the self-respect and dignity essential to their well-being.

This approach was based on the idea of 'functionings and capabilities' pioneered by Amartya Sen and elaborated in sub-

Because capabilities are defined in relation to the individual – unlike the poverty line, which is defined in relation to the household – they can also be interpreted and measured in gender-disaggregated ways.

sequent work by Dreze and Sen. Income and commodities were seen as important only in as much as they contributed to people's capabilities to achieve the lives they wanted (their 'functioning achievements'). Capabilities included not only basic individual ones such as nourishment and health but also more complex social ones, such as taking part in the community and achieving self-respect. A capabilities approach blurs the distinction between 'means' and 'ends'. Health and education, for example, are both functioning achievements in themselves as well as capabilities that allow people to achieve other valued functionings. Since capabilities are not only about what people 'choose' but what they are able to achieve, they depend partly on personal circumstances and partly on social constraints.

While these achievements relate to the individual, they can be measured at the community or national level. One attempt to do this is UNDP's Human Development Index (HDI), which combines country-level data on income, life expectancy and educational attainment. The HDI defined the following three abilities as more basic than any others:

* to live a long and healthy life;

* to be knowledgeable; and

* to have access to the resources needed for a decent standard of living.

These were seen as a 'measure of empowerment' and the foundations that would enable people to gain access to other opportunities as well.

Gender inequality and human development

Because capabilities are defined in relation to the individual – unlike the poverty line, which is defined in relation to the household – they can also be interpreted and measured in gender-disaggregated ways. This was attempted by UNDP in the 1995 *Human Development Report* (HDR), which introduced two important new indices for measuring gender inequality at the national level:

1. *The Gender Development Index (GDI)* focuses on the same three indicators as the HDI. Life expectancy at birth represents overall health status; a composite indicator of educational attainment (adult literacy rate and combined gross school enrolment ratio) represents knowledge; and real per capita Gross Domestic Product (GDP) represents standard of living. Gender-disaggregated data for each indicator are given a single social value and combined to calculate the GDI for each country. If the rationale for the HDI is extended to the GDI, it endorses the view that a precondition for the empowerment of women in any context is closing gender disparities in returns to labour efforts, in levels of education attained and in life expectancy.

2. *The Gender Empowerment Measure (GEM)* moved the focus of gender inequality from basic capabilities to disparities in wider opportunities and choices. It combined national data on gender inequalities in income earned in professional, managerial and technical occupations and in parliamentary representation. Although this broader definition of gender equality is critical to the overall goal of equitable development, it is not immediately relevant to the gender dimensions of poverty. There is no correlation between the GEM index and measures of basic needs and capabilities, including the HDI and GDI.

The GDI is closely linked to per capita GDP and increases as the latter does. It thus does not provide a measure of gender inequality as such. In fact, all the countries ranked in the top ten by the GDI are also all high-income economies while all those ranked in the bottom ten are also all low-income economies. Dijkstra and Hanmer have therefore developed another measure, called the Relative Status of Women (RSW), using the same indicators. This provides information about gender inequality in a country that is independent of its per capita GDP. Not only is the correlation between the per capita GDP and RSW of the 136 countries considered much weaker than when GDI is used, but also the ten best and worst performers no longer correspond to high and low-income countries (*see box 4.2*).

The capabilities approach has important advantages over the poverty line approach in revealing the gender dimensions of poverty. Gender-disaggregated measurements of basic aspects

[A] precondition for the empowerment of women in any context is closing gender disparities in returns to labour efforts, in levels of education attained and in life expectancy.

[G]ender inequalities cannot be attributed to poverty or patriarchy alone. They represent some combination of poverty, patriarchy and public policy.

> **Box 4.2 The Importance of Public Policy to Gender Equality**
>
> The ten best performers measured by the Relative Status of Women (RSW) include two high-income Scandinavian countries (Finland and Sweden), one upper middle-income, previously socialist, country (Hungary) and seven lower middle-income countries, of which six were previously socialist (Estonia, Latvia, Lithuania, Poland, the Russian Federation, the Slovak Republic and Jamaica). The ten worst performers include one upper middle-income country (Saudi Arabia), one lower middle-income country (Algeria) and a number of low-income countries (Afghanistan, Chad, Egypt, Mali, Nepal, Pakistan, Sierra Leone and Yemen Republic). While there is a strong 'Muslim' majority country presence in this group, they are also largely countries drawn from the belt of extreme patriarchy along with three from the West African region. These two regions also account for the next ten worst performing countries.
>
> This ranking shows the importance of public policies in enabling countries to achieve greater gender equality in ways that are not captured by their income levels. Among the best performers, both the Scandinavian and socialist countries are associated with strongly egalitarian 'welfare regimes'. The presence among the worst performers of middle-income countries like Algeria and Saudi Arabia, and the absence of low-income Muslim countries like Bangladesh or the Gambia, shows that gender inequalities cannot be attributed to poverty or patriarchy alone. They represent some combination of poverty, patriarchy and public policy.

of human capability (such as life expectancy, education and labour force participation), as well as more complex aspects (such as political participation and professional achievements) help build a comprehensive picture of the extent, scope and distribution of gender inequality in both developed and developing countries.

At the same time, it is clearly important to keep improvements in human capabilities due to overall improvements separate from those that reflect a reduction in gender inequalities. While the absolute level of well-being matters, gender inequality is an ethical problem that governments should be concerned about. There are also policy reasons for investigating women's absolute levels of deprivation as well as their deprivation relative to men as these are relevant for different human development outcomes.

In 1995, UNDP reported that women's wages on average were 75 per cent of male wages.

Gender inequality and the GDI indicators

There is a relationship between each of the dimensions making up the GDI (and the RSW) and income, growth and the structures of patriarchal constraint. Countries that perform well on one dimension may perform badly on another. Looking at the reasons for these divergences highlights those aspects of gender inequality that are responsive to economic growth and those that may need to be addressed through additional policy measures. It also helps identify the aspects of inequality that are most resistant to change.

Wages and labour force participation

The first of the three basic human capabilities identified by the HDR relates to economic opportunity and is measured by per capita GDP. This indicator reveals inequalities in labour force participation and in wages earned.

As noted in the previous chapter, female labour force participation in developing countries appears to be more strongly related to regional differences in kinship and gender relations than to differences in per capita income or incidence of poverty. Variations in female-to-male wage ratios have a less clear-cut regional pattern. In 1995, UNDP reported that women's wages on average were 75 per cent of male wages. The three countries with the lowest disparities were Australia, Tanzania and Vietnam, while the three with the highest were Bangladesh, China and the Republic of Korea.

However, there are problems with international estimates of wage disparities – greater perhaps than those of labour force participation. The data used in the GDI have not been standardised for skills, although there are likely to be gender differences in this area. Also, the GDI only looks at formal sector wages. Yet disparities in the informal sector are likely to be

Women are able to move into better-paid jobs as their education increases and as their attachment to the labour force becomes stronger.

quite different, especially in lower-income, agrarian economies. This is because: (a) the former accounts for just a small fraction of total employment in these countries; and (b) the work force in the informal economy – including the agricultural sector – tends to be less well organised, meaning that wage disparities are probably greater (*see box 4.3*). In addition, data from the formal economy tends to be dominated by the public sector, where wages are set administratively rather than competitively. Disparities thus tend to be lower than in the rest of the economy (including the rest of the formal economy).

Box 4.3 Wage Differences in the Gambia

The 1998 Household Expenditure Survey in the Gambia showed that the majority of the economically active population was concentrated in the agricultural sector: 57 per cent of men and 73 per cent of women. Annual agricultural wage earnings for women were less than half those of men. Only 2.4 per cent of the male labour force and 0.6 per cent of the female labour force was in public sector employment. Here median wages varied only slightly by gender.

While available data suggest that wage differences are decreasing, it is not always clear whether this is because female wages are rising or male wages are declining. One study of female-to-male wage ratios for 12 developing countries reported that female wages went up relative to male in all of them. The increase ranged from around 0.6–0.7 per cent annually in Brazil, Chile, Colombia and Venezuela to 2.4 per cent in Côte d'Ivoire and as much as 5 per cent in the Republic of Korea. There was a small decline in male wages in five of the seven countries for which data on the relevant explanatory variables were available. Another study indicated that the trend in male-female wage differentials is only positive for countries that have attained some level of economic growth. Women are able to move into better-paid jobs as their education increases and as their attachment to the labour force becomes stronger.

In Latin America, where women's labour force participation has been rising faster than men's, recent analysis focusing on its three larger economies (Argentina, Brazil and Chile) also reports that women's earnings are improving relative to men's. For all three countries, education levels appeared to be more important than either sex or sector in explaining variations in monthly earnings. At the same time, however, women in all three countries remain over-represented in the lower paid and less well-protected segments of the labour market. They are also likely to express much greater insecurity in relation to basic household survival and well-being than men. The researchers suggest that the most vulnerable section of the working population is those women classified as 'unpaid family workers' who have no access to an income of their own.

Despite some positive trends, gender segregation remains a feature of labour markets. The pay gap also remains larger than can be explained by differences in skills or labour market segmentation and suggests some degree of direct discrimination.

Despite some positive trends, gender segregation remains a feature of labour markets [and] the pay gap ... suggests some degree of direct discrimination.

Life expectancy

The second component of the GDI relates to life expectancy, which represents gender differences in health and physical well-being. Age-specific death rates favour women:

* although more males than females are conceived, males are more vulnerable both before and after birth. More girls are born and more boys die in the early years of life; and

* women on average live longer for hormonal reasons.

A reversal in this pattern usually means there is gender discrimination against females. On the other hand, a greater than average disparity in favour of women indicates male disadvantage.

Life expectancies overall roughly approximate the regional distribution of income. They exceed 75 years in the OECD countries, while in the rest of the world they range from 64–72 in Latin America and the Caribbean to around 55 in South Asia and 46–53 in sub-Saharan Africa. Those of women also conform to the regional distribution of per capita GNP. In 1970, sub-Saharan Africa had the lowest levels of female life expectancy (around 45 years) followed by South Asia (47), the Middle East and North Africa (54). East Asia and the Pacific and Latin America and the Caribbean have higher levels. By 1997, there had been worldwide increases in overall life expectancy, but with least change occurring in the poorer

The gap between developed and developing countries is wider in terms of maternal mortality than for any other health indicator.

countries of sub-Saharan Africa. Absolute levels of life expectancy, including absolute levels of female life expectancy, thus differentiate the richer from poorer countries of the world. Among the poorer countries, they differentiate the less from the more poor.

One of the factors that lead to variations in women's life expectancy is maternal mortality. There are two ways in which it is measured:

(a) The maternal mortality *ratio*. This measures a woman's risk of dying from a given pregnancy. It is expressed as the number of maternal deaths per 100,000 live births a year. The Millennium Development Goals (MDGs) include a commitment to reducing this.

(b) The maternal mortality *rate*. This measures the number of maternal deaths a year per 100,000 women of reproductive age. It takes account of the risks of becoming pregnant and of dying from pregnancy-related causes. Clearly, it goes down as fertility declines.

Like overall and female life expectancy, maternal mortality appears to be strongly correlated with per capita GNP (*see box 4.4*). The gap between developed and developing countries is wider in terms of maternal mortality than for any other health indicator. This includes infant mortality, the most commonly used measure of comparative disadvantage.

> ### Box 4.4 Estimates of Maternal Mortality Ratios
>
> Government estimates of maternal mortality ratios reported by the World Health Organization (WHO) show them to be highest in Africa, particularly West Africa. Figures of up to 1,750–2,900 per 100,000 births are reported for Mali and 500–1,500 for Ghana. In Asia, they vary between 600 for Bangladesh and 900 for Papua New Guinea, on the high side, and around 10–50 for China and 9–42 for the Republic of Korea. Ratios in Latin America and the Caribbean also vary considerably but tend to be lower than sub-Saharan Africa and South Asia.

Gender inequalities in life expectancy are more closely linked to regional patterns in kinship and family organisation than to regional levels of poverty. There is a close correlation between the ranking of regions of the developing world by female-to-male economic activity ratios and by female-to-male life expectancy ratios. Despite higher levels of poverty, there is greater gender equality in life expectancy in sub-Saharan Africa than in some of the higher-income countries in western Asia, North Africa and South Asia. While the percentages of women likely to survive to the age of 65 in 1999 was higher than the percentages for men across the world, the difference was lowest in the regions of 'extreme patriarchy'. There are also sub-regional variations in gender inequalities reflecting variations in family and kinship systems within regions.

There are some limitations to using life expectancy as a measure of gender inequality. For example, a comparison between Bangladesh and the Gambia showed that the West African country reported higher female than male life expectancy while Bangladesh reported the 'extreme patriarchy' pattern of higher male life expectancy. However, more detailed analysis revealed that women in the reproductive years in both countries were at a particular disadvantage. There were high rates of maternity-related mortality and nutritional anaemia among pregnant and lactating women.

Sex ratios

Sex ratios of populations are another indicator of gender discrimination at the level of basic survival chances. Women's longer life expectancies should logically lead to more females in a population. Consequently, to have more males in a country or region is the reverse of the pattern expected on the basis of biologically determined *sex* differences. Yet *gender* disadvantage in some regions significantly outweighs and reverses biological patterns. This has led to a situation where there are over a million 'missing women' in the world.

An examination of regional sex ratios in the 1980s found that the populations of the Middle East, northern areas of Africa, the Indian sub-continent and China were all characterised by 'masculine sex ratios', i.e. ratios of more than 105 males per 100 females. Countries in North America and Europe had an average of 105 females for 100 males while sub-

Gender inequalities in life expectancy are more closely linked to regional patterns in kinship and family organisation than to regional levels of poverty.

Countries in North America and Europe had an average of 105 females for 100 males while sub-Saharan Africa had 102 females. However, there were far fewer females to males in middle eastern . . . , South Asian . . . and East Asian countries.

Saharan Africa had 102 females. However, there were far fewer females to males in middle eastern countries like Turkey (95), Egypt and Iran (97) and Saudi Arabia (84); in South Asian countries like India (93) and Pakistan (92); and in East Asian countries like China (94).

Masculine sex ratios are associated with high levels of excess female mortality in the younger age groups. This has been made worse in some countries by high rates of mortality among women of reproductive age. For instance, analysis from 40 developing countries (excluding India and China) showed that excess female mortality among children is most marked in the Middle East belt and close to the median value in Latin America and sub-Saharan Africa. The 'geography of gender' of sex ratios is mirrored in the regional distribution of strong son preference. Patterns of gender discrimination appear to be particularly intransigent in South Asia.

Educational attainment

Education is the third of the capabilities included in estimates in the GDI. It is also central to the MDGs, both in 'absolute' terms (increasing overall attainments, particularly at primary level) as well as relative ones (closing the gender gap in adult literacy and education at all levels). The challenge of achieving universal education at even the primary level remains formidable, however, and has a strong gender component. According to UNICEF, over 130 million children of school age in the developing world are growing up without access to basic education. Nearly two of every three children in the developing world who do not receive a primary education are girls. Sub-Saharan Africa has the lowest rates of net primary enrolment at 57 per cent, followed by South Asia with 68 per cent, the Middle East and North Africa with 81 per cent, and Latin America and the Caribbean with 92 per cent.

The GDI shows a regional pattern to female (and overall) primary, secondary and tertiary educational attainment that reflects levels of wealth and poverty. Overall educational attainment is highest, and gender inequalities have also been largely eradicated, in the OECD countries. Female-to-male enrolment rates there were 99 per cent in 1990, while they still stand at around 84 per cent in the least developed countries.

The regional pattern of gender differences in adult literacy

– the product of past educational attainments – suggests the influence of local patriarchies. Female literacy as a percentage of male in 1992 was highest in Latin America and the Caribbean (97%), followed by South-East Asia/Pacific (90%), East Asia (80%), sub-Saharan Africa (66%), the Arab states (62%) and South Asia (55%). However, the regional pattern in current educational attainments, as measured by primary enrolment ratios, suggests that this influence may have been lessened by economic growth. All these regions except sub-Saharan Africa and South Asia report high rates of female-to-male enrolment (92 to 98%). This supports the finding that economic growth among countries that have reached a certain level of income helps close the gender gap in education, regardless of regional differences in gender relations.

Differences in regional patriarchies may explain the disparity between South Asia and sub-Saharan Africa. Poverty reduction and educational attainment for both girls and boys at the primary levels have been greater in the former. For example, female primary enrolment rates had risen to over 80 per cent in South Asia by 1995, compared to 60 per cent in sub-Saharan Africa. However, gender inequalities continued to be higher in South Asia. Female-to-male attainment at primary level was 75 per cent there compared to 85 per cent in sub-Saharan Africa. At the secondary level, where rates are generally lower, female-to-male ratios were around 14 per cent in the former and 40 per cent in the latter.

Rapid growth, urbanisation and industrialisation in East and South-East Asia appear to have led to both rapidly declining fertility rates as well as rising levels of educational attainment for girls as well as boys. However, there is evidence that the education of male children in some East Asian countries was achieved at the expense, and often through the contribution, of female children. Daughters in Taiwan, for example, were given the minimum level of education necessary to allow them to take up 'female' jobs in factories or white-collar clerical work and their wages were then used to subsidise greater investment in sons' education.

Male disadvantage

Marked deviations from expected patterns of gender difference can reveal not only female but also male disadvantage. Some

[E]conomic growth among countries that have reached a certain level of income helps close the gender gap in education ...

Marked deviations from expected patterns of gender difference can reveal not only female but also male disadvantage. [e.g. in life expectancy and education].

examples are provided below in terms of life expectancy and education.

Life expectancy

Situations of possible male disadvantage in life expectancy are illustrated by the following:

1. Unusually high female-to-male ratios were found in the 5–9 age group in some of the poorest regions of India among the most socially excluded groups (scheduled castes and tribes). Extremely poor health services and infrastructure in these areas led to fewer boys surviving.

2. Male life expectancy has declined more dramatically than female in Eastern Europe since countries embarked on economic transition. This is probably due to the stress caused by traditional expectations of men being the dominant breadwinners and decision-makers in their families. Rates of cardiovascular diseases, suicide and alcoholism in Russia, for example, are significantly higher for men than women.

The first example suggests the need to improve access to, and provision of, health care facilities in the poorer, more isolated areas of South Asia. The second shows the 'costs' that rigidities in gender identities can impose on men. More egalitarian models of gender relations might have allowed the costs of transition to be shared more equitably. Unfortunately, women seem to find it easier – or more imperative – to share the burden of economic provisioning than men appear to find sharing the burden of domestic work.

Education

There is also evidence of male disadvantage in educational attainment in some regions, particularly the English-speaking Caribbean. Women make up 70 per cent of graduates from the University of the West Indies. In Jamaica, the lower achievement of boys is already evident at the primary level and widens subsequently. Prevailing ideas of masculinity and femininity see men as dominant, appropriate to the public sphere, strong, etc. and women as submissive, appropriate to the private sphere, sensitive and so on. These values are internalised by children and structure their interactions at home, school and work and in the community. The reality, however, is that women have always worked outside the home. Thus while socialisation processes equip women for the discipline of school life, their relative independence allows them to take advantage of labour market and political opportunities. However, there is little to encourage men to participate in an educational system based on values and a language that is perceived as 'effeminate'.

While male underachievement in education is clearly a matter of concern, it should be noted that it does not translate into male disadvantage in the market place. Data from the 1990s shows that women's participation in the labour force, and in the formal sectors of their economies, is lower than that of men. They have higher rates of unemployment and tend to be among the lowest paid.

More comprehensive data on gender disparities in wages across the economy, rather than only in the formal sector, would provide a better measure of economic opportunity.

Summary

The measures of human capabilities discussed in this section make a number of useful contributions to understanding gender and poverty:

- they help monitor differences in basic achievements across countries and over time;

- they draw attention to regional differences in kinship and gender relations – and associated patterns of gender inequality – that are not necessarily the same as regional patterns of income or poverty; and

- they reveal some aspects of gender inequality that seem to be resilient over time or impervious to economic growth and others that do not.

At the same time, GDI indicators could be made more sensitive to gender disparities in poorer countries. More comprehensive data on gender disparities in wages across the economy, rather than only in the formal sector, would provide a better measure of economic opportunity. In addition, while overall life expectancy may be a useful measure of development, it disguises age-specific differentials in mortality. It also conceals gender disadvantage in the reproductive age groups.

A growing body of work explores the experience of poverty from the perspective of the poor.

Participatory Poverty Assessments (PPAs)

Poverty from the perspective of the poor

A growing body of work explores the experience of poverty from the perspective of the poor. Such participatory poverty assessments (PPAs) use a variety of largely qualitative methods (including focus groups, in-depth discussions with key informants and various visual techniques such as matrices, mapping, transects and venn diagrams). They originated in earlier attempts by practitioners in the field to promote 'bottom-up' appraisal and evaluation of development projects through a range of techniques collectively known as Participatory Rural Appraisal (PRA). Participatory approaches are increasingly prominent in national poverty assessment exercises carried out by international development agencies. However, they generally use focus group discussions rather than the range of methods mentioned above.

Key contributions that PPA approaches have made in relation to the discussion here include showing that:

* Poverty is multi-dimensional and includes not only economic deprivation but also various forms of vulnerability (*see box 4.5*).

* Poor people are not only concerned with meeting their immediate food needs but also have a variety of longer-term goals such as security, accumulation, social standing and self-respect (although poverty may force them into humiliating patron-client relationships, extremely exploitative forms of work or other equally painful situations).

* Poor people use a variety of ways and means in seeking to achieve their goals, including casual waged work, bonded labour, care of cattle and livestock, micro-cultivation, seasonal migration, sex work, begging and theft.

* Poor people rely on a variety of resources other than their labour, including:
  (a) human resources – which tend to be basic unskilled labour among the very poor;
  (b) material resources – physical assets and inventories, loans in cash and kind and common property resources; and

(c) 'social' resources – claims they can make on others as a result of their membership of various social networks, associations and relationships. They depend on informal safety nets of kin and community to tide them over in times of crisis.

Box 4.5 Insecurity and Vulnerability

The World Bank's *World Development Report* in 2000 included 'insecurity' as one of the three key dimensions of poverty. The Bank designates certain percentages of the population above the poverty line as 'vulnerable' because they face a high likelihood of falling below it. Vulnerability has now become an integral aspect of poverty analysis, and is both:

* objective, i.e. the exposure to risks, shocks and stress and the inability to deal with them without sustaining damaging loss (e.g. becoming less healthy, selling off productive assets or withdrawing children from school); and

* subjective, i.e. the sense of powerlessness in the face of threats.

Vulnerability looks at fluctuations in the well-being of the poor and at movements of household into – and out of – poverty over time. For example, among vulnerable groups in the UNICEF critique of structural adjustment were the 'newly poor' – those who had been retrenched from the public sector as it was downsized.

A review of 22 national poverty assessments undertaken in sub-Saharan Africa by the mid-1990s identified the following among the dimensions of poverty:

* food insecurity (irregular meals and periods of food shortage);

* exclusion from social services (for financial reasons, but also due to a lack of infrastructure and/or the behaviour of providers);

[P]overty tended to be associated with dependence . . . [and] the extreme poor were the elderly, the disabled and, in some cases, female-headed households.

* lack of ownership of productive assets (e.g. grinding machines, cattle, credit, ox-carts, fishing nets, radios, bicycles and land);

* poor quality housing;

* irregularity of income flows; and

* powerlessness (not being heard in the community).

In addition, poverty tended to be associated with dependence. Poor people sought to bind themselves into patron-client relationships, often on demeaning terms, in order to assure some degree of protection in the face of crisis. The extreme poor were the elderly, the disabled and, in some cases, female-headed households. These were totally dependent on the support of others for their survival.

Box 4.6 The Need for Comprehensive Policies to Address Poverty

PPAs have highlighted how different aspects of poverty are connected. This has underlined the need for a comprehensive approach to poverty reduction. Ill-health, for example, was shown to be both a major cause and a consequence of poverty. However, health policies that are independent of measures providing clean drinking water are unlikely to be very effective where there is a high incidence of water-borne diseases. Similarly, hunger undermines school attendance as well as the capacity to learn, while food-for-education schemes help to address both.

Context-specific and qualitative approaches to poverty assessment can enrich poverty analysis in the following ways:

* The information they provide is not determined in advance but emerges out of the process of data collection. This allows findings from quantitative surveys to be verified and interpreted. It can also help to correct entrenched misconceptions.

- They can provide a more dynamic analysis of poverty as they draw attention to its underlying causes and processes as well as to its description.

- They illuminate the factors that connect policy measures at the macro-level and outcomes at the level of individuals, households and communities.

Participatory assessments and gender

PPAs have great potential for capturing some of the gendered aspects of poverty such as the following:

a. Forms of disadvantage that affect poor women more
They provided a number of examples, including:

- women's greater time burden – or 'time poverty' – in Africa;

- the costs of dowry in Bangladesh; and

- domestic violence, unequal decision-making power and disproportionate workloads in Vietnam. Women were also seen as 'tools' in coping with hardship (e.g. girls were sold to foreigners in order to pull the rest of the family out of poverty).

b. The connections between production and reproduction
They made the connections between production and reproduction more visible. For example, the ability of the poor to generate income in Guinea-Bissau is reduced because environmental degradation forces them (especially women) to spend so much time on routine household tasks such as fuel wood collection and fetching water.

c. Variations in household relationships
They made it clear that in some countries (e.g. Ghana and Zambia) women and men had:

- substantially different bases for their livelihood activities;

- a high degree of separation of income streams in the household; and

- an associated separation of family responsibilities.

Anthropological work has already documented this but it had barely registered in mainstream economic analysis, which had

PPAs have great potential for capturing some of the gendered aspects of poverty ...

The Consultations with the Poor carried out across the world in preparation for the 2001 World Development Report (WDR), reported that state institutions were not responsive or accountable to the poor.

continued to treat households as characterised by the pooling of resources.

d. The vulnerability of female-headed households

They identified female-headed households as more vulnerable to poverty in some parts of Africa: Benin, Kenya, Rwanda and Sierra Leone. Remittances from absent (male) members emerged as an important factor in whether or not female-headed households were poor in Cape Verde, Mauritania and Uganda. In Ghana, female headship was associated with poverty in the north but not in the south.

e. Gender differences in priorities

They showed that men and women often had different concerns and priorities. The Zambian study found that women emphasised basic needs while men emphasised ownership of physical assets. In the Gambia, both women and men prioritised income. However, while women gave second priority to health, men prioritised education. Distance from and quality of drinking water sources were concerns almost exclusively voiced by women in sub-Saharan Africa, reflecting their primary responsibility in this area. Awareness of different priorities is necessary to predict the effects of, for example, increasing male cash flows (will they buy more cattle or meet current food needs?) or of imposing user fees on health or education.

f. Policy-related inequalities and unequal treatment

They showed how policy-related inequalities reinforce women's economic disadvantage in earning a livelihood. In Guinea-Bissau, South Africa and Zambia, women had often been bypassed in the distribution of credit, agricultural extension, etc. Kenya was the only country where agricultural extension services appeared not to have discriminated against women.

The Consultations with the Poor carried out across the world in preparation for the 2001 *World Development Report* (WDR), reported that state institutions were not responsive or accountable to the poor. On the contrary, they treated poor people with arrogance and disdain. A PPA from Tanzania, for example, noted the widespread rudeness of health staff. This is partly explained by the fact that those employed in public service tend, almost by definition, to be the better-off, better-educated or better-connected members of society. They often reproduce inequalities of class, gender, caste and status from the private domain through their actions and interactions in the public domain.

g. Women's lack of access to resources

They highlighted the problems faced by women in obtaining access to land. In Vietnam, despite the 1993 Land law which protected women's right to inheritance, sons were inheriting land in accordance with earlier custom. In Kenya and Tanzania too, where women had been granted legal rights to land, customary law continued to prevail and few women took advantage of these rights. In Cameroon, the trend towards privatisation was undermining women's traditional rights of usufruct. The Guinea-Bissau report, on the other hand, identified lack of credit and other inputs, rather than access to land, as key gender-related constraints. These in turn are a major constraint to the country's socio-economic development.

Limitations of participatory assessments

Insights from participatory assessments have increased understanding of the gender dimensions of poverty. However, they have done so unevenly, and often incidentally. Many lack any reference to gender issues while, in others, gender is used simply as a synonym for women. Two key explanations for this are: (a) various kinds of biases in the process by which poverty profiles are compiled and translated into policy; and (b) the fact that 'poor people's perceptions' reflect the norms and values of society to which both women and men subscribe.

a. Various kinds of bias in the process

PPAs, like any other methodology, are as gender-blind or as gender-aware as those who conduct them. The types of questions asked, the issues explored and the range of information obtained depend on what is considered relevant. For example, an analysis in West Bengal talks about the violence experienced by the poor, but does not mention gender-specific forms of violence. Data suggest, however, that sexual assault and harassment of women in the public domain and violence from husbands or other family members in the domestic sphere are

PPAs, like any other methodology, are as gender-blind or as gender-aware as those who conduct them.

Even when participatory assessments generate the relevant information, 'transmission losses'... may occur when the analysis is turned into a policy document... The [World] Bank sometimes seems to be imposing its own ideas about poverty as seen in the 1990 WDR rather than basing its actions on the results of the studies.'

frequent occurrences and often related to frustrations born of poverty.

Even when participatory assessments generate the relevant information, 'transmission losses' can occur. The research team may lack the skills to interpret and incorporate the information into the analysis on which policy measures will be based. For example, despite frequent references to alcoholism as a cause of poverty in the assessments, it was never taken up in the analysis because it did not fit the model of poverty that was used. Yet alcoholism, usually a male phenomenon, often goes with male unemployment and domestic violence against women, while brewing alcohol is an important source of livelihood for women in the countryside.

Further transmission losses may occur when the analysis is turned into a policy document. A World Bank peer review process determines what aspects will be included and how these will be translated into practical measures. The Bank sometimes seems to be imposing its own ideas about poverty as seen in the 1990 WDR rather than basing its actions on the results of the studies. For example, female education – particularly primary school enrolment for girls – is often the main policy recommendation relating to gender issues. Yet this appears to reflect the Bank's own position rather than any priorities suggested in the PPAs. Indeed, rural parents often express their reluctance to educate their daughters.

b. 'Poor people's perceptions' reflect social norms and values

The findings of PPAs may also fail to include gender issues because of 'poor people's perceptions'. These perceptions often reflect norms and values that do not attach any weight to gender inequalities or to violations of women's human rights. Moreover, women frequently subscribe to these value systems and accept that they have lesser worth as human beings. For example, both men and women in Guinea saw women's heavier workloads as well as male domination in private and public decision-making as 'natural' to the organisation of gender relations rather than unjust.

Relying on poor people to define their condition can also conceal major issues of inequality, many of which implicate women. These include female foeticide and infanticide, biases in the distribution of health and nutrition in the family and exploitative treatment of younger women by older (e.g. their mothers-in-law). Another example is female circumcision. This is not only a means of controlling women's sexuality and a considerable threat to their health and well-being but also a way in which mothers prepare their daughters for womanhood. However, there is little reference to the issue in PPAs carried out in countries where it is widely practised. The Gambian PPA, for example, does not mention it despite the fact that 99 per cent of adult women have been circumcised and it has been taken up as a health as well as a rights issue by local women's groups.

While violence against women is mentioned in some assessments, they do not capture the scale on which it occurs. The use, or threat, of violence is clearly an important factor in maintaining power relations in the household. Reasons for domestic violence given in PPAs range from a husband not getting his meals on time to a mother-in-law asserting her authority over her son's new wife. Violence is also reported in situations where women were seeking some degree of independence, such as when they gained access to loans or to paid work. However, there is also a poverty dimension to domestic violence since scarcity and economic crisis intensify frustrations in the family.

Many aspects of gender discrimination are embedded in unquestioned and largely unnoticed traditions and beliefs that are seen as biologically given or divinely ordained. Subordinate groups are likely to accept, and even collude with, their lot in society where:

a) powerful cultural or ideological norms explain and justify inequality; and

b) the possibility of challenging these norms is both limited and likely to carry heavy personal and social costs.

Women may think that violence at the hands of their husbands is an acceptable part of marriage or a legitimate expression of male authority. They may not perceive or complain about gender discrimination in the household, and indeed may practise it against their own daughters. These aspects of deprivation, while they may reflect society-wide beliefs and practices,

Many aspects of gender discrimination are embedded in unquestioned and largely unnoticed traditions and beliefs that are seen as biologically given or divinely ordained.

The three ways of thinking about poverty outlined ... offer different insights and, taken together, provide a more comprehensive understanding of the gender dimensions of poverty than any would on its own.

can be exacerbated by poverty. At the same time, values and beliefs can be changed. As communities become exposed to new realities, they see possible new ways of 'being and doing' and start to question what was previously taken for granted.

Conclusion

The three ways of thinking about poverty outlined above are complementary rather than competing. They offer different insights and, taken together, provide a more comprehensive understanding of the gender dimensions of poverty than any would on its own. The evidence they provide of gender inequalities in the distribution of basic needs and capabilities in the household – together with studies showing that households do not necessarily pool their incomes – presents a serious challenge to the unitary model of the household favoured by conventional economists. This model had previously dominated economic approaches to poverty analysis and informed many of the policies intended to address poverty.

There has thus been growing attention by economists to other ideas of the household. In 'bargaining' models, for example, household members are assumed to 'co-operate' in production and reproduction because the returns to this outweigh those to individual efforts. Should there be conflict over the terms of co-operation or the distribution of its gains, decisions are arrived at through either: (a) bargaining and

Women working in the fish canning industry in Thailand
INTERNATIONAL LABOUR ORGANIZATION

Box 4.7 The Need for a Multi-faceted Response to Gender Disadvantage

Women, particularly poorer women, face extremely unfavourable access to land and other valued resources. Also, the terms on which they participate in paid work, including the returns to their efforts, do little to improve their subordinate status in the family. They may be actively discriminated against in access to important resources such as credit, agricultural inputs, extension services, marketing outlets and so on. Clearly, dismantling such 'imposed gender disadvantages' could play an important role in addressing gender inequalities in the household as well as the economy. Formal legislation on gender equality is one way to address deeply-entrenched forms of discrimination in marriage and work. At the same time it is important to note that legislation alone will not ensure women's rights if customary laws and community beliefs prevent it from being implemented. Education and information on these rights is needed, together with an effective enforcement machinery and an active civil society prepared to undertake public action to ensure their enforcement.

negotiation; (b) the covert or overt exercise of threat, including the threat of violence; or (c) compliance on the part of subordinate members. Alternatively, unresolved conflicts can result in the break-down of co-operation as a member (or members) exercise the 'exit' option and withdraw from household membership altogether. The extent to which household members can promote their own preferences or interests will reflect their bargaining power in relation to other members.

These new approaches thus accommodate the possibility of unequal power relations in the household in a way that previous models did not. An important contribution of this literature is the idea of a 'fall-back' position as something that determines bargaining power in the household. This refers to the resources that women and men are able to command (fall back on), independent of their membership of that household. Women are likely to make fewer claims on household and community

As women gain access to new forms of resources, previously accepted aspects of deprivation and discrimination are likely be increasingly questioned.

resources in cultures where they are defined as inferior or less deserving than men. Also, women are much more likely to see themselves, and be seen by others, as of less worth in situations where their contribution to the household is confined to unpaid family work and hence less visible. Improving women's access to resources outside the household can thus provide them with leverage to challenge power relations inside it (*see box 4.7*).

As women gain access to new forms of resources, previously accepted aspects of deprivation and discrimination are likely be increasingly questioned. Policies that seek to address the gender dimensions of poverty, and to tackle gender discrimination in a society, have an important role to play in this process of change. They can promote new models of gender relations that help to expand the range of possibilities available to women and men in organising their lives.

5. Gender Inequality and Poverty Eradication: Promoting Household Livelihoods

Introduction

The eradication of extreme poverty is the first – and overarching – Millennium Development Goal (MDG). It is expressed in terms of two targets:

* halving the proportion of people in extreme poverty, and

* halving the number of people suffering from hunger.

The first target focuses on increasing household *income* as an important means of achieving the goal. The second deals with reducing hunger as a measure of the desired *outcome*. This chapter is mainly concerned with the former – the 'means' dimension of poverty reduction – while issues of hunger and malnutrition are explored in the next chapter. The powerful place held by the idea of the male breadwinner in development studies and policies has meant that the importance of women's breadwinning role has been neglected, particularly among the poor. This chapter aims to make good this omission. Two other indicators that are part of the MDGs should be borne in mind in this discussion:

* the expansion of women's waged employment in the non-agricultural sector (an indicator associated with the goal of women's empowerment); and

* security of land tenure (an indicator associated with the goal of environmental sustainability).

While previous chapters have looked at the relationship between gender inequality and income poverty at the broad, regional level, this chapter focuses on the relationship at the

The powerful place held by the male breadwinner in development studies and policies has meant that ... women's breadwinning role has been neglected.

level of the household. Much of the empirical material is drawn from sub-Saharan Africa and South Asia (although there are examples from other parts of the world in the concluding section). The focus on these two regions provides some useful comparisons and contrasts:

1. They have the highest incidence of poverty in the world and account for the largest numbers of poor people.

2. They are both rural agrarian economies, with agriculture being a major source of employment for the poor, particularly poor women.

3. They have very different resource endowments:

   * South Asia is usually described as labour-abundant – it has a high person to land ratio and a large class of landless households.

   * Sub-Saharan Africa is usually described as land-abundant and labour-constrained – it has a low ratio of people to land and landlessness is still insignificant.

4. They provide contrasting models of gender relations (although there are considerable internal differences within the two regions):

   * South Asia is in the male farming system category and part of the belt of 'classic' patriarchy characterised by extreme forms of gender discrimination.

   * Sub-Saharan Africa is in the female farming system category, with less corporate forms of household arrangements and a less strict public-private divide.

Gender Inequality and Household Poverty in South Asia

Women's work and household survival

As noted earlier, female seclusion in regions of extreme patriarchy explains women's generally low levels of labour force participation. Work in the public domain, particularly in waged employment for others, means a loss of status for women and their households. Thus while poverty may force women to work outside the home, increased household prosperity may lead to their withdrawal into it again. An exception is work in the public sector, an acceptable source of employment for educated women. At the same time, the active role that women, including those from better-off households, play in home-based economic activities tends to be socially and statistically invisible. It is treated as an extension of their domestic chores. This leads not only to extremely low levels of labour force participation, using the narrow International Labour Organization (ILO) definition (i.e. including only activities done for pay or profit) but also to a strong relationship between paid work by women and household poverty. A discussion of studies from India and Bangladesh illustrates this, as well as highlighting some of the constraints poor women face in their ability to contribute to household income.

[T]he active role that women, including those from better-off households, play in home-based economic activities tends to be socially and statistically invisible.

The gender distribution of work in rural areas

Rural poverty in South Asia is closely connected with landlessness, rural wage labour and, in India, with caste. Partly as a result of increasing landlessness, there has been a steady decline in 'own cultivation' as a source of rural employment during the twentieth century. Men have diversified into wage labour in the agricultural sector, as well as various forms of non-agricultural activities in the rural sector economy. They have also migrated into the urban economy. Women, however, remain largely concentrated in rural areas.

India

According to official estimates, landless and land-poor households made up over 50 per cent of rural households in India in 1992. The landless poor are mainly drawn from 'untouchable' castes that also make up the bulk of the agricultural wage labour in the countryside. In addition, they are found in a variety of off-farm activities – such as non-agricultural wage labour, small commodity production and informal, caste-based services (sweepers, midwives, barbers, etc.) – and migrating into urban areas.

Women from these groups do not face the same restrictions as women from higher castes and they have higher rates of labour force participation than the rest of the female population. However, they are mainly found in agricultural waged employment, among the least well-paid forms of work available in the economy. Only 19 per cent of female labour from the poorest households was involved in 'statistically recognised' off-farm activities (wage labour in the non-agricultural sector and self-employed traders and vendors). There is also a marked regional pattern to female labour force participation that partly reflects the 'north-south' gender divide noted earlier.

Several explanations have been offered for the 'feminisation' of agricultural wage labour. These include:

* the loss of land for subsistence cultivation and inadequate growth of productive employment opportunities on family farms;

* low incomes of agricultural households and inequality in land distribution;

* the spread of Green Revolution technology since the 1960s, which led to some labour displacement (as a result of mechanisation) but increased the productivity of agriculture and the overall demand for labour. It also led to a greater increase in female than male labour use;

* a decline in rural non-agricultural employment and a shift back into agriculture, particularly into 'subsidiary' forms of employment by women, since the early 1990s. This followed the collapse of government programmes, designed to benefit rural areas, that had been financed by external debt. There has also been a sharp increase in female casual employment.

Bangladesh

Bangladesh has also experienced growing landlessness, declining farm size and diversification out of agriculture into various off-farm activities. The share of agriculture in the rural labour force has fallen dramatically – from 85 per cent in 1974 to 66 per cent in 1984/85. This shift has been accompanied by an increase in other occupations, including construction (33%), trade (17%) and transport (9.9%). However, female labour force participation rates remain low – much lower than India.

In the countryside, it has risen very gradually, from 7 per cent in the early eighties to around 17 per cent in 1996.

Village studies from the 1970s and earlier noted that women's contribution in the agricultural process was largely in post-harvest processing. This used manually operated technology and was carried out in the home, usually as unpaid family labour. Larger land-owning households, however, did hire female labour from landless groups to substitute for the labour of women within the family. Moreover, women's employment often eludes official statistics. For example, official estimates in 1981 were of 3 per cent female labour force participation. However, a study based on 1985 data from four villages found that 8–20 per cent of households sent their women in search of wage employment. Among landless households, the figures rose to 50–77 per cent. Information from 46 villages in the same district confirmed that 11–24 per cent of households – and around 60 per cent of landless households – had women in wage employment. This may have reflected: (a) a gradual lessening of restrictions of female labour force participation due to poverty; and (b) new employment opportunities for women in field-based tasks due to the Green Revolution. While some of this female agricultural labour is in own cultivation, some of it is for wages.

A re-survey in 1994 of eight villages first surveyed in 1980 showed a significant increase in women's income contributions in poor households, evidence of increasing participation in paid work. Whereas the earlier study had estimated that women contributed 24 per cent of household income, the more recent study suggested that they now contributed around 45 per cent. Children's contribution had declined from 29 per cent of household income to 6 per cent, partly because many more now attended school.

Studies of micro-credit programmes that target women in poor and landless households report their increased participation in market-oriented work as well as increases in the size of their contributions. Yet this increased participation continues to follow the traditional gender division of labour in the informal economy. There has also been a increase in female migration into towns in recent years, partly in response to the pull exercised by the rise in export garment manufacturing.

[W]omen's employment often eludes official statistics.

[P]oor women are paid even less than poor men. Thus while their earnings are used to meet basic needs in the household, they are not sufficient to pull households out of poverty.

Household poverty and women's paid work

Apart from restrictions on women's mobility noted, another reason for the strong association between household poverty and women's work is that poor women are paid even less than poor men. Thus while their earnings are used to meet basic needs in the household, they are not sufficient to pull households out of poverty. This is particularly so when there is no male earner in the household. Statistics at the end of the 1980s show that women in both India and Bangladesh were commonly paid approximately half the male wage for the same employment – although there are regional variations in overall wages as well as in gender wage disparities.

India

The National Sample Survey (NSS) in 1983 showed that women from landless and land-poor households had the highest levels of participation in paid work, while women from landholding households had higher levels of participation in various unpaid forms of productive activity. This unpaid work played an important 'expenditure saving' or 'income replacing' role. However, there is an important distinction between those activities based on ownership of resources (livestock rearing, homestead farming) and those involving common property resources (fuel and fodder). The former were largely done by women in landowning households, while the latter were undertaken by poorer women. The importance of this latter category of activity is shown by a study in Rajasthan, which found that 42 per cent of the income of labouring and land-poor households came from common property resources compared to 15 per cent for larger landowners.

Most women combined their productive activities, whether paid or unpaid, with domestic chores. For example, time allocation data collected in rural Madhya Pradesh found that domestic chores averaged 58 per cent of women's work time across the sample of 155 households. This rose to 79 per cent among middle income and 96 per cent among wealthy households. Around 50 per cent of women's work time went into unpaid family labour in agricultural production among middle income farming households. This compared to just 5 per cent among landless wage labouring households. Wage labour

Young woman selling food products in India
INTERNATIONAL LABOUR ORGANIZATION

accounted for around 40 per cent of women's working time among this latter group, but was negligible among middle and wealthy farmers.

Along with a general rise in wages in the country, there was a faster rise in real agricultural wages for women than men in almost every state. Gender wage disparities have declined. Overall, rural women's earnings were only 52 per cent of their male counterparts in 1972 but had risen to 69 per cent by 1983. In West Bengal, female farm wages rose from 75 per cent of male wage rates to 86 per cent between the mid-1960s and the early 1970s. The gap between male and female wages was highest, and fluctuated most, in the least agriculturally developed areas.

Studies suggest that women's ability to translate their

Cross national data covering over 40 high, middle and low-income countries shows that many more women are to be found in 'male' occupations outside agriculture than men are to be found in 'female' ones. However, women continue to be paid a 'female' wage.

education into higher wages has increased over time. Earlier studies, based on data from the 1970s, had shown that the effect of extra education, even among unskilled farm labourers, was substantial for men but insignificant for women. However, a later study in West Bengal found that returns to education were positive for both women and men and actually higher for women. One explanation may be the growing need for skilled labour stemming from the spread of Green Revolution technology. Another may be connected to the increase in public sector employment, though this largely benefited the better-off households (and men more than women). Gender differentials persist, however, and have been slower to change in some regions than others (*see box 5.1*).

Box 5.1 Male and Female Tasks and Pay Levels

A study in rural Tamil Nadu showed a marked gender division of labour in agriculture among the landless 'untouchable' castes. Men traditionally did the ploughing, digging and sowing while women did the carrying and weeding. Women earned around half as much as men for the same number of hours. Both women and men agreed that men should be paid more because their work was 'harder' and because it would be humiliating for a man to be paid the same as a woman, even for the same work. When the mechanisation of ploughing led to the displacement of large numbers of men, they preferred to remain unemployed than do 'female' work for fear of losing face (although women sometimes took on men's jobs).

This reluctance on the part of men to take up 'female' work appears to extend far beyond rural Tamil Nadu. Cross national data covering over 40 high, middle and low-income countries shows that many more women are to be found in 'male' occupations outside agriculture than men are to be found in 'female' ones. However, women continue to be paid a 'female' wage.

Bangladesh

In Bangladesh, studies since the 1970s have showed a strong connection between female paid activity and household poverty. There was greater poverty in households with female wage earners, most of whom came from landless households and had started work either because their husband's income was insufficient (due to sickness, disability or underemployment) or else because of divorce or separation. Such women contributed around 24 per cent of their households' total annual income, compared to around 1 per cent of household income by women who did not undertake waged work.

Household survey data from 1994 and 2000 indicated that paid work in the countryside continued to be undertaken by women from poorer households, particularly those from female-headed households. A large-scale national household survey found that share of household income from female earnings was significantly higher in poorer households.

As in India, common property resources play an important expenditure-saving function for poor households. This includes collecting fuel and fodder, house-building materials and various wild fruits and vegetables; fishing; and crop gleaning. National household surveys in 1990 showed that such activities accounted for around 4 per cent of the total income of large landowning households but around 22 per cent for landless and land-poor households. Micro-level studies confirm that women and children make an important contribution to this work.

Gender and work in urban areas

Poverty also has a marked gender dimension in urban areas in South Asia. Urbanisation is growing across the sub-continent, partly driven by the rural poor's search for employment. The percentage of women living in urban areas has risen from around 19 per cent in 1970 to around 25 per cent in recent years.

India

In India, workers in the organised sector are largely drawn from skilled castes and better-off families. Gender reinforces this caste and class segmentation. Not only are organised sector workers overwhelmingly male, but also poor women tend to be concentrated in the most casualised segments of the informal economy. Indian census data shows that women's labour force

A large-scale national household survey [in Bangladesh] found that share of household income from female earnings was significantly higher in poorer households.

Large and medium-sized enterprises in India have increasingly subcontracted work to women based at home or in small workshops ... Female workers became 60 per cent of the workforce.

participation in urban areas is lower both than men's and than that of women in rural areas. It also appears to have been declining since the 1970s. This may be because it is easier to combine subsistence and paid work in rural areas. Access to some form of productive resource – a homestead plot, livestock and poultry or ecological reserves – allows women to feed the family as well as earn an income. In urban areas, on the other hand, earning a living requires more mobility, financial capital and skills, including skills in dealing with officials. This places women at a greater disadvantage.

On the other hand, official statistics may be even less able to capture the nature of women's paid activities in the urban informal economy than they are in the rural. For example, one study found that sub-contracting had increased from 9.36 per cent in 1970 to 25 per cent in 1993–1994. This has led to an expansion of women's participation in various kinds of labour-intensive technologies, largely located in the informal economy.

Yet this had gone largely undetected in macro-statistics. A great deal of this increase seems to be associated with export-oriented manufacturing and with multinational companies (*see box 5.2*).

Box 5.2 The 'Feminising' of Export-oriented Work

Large and medium-sized enterprises in India have increasingly subcontracted work to women based at home or in small workshops. For example, textile production in Tirpur was originally carried out in mills employing only male workers. With the fragmentation of the production process, however, women workers began to be drawn in as 'helpers', often from the home. The expansion of exports led to a rapid acceleration in subcontracting and informalisation. Female workers became 60 per cent of the workforce. They were hired on casual piecework contracts and earned daily incomes that were barely above the official minimum in the area. Similar increases in sub-contracting were also observed in other export sectors (e.g. garments, plastics, and cashew and coir processing). These trends indicate that, as in other countries, export-oriented employment in India has been 'feminised'. However, this is often not visible since it is largely located in the informal economy.

Bangladesh

Bangladesh has also experienced both a rise in urbanisation and an increase in the percentage of the female population living in urban areas (from 8 per cent in 1970 to 14 per cent in recent years). Because restrictions on women's mobility in the public domain tend to be more strictly enforced in rural areas, poorer women have been migrating to the relative anonymity of towns since the 1970s to earn a living. Small-scale studies from the 1970s and 1980s, for example, noted the high proportion of destitute women, often female heads, among slum dwellers in Dhaka. These women mainly worked in the informal economy as domestic servants or in a range of casual or marginalised forms of work (e.g. prostitution).

Unlike India, official statistics document a fairly rapid rise in urban female labour force participation over the last decade or so. This work is in a range of export-oriented industries, particularly the garment industry, which took off in the 1980s. In other words, the 'feminisation' of export-oriented manufacturing has taken a far more visible form in Bangladesh than it seems to have done in India. High percentages of female rural migrants are employed in these factories, often drawn from the poorest parts of the country. Clearly, the pressures of poverty have combined with the 'pull' of new opportunities to erode some of the previous restrictions on women's public mobility.

Household poverty and women's work in urban areas

The association found in rural areas between women's participation in paid work and household poverty is also found in urban areas.

India

Activities in which women from low-income households are involved are low paying, require low skills and are extensions of domestic work. The main exception to this pattern is the information technology (IT) sector, which provided well-paid jobs but largely benefited educated urban women. A National Institute of Urban Affairs (NIUA) survey of six cities in 1988 found that 31 per cent of the working women were self-employed, 25 per cent were piece rate workers and 18 per cent were casual labourers. Predictably, they were concentrated in

[In Bangladesh] because restrictions on women's mobility in the public domain tend to be more strictly enforced in rural areas, poorer women have been migrating to the relative anonymity of towns since the 1970s to earn a living.

Homeworkers often receive the lowest labour returns. This family is from Nepal

INTERNATIONAL LABOUR ORGANIZATION

the lowest paying and least skilled occupations. Homeworkers received the lowest returns, lower even than casual wage workers. The very low returns to women's work in the informal economy, where they tend to be concentrated, explains the strong association between women's economic activity and household poverty in urban areas.

The same survey showed that female labour force participation was higher among low-income households than census estimates for all the cities, and considerably higher for younger age groups. 62 per cent of low-income households had at least one working woman; percentages were much higher in cities based in the south. Female work force participation was highest in households where the head was employed in casual labour, and these were likely to be the poorest. A study based in Faridabad noted the extreme poverty of female-maintained households: 14.2 per cent of those sampled depended entirely on female earnings and these were 'the poorest of the poor'.

However, despite the low pay women receive, their economic contributions have been shown to be the single most important element of the survival strategy of poor urban households. The NIUA study confirmed that 11 per cent of households relied entirely on female earnings, while women contributed 25–50 per cent of earnings in around a third of the households.

Bangladesh

Studies of the urban economy in Bangladesh also reveal the association between female labour force participation and household poverty. Household survey data from 1992 gave overall male labour force participation rates of 68 per cent, compared to 34 per cent among women. While increases in per capita household income led to a decline in participation rates for both women and men – partly reflecting more younger household members currently studying – the decline was very much steeper for women. This was probably because many more women, particularly married women, gave up work.

A recent study of the livelihoods of poorer urban households provides more details about women's activities and confirms the gender segmentation of the informal economy:

* Women were largely found in garment factories, domestic service, street-selling and trading (on a petty scale and within a restricted area) and manual labouring, mainly in the construction industry.

* Men were found in the transport sector (e.g. rickshaw pulling and taxi driving); skilled crafts (e.g. carpentry, mosaic laying and metal work) and the service industry or retail sector (e.g. shop/restaurant/hotel workers, barbers and cooks).

The rise of export-oriented manufacturing, particularly garments, has provided an opening into the formal economy for women, many of whom come from poor households. It has also made some degree of improvement in their circumstances

[D]espite the low pay women receive, their economic contributions have been shown to be the single most important element of the survival strategy of poor urban households.

A study of urban slum households [in Bangladesh] found that those with a female garment worker ... were more likely to be able to meet their daily needs and even to save than those without.

possible (*see box 5.3*). However, the extent to which women's contributions have changed their position in the household is severely limited by differences in female and male earnings, obstacles to their advancement and men's control over whether they work outside the home or not.

Box 5.3 The Garment Industry and Improved Possibilities for Women

The garment industry pays higher wages than most activities available to women in the informal economy in Bangladesh (though it has many of the features of informalisation discussed in Chapter 3). Micro-level studies show that women day labourers earn around 11 *takas* a day while domestic servants earn around 690 *takas* a month. By contrast, one study found that, although around 25 per cent of female garment workers earned less than 500 *takas* a month, 25 per cent earned more than 1,500 a month. Gender differences in wages are less than in other manufacturing industries. In addition, women's wages more than doubled between 1990 and 1996, making it possible for women to improve their situation. A study of urban slum households found that those with a female garment worker amongst their members were more likely to be able to meet their daily needs and even to save than those without. However, households which reported a female manual labourer as a member were much less likely to meet their needs than those where women did not work. This supports the view that manual labour, particularly for women, is a low-status option, resorted to only in times of extreme hardship.

Gender Inequality and Household Poverty in Sub-Saharan Africa

There are fewer cultural restrictions on women's mobility in the public domain in sub-Saharan Africa and consistently high estimates of female labour force participation. The biases that have led to women's work being underestimated in national statistics in other regions do not seem to have done so here.

However, due to various constraints, poor women have a far more limited set of economic options than men from equivalent social groups. The *kind* of work that women do may thus be a more powerful indicator of poverty than the fact that they work. Once again, though, flawed models, inappropriate concepts and unreliable statistics fail to reveal all their different productive activities. Moreover, while its low density of population leads to the region being characterised as 'land-abundant', this is misleading. Only a third can be classified as 'land-abundant' and even this is declining.

These flaws have also obscured how the poor earn their livelihoods in general. There has been an overemphasis in the region on subsistence farming combined with a lack of attention to markets. There appears to be a view among many economists that labour markets in rural Africa are very thin and are only now emerging in some areas in response to population growth and external trade opportunities. There are, of course, variations across the subcontinent that reflect differences in the climate and in 'local histories of impoverishment and accumulation'. Yet it can be safely said that most people in rural areas cannot depend for their livelihood on farming alone. The poorest groups are thus those without access to off-farm income (*see box 5.4*).

There has been an overemphasis in [sub-Saharan Africa] on subsistence farming combined with a lack of attention to markets.

Box 5.4 The Importance of Off-farm Income to Rural Households

A comprehensive review of 23 field studies across sub-Saharan Africa noted that, on average, 45 per cent of rural households' income came from the non-farm sector. This was so despite wide variations in the source of the contributions – whether from waged work, self-employment in off-farm activities or migration. In many cases:

- non-farm income activities were more important than on-farm ones;

- within the non-farm sector, wage labour was more important than income from self-employment; and

- except in districts near mines and urban markets, local employment in the non-farm sector produced more income than income from migrants.

The very poor have long diversified their activities because no single source of income can sustain household members. Unable to buy the inputs needed to improve farm yields, their only option is to enter off-farm activities that require little capital and few skills. Off-farm activity can also be driven by the need for capital to invest in farm productivity or to smooth seasonal ups and downs in agricultural production. More recently, it has been accelerated by the economic liberalisation that led to the removal of seed and fertiliser subsidies and of government-regulated food pricing. This undermined peasant production of food and cash crops, particularly in regions with poor transport links. At the same time, the price of consumer goods went up and there were cut-backs in public funding of various social services. Rural households therefore had to search for new, more remunerative activities outside agriculture.

Men appear to be moving into the off-farm sector faster than women, leading to a higher concentration of women on the land. In most of the region, men make up the majority of migrants to mines and cities in search of employment, leaving women to take up male tasks in agriculture. With the spread of market relations, agriculture in sub-Saharan Africa, as in South and West Asia, is becoming increasing 'feminised'.

Gender and economic activity in the rural economy

While it is widely acknowledged that women play a major role in agriculture in Africa, there has been a tendency to associate them with food crops and men with cash crops. The reality is much more varied not only across the region but also often between neighbouring areas. In some parts of the sub-continent, women grow the staple food crop for family subsistence while men grow food for sale; in others, men grow industrial or export crops, perhaps in addition to the food staple. There is also a range of other possibilities.

Women certainly contribute a high percentage of labour in food production – for household consumption as well as for sale. This ranges from 30 per cent in Sudan to 80 per cent in the Congo. The percentage of women in the economically active labour force in agriculture ranges from 48 per cent in Burkina Faso to 73 per cent in the Congo. This means that men are often heavily involved in food production. Women also produce and sell crops to buy other food. The poorest house-holds often have a deficiency of cereals because of the small size of their holdings. A 'time-honoured' survival strategy is thus the sale of higher economic and nutritional value foods, such as pulses and legumes, in order to purchase lower-value cereals. If women grow secondary crops while men grow the staple cereal, their production may be more market-oriented than men's.

Livelihoods based on land in the region depend on other factors of production, including labour and various productive inputs, animal traction and improved implements. They also depend on the ability to cultivate high-value crops and have access to marketing outlets. While women may have access to land, they do not usually have title to it, resulting in insecurity of tenure. This leaves widows, divorced and deserted women in a difficult position, particularly in patrilocal societies. Lack of access to agricultural credit by rural farmers affects both men and women. However, state marketing boards and agricultural co-operatives have tended to buy from – and distribute supplies, credit and extension services to – male household heads. Women often need husbands' permission before being granted loans.

While women may have access to land, they do not usually have title to it, resulting in insecurity of tenure.

Women picking tea in Tanzania
UN/DPI

[NTAE] contracts are provided on the understanding that male household heads can mobilise the labour of women and children in the family.

Contract farming

The problems of women farmers have been worsened by the increasing commercialisation of agriculture. New non-traditional agricultural export (NTAE) crops are mainly produced in large-scale plantations and packing plants. However, certain export crops – particularly horticulture – are grown by smallholder farmers, often on a contract basis. Generally it is the better-off farmers who have benefited because land, equipment and other capital requirements were needed to qualify for the contracts. In Kenya, for example, smallholders growing export vegetables were found to own twice as much and better quality land those that did not, and their land was also more likely to be irrigated.

Box 5.5 The Expansion of NTAEs in Uganda

In Uganda, the slump of coffee prices in the early 1990s led to a move, strongly promoted by the World Bank, into non-traditional agricultural export (NTAE) crops. A recent study set in two villages found that men and women expressed different preferences in their choice of crops and different concerns in relation to household livelihoods. Women emphasised food security while men emphasised income generation. While the two are clearly related, the difference may reflect women's lower confidence in, and poorer access to, markets. The importance of market access is also supported by evidence that the poorer and more isolated village focused primarily on food crops while the village closer to Kampala had begun to specialise in cash crops.

Labour was the biggest constraint on the ability of households to respond to improvement in prices for their crops. Female-headed households relied heavily on (predominantly male) hired labour. Women's labour supply was also less elastic than men's due to the other demands on their time. Other constraints included lack of access to agricultural inputs. The study found greater flexibility in the actual division of labour than might be expected, suggesting that men would be willing to participate in all stages of agricultural production if the incentives were right. However, they were not necessarily willing to increase their contribution to domestic labour.

The contracts are also provided on the understanding that male household heads can mobilise the labour of women and children in the family. Men have thus taken on the management of cash crops, while women are expected to contribute labour to these crops as well as their own. For example, women in Kenya provide the primary labour in the production of French beans for export, and experience an increase in their workloads, but men sign the contracts and hence receive the payments. In addition, men have begun to encroach on land that had previously been used by women for household food production and for sale in local produce markets, thereby eroding independent spheres of activity by women.

Off-farm activities

There has been limited research on women's off-farm activities because of the strong association of women with subsistence farming. However, there is evidence of significant levels of involvement. A study in Zimbabwe, for example, that looked at the income from activities in 12 villages found 58 per cent of men and 42 per cent of women engaged in home-based industries. The work undertaken was gender specific, however, and women's was generally less remunerative. For example, the lowest annual income for a male home industry – brick-makers – was at least seven times as much as that for beer brewing, a female occupation.

A re-study in 1989 of an area in north-east Ghana originally studied in 1975 found many more women engaged in generating income through off-farm activities than previously. However, the actual range of activities had not changed much. The most important source of income was trading, primarily in cooked food and various kinds of petty trade. Women's contribution to household livelihoods thus combined their reproductive work, their productive work for male household members and some independent economic activity.

Waged labour

The other under-reported, and under-researched, aspect of women's work is wage labour, particularly casual wage labour on smallholder farms. This is part of the larger failure noted above to recognise the importance of rural labour markets in Africa. Nevertheless, employment by the day, for cash and for

[In Zimbabwe] the lowest annual income for a male home industry – brick-makers – was at least seven times as much as that for beer brewing, a female occupation.

payment in kind, is widespread. It is a critical source of labour supply to the more successful farmers in smallholder areas. Female waged labour is also of growing importance for very poor households, though to a varying degree across the sub-continent.

For example, a study in Zambia in the late 1980s found that around two-thirds of the sampled households hired labour for growing hybrid maize and that the regular supply of locally hired casual labour was largely female. On the other hand, studies in Uganda found wage labour mainly provided by men, particularly younger, single men. They entered the labour market to establish themselves financially or to support a young family, and left it when their households were more established. Women seeking waged employment were generally divorced or widowed.

Wage labour opportunities have expanded in many parts of the region as a result of the increased cultivation of NTAE crops. Women make up a significant percentage of the workforce in the large-scale enterprises organised along quasi-industrial lines. In Kenya and Zambia, for example, over 65 per cent of workers in vegetable packing plants and on farms are women. In Zimbabwe, women make up 91 per cent of horticultural employees. These women tend to be young and often unmarried, but there is also a high proportion of women heads of households. In Kenya, for example, they made up over half of those participating in export vegetable production. Ninety per cent of women working in South African fruit production were married.

The majority of women who take up these jobs have few asset holdings and limited wage-earning opportunities in agriculture. The export horticulture industry attracts large numbers of individuals from landless and land poor households who migrate from rural areas to work in packing sites in the cities. A recent study in Kenya found that 100 per cent of wage workers in packinghouses and 86 per cent of those on farms had migrated from other parts of the country, often leaving their children behind. One major difference for women working as waged labour in the NTAE sector is that they are paid cash in direct exchange for their labour in contrast to the unpaid labour they provide on family farms.

Household poverty and women's economic activity

Given the generally high rates of female labour force participation in sub-Saharan Africa, there is no clear-cut association between household poverty and women's labour force participation of the kind noted in South Asia. Nor, however, is there necessarily any relationship between the income of the household and the poverty of its women members. Indeed, since income pooling is not practised in many parts of Africa, it is quite possible for married women to be much poorer than their husbands if they do not receive any support from them. They must then survive largely through their own efforts.

The gendered structure of authority and incentives within the household has been shown by several studies. For example, a study in Cameroon noted women's reluctance to provide their labour to crops when the proceeds would be controlled by men. They preferred to use their labour on crops that were under their control. It also pointed to the use of violence by men to coerce their wives into providing the necessary labour. A number of well-known studies in the Gambia also highlight struggles in the household over the allocation of women's labour and provide examples of project failures that resulted from this. Analysis from Burkina Faso shows how senior males in the household control labour and other inputs on holdings, to the relative neglect of holdings controlled by junior men as well as female members.

These studies have drawn attention to 'allocative inefficiencies' (i.e. the fact that resources are not distributed in an efficient way) because of inequalities in household relations. However, they generally neglect gender inequalities external to the household. These include a lack of agricultural inputs (fertiliser, plough, etc.) that is more common among female-headed households. Moreover, as noted earlier, poverty in the region is increasingly associated with the inability to obtain an income from off-farm activities. These often provide the funds to invest in raising agricultural productivity. With their smaller holdings, women farmers are unlikely to generate enough surplus from their farming activities to provide the start-up capital for off-farm enterprise and many rely on male household members to assist them. However, poorer women are least likely to have such support. With little start-up capital and

With their smaller holdings, women farmers are unlikely to generate enough surplus from their farming activities to provide the start-up capital for off-farm enterprise ...

[In north-east Ghana] women might suffer from poverty even when their husbands did not, but ... poor male household heads did not have wives with high incomes or secure assets.

poorer access to land, the kinds of options available to them are likely to yield low returns. Women's scarce labour time is thus spent in low productivity, low-income activities.

This may also be true for men to some extent. However, men tend to have more capital, skills or education, which enable them to escape. For example, research from rural Tanzania shows that men were far more successful than women in translating educational achievements into off-farm employment. A 36-year-old man with secondary education had a three in four chance of such employment while a woman of the same age and educational level had only half that chance. With completed primary education she had a quarter of the chance, and with partial primary education only a fifth.

> ### Box 5.6 Women's Poverty Status in Households in North-East Ghana
>
> In the large, complex households of north-east Ghana, there could be several married female members with a wide range in their incomes and savings. The wife's poverty status was not the same as her husband's. It depended instead on the transfers made by husbands to assist their wives and the wider set of relationships that women drew on for start-up capital for their own enterprises. These included those of their natal families. The women likely to be poorer were those who: (a) were prevented by their age from working and could not rely on kin for their material needs; or (b) were in poor health and therefore forced to depend on husbands/fathers. In other words, women might suffer from poverty even when their husbands did not, but the converse did not seem to be true – i.e. poor male household heads did not have wives with high incomes or secure assets.

Research in Ghana, where off-farm opportunities for women were few and poorly paid, highlights how poverty might be unequally distributed in the same household (*see box 5.6*). Labour markets appeared to be very underdeveloped in this area, although many women worked for others for in-kind returns. Where wage labour markets were more developed, studies suggest that women's participation in agricultural wage labour – particularly casual wage labour – can be taken as an important indicator of both household and female poverty. While casual wage labour is generally poorly paid, women receive between one third and half the male rate for a day's work.

Women's lower wages in Uganda, for example, reflected a combination of their domestic workloads, their responsibility for the food needs of the family and their lack of bargaining power, given the lack of or limited alternatives. There was a higher frequency of 'distress' sales on the part of women due to their responsibilities for meeting basic needs within the household (i.e. they accepted less than the going rate of pay because of urgent need for food or income). This undermined their bargaining position.

Small farmers in Nigeria, some of them women, generated less employment per farmer than large farmers but paid higher daily wages. One reason was that small-scale farmers hired their close female relatives and friends and needed to keep their good will while larger farmers had less personalised relationships. However, the lowest wages and strictest terms of work were found in agribusiness units. Consequently, agribusiness workers tended to be poorer, foreign migrants or in urgent need of cash. None of these women had a farm of their own so land shortages may have been developing in the area.

In areas of rural Zimbabwe, female wage labour was low paid because it tended to be undertaken by female household heads who had no source of male support and less bargaining power with employers. There was a difference between *de jure* and *de facto* female heads.[1] The former were much poorer, less likely to receive remittances and owned less land and assets than male-headed households or *de facto* female-headed households. The overwhelming majority of the women in casual labour in the country's largest agri-industrial enterprise were *de jure*

There was a higher frequency of 'distress' sales on the part of women due to their responsibilities for meeting basic needs within the household ...

---

[1]In Africa, *de jure* female heads are those who become heads of their own households as a result of divorce, widowhood or abandonment or else as wives in polygamous marriages while *de facto* female-headed households are those where male family members are absent, usually because they have migrated in search of work.

Better functioning labour markets are important in easing the labour constraints faced by women-headed households.

household heads (while the majority of male casual labourers were married). The children of female casual workers suffered from higher than average levels of malnutrition.

Box 5.7 The Importance of Labour Markets to Economic Growth

Better functioning labour markets are important in easing the labour constraints faced by women-headed households. They also provide labour opportunities for women from poorer households who rely on this as a source of income. A survey in rural Tanzania, for example, found that the poorest households were predominantly female-only and had smaller holdings. They were also the main source of agricultural manual wage labour. Around 80 per cent had at least one agricultural wage labourer compared to households that were either headed by men or received male support. In the latter group, there was evidence that men prevented their wives from taking up waged work and women often gave this up when they got married. Marriage was thus a major constraint on women's ability to provide wage labour. On the other hand, the availability of this work allowed many women to leave violent marriages. In this example, labour shortages constrained economic accumulation in a potentially dynamic sector of the rural economy. This shortage partly reflected the exercise of patriarchal authority within the household. It prevented a female wage labour force emerging in a situation where the availability of labour would have contributed to economic growth.

A more recent study of rural poverty in South Africa selected a sample of households based on female involvement with wage labour. These households were compared with a national survey of rural households and found to have higher levels of poverty. However, there were variations in their poverty levels. Households that had ratios of adult resident men to women below the mean for all black rural households were also poorer, and households made up entirely of females were the poorest. Very few of these women were able to earn a living through

self-employment in cultivation or livestock-raising. Instead, they relied for survival on selling their labour, with agricultural wage labour accounting for around 60 per cent of such employment. This and domestic service were the least well-paid jobs in the labour market. According to the national survey, 58 per cent of households received 90 per cent or more of their income as wages or remitted wages.

The study explores variations in the levels of poverty among sample households to identify: (a) the characteristics of poor women who had been able to escape from the worst aspects of deprivation; and (b) barriers that blocked the escape routes of others. The former were mainly women who earned relatively high wages in stable employment on large-scale, state-run farms. They had:

A woman does the family washing in a river in Zimbabwe
UN/DPI

* completed a relatively large number of years of schooling;

* avoided too early and too frequent pregnancies; and

* not allowed male family members to prevent them from seeking wage employment.

[E]vidence from urban areas in sub-Saharan Africa shows that women are more likely to be found in the informal economy than in the formal, and in self-employment within it.

They thus had longer and less interrupted work experience. Part of their success stemmed from advantages derived from parents, particularly from highly motivated mothers.

Gender and economic activity in the urban economy

In general, evidence from urban areas in sub-Saharan Africa shows that women are more likely to be found in the informal economy than in the formal, and in self-employment within it. Men, on the other hand, are more likely to be found in the public sector and in various forms of formal as well as informal waged employment.

Education has an important role to play in access to better-paid jobs outside farming in many parts of the region. However, it appears to have a greater significance in formal rather than informal employment and in urban rather than rural contexts. It has been found to increase the likelihood for both men and women to enter public sector employment. Yet studies in several countries (Côte d'Ivoire, Ghana, Guinea and Uganda) show that, for every level of education, men were more likely to obtain public sector employment than women, and to earn higher wages. The effect was least in evidence in the self-employed sector where most women were located. Schooling in Ghana was found to be positively associated with entry into wage employment and, among wage employees, with entry in the public sector. Similar findings were reported for Côte d'Ivoire, Guinea and Uganda.

While women gained more limited entry into public sector employment than men in much of Africa, many more women were also affected by the cuts in public sector employment as a result of structural adjustment policies (SAPs). This is because they were concentrated in the lower skilled and lower paid jobs where the majority of the cuts were made. For example, women made up 26 per cent of public sector employment in Ghana but 35 per cent of those downsized. Moreover, a study from Guinea noted that of the thousands who were retrenched from public sector employment, women were less able than men to find jobs in the private sector. However, this is likely to refer to formal sector employment as their share of informal employment appears to be on the increase.

Earlier ideas about the urban informal economy in Africa saw it as made up of those who had not been able to find more better paid formal employment with possibilities for upward mobility. However, these have had to be revised in the light of a dramatic decline in real wages in the urban formal sector (from an index of 100 in 1975 to 52 in 1985) and the emergence of a highly profitable 'parallel' economy. The share of the female labour force in the informal sector rose from 10 per cent in 1970 to 18 per cent in 1990 (and consequently the percentage of women from 29 to 35%). At the same time, increasing numbers of men are also seeking opportunities in the informal economy because of the higher earnings there.

However, men and women from poorer households – who lack skills, education and capital – have always been found in the informal economy. There they engage in a wide range of income-generating activities. As noted earlier, women are particularly concentrated in the self-employed sector. This offers not only relative ease of entry to those with little or no education but also some degree of flexibility in managing domestic activities. Male enterprise tended to be more capital-intensive, although returns to capital inputs were positive and significant for both men and women, and perhaps more so for the latter. Vocational training had little effect on productivity but may have eased entry into certain sectors.

Within the category of self-employed workers, women make up 62–87 per cent of those in trading. As traders, aside from market women in areas of West Africa, they tend to be confined to the less profitable niches. For instance, one study found that 75 per cent of traders in urban food markets in Tanzania were men and that they controlled almost all the maize wholesale and intermediary trade. Women were generally concentrated in the low-profit retail trade. Similarly, a study of the rice market in eastern Guinea found that female traders tended to be small-scale whereas male traders were generally wholesalers. Gender also differentiated the scale and type of products. Women were more likely to trade in perishable goods (fresh fruit and vegetables) and in smaller quantities. This is seen as an extension of their role in household food provisioning and so does not challenge prevailing gender ideologies. According to one study carried out in Burkina Faso, there is a clear correlation between income and scale of trade. Wholesalers in fruits and vegetables earned five times more income than retailers.

Data from South Africa showed that the net monthly income of self-employed women in 1990 was about 44 per cent of that earned by men in the same category. In Abidjan, women heads of business in the informal sector also earned less than half of the amount earned by men. Among independent marginal workers (i.e. those with no capital) women earned half that of men in the same situation in Burkina Faso, 30 per cent in Cameroon, 38 per cent in Côte d'Ivoire and 68 per cent in Mali. However, in Guinea they earned 60 per cent more. Gender differences in returns to business activities are illustrated by a 1992 study of the informal sector in a town in northern Nigeria (*see box 5.8*).

Box 5.8 Gender Differences in Returns to Business Activities in Northern Nigeria

A study of Zaria, a town in northern Nigeria, found that women made up 45 per cent of enterprise heads. Divided into low- and high-income sectors, it found that 84 per cent of enterprise heads were in low income earning activities. These had very low entry requirements in terms of either start-up costs or skills and most such entre-preneurs had at least one other income-generating activity. 96 per cent of female entrepreneurs were low income compared with 76 per cent of males. The incomes of female heads were considerably lower than those of male heads. The study also showed that 57 per cent of the informal sector workers were employees, not independent entrepreneurs.

Between the 1970s and 1991/92, the informal sector expanded and the gap between the high- and low-income sectors and between male and female incomes widened. There had been a large rise in the proportion of women working as cheap labour in the informal sector. Their average wage was 32 per cent that of males. This is around one sixth of the official minimum wage, which itself had been pegged at less than the 1975 minimum.

Other insights into the link between household poverty and women's work can be found in studies that explore household responses in times of crisis. One such study looked at Tanzania in 1988 at a time when the country was undergoing crisis and economic reform. This had led to sharply declining real wages in the formal sector and increasing pursuit of informal income-generating activities, primarily by women. That women's increased involvement in income generation was largely a response to crisis is shown by the fact that 80 per cent of them had started their businesses in the five years prior to the survey compared to 50 per cent of the men. The number of self-employed urban women had risen from 7 per cent in the 1970s to over 60 per cent. In many cases, it was their husbands who provided them with start-up capital. Households maintained their attachments to formal employment where possible because of the security, rather than the amount, of earnings. Women were more likely to combine activities, the most common being small businesses and urban farming, usually on plots in peri-urban areas.

A focus on urban formal employment obscured a major consequence of economic reform: the role of women's informal incomes in the widening gap between income groups and the reasons for it. Such a focus suggests that women from upper and middle-income households earned only two or three times the income made by an average working woman. A look at these same women's earnings in the informal economy, however, shows them making about 10 times what poorer women made from their small businesses, and an average of 10 times their own formal salaries as professionals. Their advantage lay in their access to greater capital, know-how and resources to enter major businesses.

Links between Gender Inequality and Income Poverty: The Wider Picture

This chapter has drawn largely on material from South Asia and sub-Saharan Africa to highlight:

* women's role as economic actors;

* the critical importance of their economic contributions to the household; and

It is clear that women's work is critical to the survival and security of poor households and an important route through which they are able escape out of poverty.

- the particular importance of this contribution in the livelihood strategies of the poor.

This final section makes some generalisations about the links between gender inequality and household poverty and their implications for the goal of poverty reduction, and includes examples from other regions.

Women's work and household survival

It is clear that women's work is critical to the survival and security of poor households and an important route through which they are able to escape out of poverty. Women from poor households engage in a variety of income-generating and expenditure-saving activities. In some cases, these supplement male contributions while in others they are the primary, or sole, source of household livelihoods.

However, the relationship between women's paid work and household poverty reflects variations in both local economies and local structures of patriarchy. In regions with female seclusion, women's involvement in paid work outside the home may itself indicate household poverty. In other regions, the kind of work that women – and men – do is then a more powerful indicator of poverty than the fact that they work. The type of work connected with female poverty varies, however. For example, a study comparing livelihood strategies in the north and south of Vietnam noted that different occupations were associated with greater poverty in the two study locations. The north had a far more egalitarian distribution of land and very little landlessness. Households in which women had not been able to diversify out of the cultivation of rice and various low-grade staples into other higher-value crops or off-farm activities tended to be poorer. In the south, where landlessness was more widespread, households where women (but not men) engaged in agricultural wage labour tended to be poorer.

Over the last half-century, employment in Latin America has become predominantly urban and primarily export-oriented. While women's employment has been rising consistently, public employment has shrunk in the wake of economic crisis and restructuring, deteriorating working conditions, increased numbers of people seeking work and the mounting informalisation of labour markets. While household poverty is associated throughout the region with underemployment and unemployment, women in Chile face a higher than average risk of unemployment and/or entering precarious forms of work. According to a study based on data from Argentina, Chile and Mexico, women who worked as unpaid family labour reported the greatest degree of insecurity about both their work and their family needs.

In many parts of the region, poor, unskilled women – particularly those who have migrated from rural areas – are found mainly in domestic service, often 'living in' with employers. In the early 1990s, 25 per cent of women workers in Honduras and 14 per cent in El Salvador were estimated to be in such work. A study of low-income settlements in urban Mexico found it to be the single largest category (32%) among working female household heads as well as spouses. While conditions of work within domestic service vary, wages tend to be very low for those who live in. Hours of work are long, with few opportunities for social life. It has been observed for Peru that domestic service is only slightly better than begging or prostitution.

In the Caribbean, women have always worked outside the home and this is an integral part of their identity. Here it is the absence of paid work, rather than its presence, that signals female poverty. In particular, poverty is associated with the unemployment or underemployment of female household heads. In fact, a recent Family Life Survey carried out in Trinidad and Tobago revealed that 16 per cent of female heads had never been employed. While men in poverty generally resorted to drugs and violent crime, women were more likely to get involved in prostitution.

Women's work and household responses to crisis

A second link between household poverty and women's participation in paid work relates to household responses to crisis and insecurity. As seen in Chapter 2, SAPs put pressure on women to earn more income. This chapter has also pointed to the 'distress sale' of labour by women when usual sources of household income fall short or dry up and noted the use of women's labour as a means of smoothing household income flows.

In the Caribbean, women have always worked outside the home ... Here it is the absence of paid work, rather than its presence, that signals female poverty.

Women take gravel from a river bed for the construction industry in Indonesia

INTERNATIONAL LABOUR ORGANIZATION

Women's labour plays a key role in helping households manage various kinds of contingencies.

Women's labour plays a key role in helping households manage various kinds of contingencies.

Studies following the East Asian crisis in 1997–1998 provide other insights into the gendered nature of impacts and responses. In Indonesia, for example, a study found that 46 per cent of the unemployed were women, although they made up around a third of the labour force. In Thailand, between January 1997 and February 1998, women made up 50–60 per cent of the unemployed. In the Republic of Korea, women were 75 per cent of 'discouraged workers' and 86 per cent of those retrenched from the hard-hit banking and financial sectors. Their overall employment rate fell by 7.1 per cent, compared to 3.8 per cent for men. Export processing zones laid off their regular workers, mainly women, and re-hired them on a piece rate basis. However, as men were laid off, the percentage of women in paid and unpaid work increased.

There were also knock-on effects of the crisis on children. For example, entry into school was deferred for young children in Indonesia while older ones, particularly girls, were withdrawn in order to contribute to household livelihoods. The crisis appeared to lead to an increase in child labour, prostitution and domestic violence. In Jakarta, it is estimated that 2–4 times more women became sex workers in 1998 than in 1997.

Interestingly, the effect of crisis in some cases may be breaking down earlier barriers. One of the impacts in Indonesia, along with many more women seeking paid work in order to avoid taking older children out of school, was a break down in the normal gender division of occupations. Women entered traditionally male occupations, such as fishing in the open sea, while men took up 'female' occupations such as oyster shucking and fish salting.

It is clear from these studies that responses to crisis, shocks and insecurity are likely to take gender differentiated forms and to have gender differentiated effects because women and men face different constraints and opportunities. While men generally have wider labour market choices, they may also have to take up physically demanding forms of manual labour or travel long distances away from their homes and families in search of work. Women, on the other hand, face more restricted options that include personally humiliating forms of work such as domestic service, begging or prostitution. Responses to crisis also have gender-differentiated effects on other family members. For example, the withdrawal of children, particularly girls, from school is one mechanism behind the inter-generational transmission of poverty.

A concern with risk, insecurity and vulnerability has entered the policy discourse on poverty in a central way, as seen by comparing the 1990 and 2000 WDR. While the former gave a residual place to 'safety nets', the latter included 'security' as one of its three key themes. However, the extent to which the design of social protection and safety net measures seek to benefit women as well as men from poor households varies considerably. In some cases, as noted in Chapter 2, such measures may deliberately or unconsciously target men on the assumption that they are the primary breadwinners.

Female headship and household poverty

The relationship between female headship and household poverty is not clear-cut. However, looking at the kinds of processes that give rise to the association between them can help reveal the interactions between gender and poverty in different socio-economic contexts (*see box 5.9*).

It seems that what is important is not female headship *per se* but the processes by which women become heads of households. These are only partly captured by the distinction between *de jure* and *de facto* female headship. While *de jure* forms of headship might be expected to be associated with greater poverty – given the likely absence of a male breadwinner – this is not always the case. For example, a comparison of households in Malawi and Kenya often found the reverse. In Kenya, this was because *de jure* female heads were often wives in polygamous marriages who received contributions from husbands towards the care of their children. In the area of Malawi studied, it was due to local marriage practices under which husbands moved in with their wives' lineage who held the family land. Most *de facto* female-headed households were the product of male migration due to household poverty. They were the poorest category in both cases, except those whose male members had migrated to South Africa at a time when high remitted wages made receiving households the most prosperous in the sample.

[T]he withdrawal of children, particularly girls, from school is one mechanism behind the inter-generational transmission of poverty.

[T]he presence of adult able-bodied male members in the household does not necessarily signify male support.

Box 5.9 Female Headship and Poverty in Bangladesh and Ghana

Analysis of household survey data sets from 10 countries failed to find a consistent relationship between female headship and different measures of income poverty except in two: Bangladesh and Ghana. The finding relating to Bangladesh is not unexpected as an association between poverty and *de jure* female headship has been consistently reported by a large number of quantitative and qualitative studies. The finding for Ghana is more surprising, as data from 1987/88 suggested that female-headed households were generally better off than male-headed ones by a number of different criteria. However, this disguised the fact that female heads worked 10 more hours per week than male heads, were more likely to be the sole primary earners in their households and had higher dependency ratios. Men were more likely to live with at least one other adult worker, while women heads were more likely to have to combine income generation with domestic work. There were varying degrees of poverty among female heads, with widows worst off, followed by divorced women. Currently married women were relatively well-off. In addition, PPAs found that female headship was associated with poverty in the north, with its patrilineal kinship systems, but not in the south where matriliniality was more prevalent. A study in the north-east also noted the high incidence of female poverty within male-headed households.

Male support, therefore, is important for distinguishing poor from less poor female-headed households. However, the presence of adult able-bodied male members in the household does not necessarily signify male support. Indeed, it may be a drain on household resources and lead to greater poverty for women and children. In Costa Rica, Mexico and the Philippines, *de jure* female-headed households were found to be better off than male-headed households for this reason. These households were often set up by women to avoid the demands made on the household budget by irresponsible husbands and partners. In many of these cases, contributions by adult sons compensated for the absence of male partners. Female-headed households in urban Mexico found it easier to defend basic consumption levels in the face of economic crisis because females controlled basic needs.

Finally, it is worth noting that evidence from Bangladesh, Vietnam and South Africa suggests that *female-only* membership appears to be an unequivocal indicator of household poverty.

Studies of household livelihoods strategies show that time is a gender dimension of poverty. Most poor women have longer working days than men.

Box 5.10 Time Poverty and Household Survival

Studies of household livelihoods strategies show that time is a gender dimension of poverty. Most poor women have longer working days than men. Their need to contribute economically to household productive efforts is combined with the resilience of the gender division of labour in reproductive activities. Variations in this depend on the extent to which domestic chores can be shifted to others within the household. A study in rural Vietnam found that the demands of domestic work limited: (a) the amount of time women had for other productive activities; (b) the range of such activities; and (c) the returns they enjoyed to their overall labour effort. Men could easily migrate in the slack season to search for work as carpenters, builders, cyclo drivers, traders, etc. Women were 'tied to the village bamboo groves' because of their responsibilities on the farm and in the home.

In response to persistent poverty over the past decade in Mexico, women and children increased their inputs into paid work. They worked longer hours for lower wages in worse conditions, relying increasingly on informal activities as formal ones became scarce. With the decreasing capacity of older adult men to provide for the household and the increasing migration of younger men in search for work in transnational labour markets, women have become the main providers for many urban poor households.

Gender inequality and returns to women's work

The final link between gender inequality and poverty reflects inequality in returns to labour, widely recognised as the key asset at the disposal of the poor. It is clear that these inequalities are not static. They can change in response to market forces or they can be addressed through public policy. In addition, they can also be addressed through various forms of bargain and protest, most effective when they are undertaken collectively (*see Chapter 7*).

Explanations for gender inequalities in returns to labour reflect a combination of the gender-specific, gender-intensified and imposed gender constraints discussed in Chapter 3. This chapter has provided various examples of gender-specific constraints, including:

* Powerful social norms in Bangladesh, the northern states of India and Pakistan that restrict women's movement in the public domain and confine them to activities in the home that generally carry lower returns.

* Primary responsibility for household tasks and childcare that limits the kind of activities women can undertake in terms of time as well as space even in the absence of cultural constraints on their public mobility.

* Ideas about masculinity and femininity that lead to returns to labour being differentiated by gender. In the study in rural Tamil Nadu mentioned earlier, the view that men 'should' earn more was subscribed to not only by employers and the men themselves but also by many of the women (*see box 5.1*). Such views exercised an upward pressure on the reserve price of male labour.

* The non-reciprocal forms of control that senior men exercise over the labour of women and junior males in the household in a number of countries in sub-Saharan Africa. This reduces the amount of time the latter can put into their own agricultural holdings or enterprises.

These various limits on women's mobility in relation to market opportunities help to explain why location appears to be far more important in explaining returns to women's labour than men's. For example, female-headed households in more remote areas were least responsive to price signals in the study on supply response to increases in maize prices referred to earlier. This was because they would least be able to transport their goods to the market. The importance of proximity to commercial areas also helped explain levels of women's entrepreneurial activity in urban areas in Africa. A study in Nigeria noted that improvements in transportation had vastly reduced the unpaid porterage (head-carrying) duties that women owed to their husbands and male kin. It has allowed them to take up paid work in agriculture as well as to start their own farms. Labour-saving technologies that addressed women's domestic workloads would have a similar effect.

Gender-intensified forms of disadvantage that have featured in the discussion relate to:

* gender inequalities in access to, and control over, land and property. Unequal principles of inheritance either dispossess women of any right to inherit land or mediate their access to it through male family members. Women consequently either do not have the option of farming or else farm smaller and less favourable plots; and

* gender inequalities in education. These restricted women's ability to take advantage of expanded public sector employment in India (which were generally closed off to men from poorer households as well). In Africa, educational inequalities were primarily relevant to accessing jobs in urban formal sector employment, but also made a difference to employment opportunities in rural labour markets.

Finally, various examples have been given of imposed disadvantage that help to reproduce, and often intensify, existing forms of gender disadvantage in the household and community. These include:

* the discrimination practised by employers who believe that men should be paid higher wages than women, regardless of the work they do;

* discriminatory practices by corporations that provide outgrower contracts to male farmers, bypassing women; and

Unequal principles of inheritance either dispossess women of any right to inherit land or mediate their access to it through male family members.

Unless economic growth is accompanied by a genuine effort to address the constraints that undermine returns to women's labour, women from low-income households will not be able to take advantage of the opportunities generated.

* the various forms of biases embedded in state provision of extension, credit and other services.

Conclusion

A key policy message emerging from the findings in this chapter relates to:

(a) the significance of women's contributions to household livelihoods, particularly among the poor; and

(b) the association between low returns to women's labour and extreme poverty.

Improving women's access to economic opportunities, as well as returns to their efforts, will clearly be critical to the goal of halving world poverty. However, a commitment to labour-intensive growth strategies will not achieve these objectives on its own. Unless economic growth is accompanied by a genuine effort to address the constraints that undermine returns to women's labour, women from low-income households will not be able to take advantage of the opportunities generated. This means dismantling various forms of discrimination in the public domain. It also means greater attention to women's workloads in the domestic domain. This includes support for their child-care responsibilities and the promotion of labour-saving technologies to reduce the burden of low-value, routine but necessary forms of domestic labour.

It could, of course, be argued (and frequently has been) that it is not important to focus on women's earning capacity since they are the secondary earners. Priority should instead be given to improving the earning capacity of the primary male bread-winner, since he has fewer constraints in taking up economic opportunities and his income is the main basis for meeting basic needs in the household. However, as argued above, this assumption of the primary male breadwinner has long had a detrimental influence on the design of development policy – including the design of measures specifically aimed at address-ing poverty. It has been shown that households are not, in fact, necessarily egalitarian. Rather, there is evidence of stark inequalities in the distribution of basic welfare in the household.

Greater importance should therefore be given to women's economic contributions in the design of policy because of: (a) the demonstrated significance of this contribution to the livelihoods of low-income households; and (b) evidence that improving male earnings does not necessarily lead to an equiv- alent improvement in the welfare of household members. Equalising economic opportunities to improve women's econ- omic agency and earning capacity may be an effective way of addressing the income poverty of households as well as the human capabilities of its members (including, of course, its female members). The evidence for this is discussed in the next chapter.

6. Gender Equality and Human Development Outcomes: Enhancing Capabilities

Introduction

In addition to the goal of halving income poverty in the world, the Millennium Development Goals are concerned with the achievement of a number of human development outcomes (*see Table 1.1, page 8*). These relate to:

* 'first-order' needs, such as food and health, that are basic to life; and

* 'second order' needs (e.g. access to contraception, education, economic opportunities and political representation) that improve the quality of life and the capacity for agency.

These human development outcomes, and the MDGs and their targets and indicators, are inter-related. For example, it has been shown that education helps reduce fertility through a number of different routes: (a) by making women more receptive to the idea of birth control; (b) by making it easier for them to access effective forms of contraception; and (c) because increasing investment in children's education makes large families less affordable.

Similarly, improvements in maternal mortality reflect reduced fertility levels as well as improved access to reproductive health facilities. Each of these in turn is facilitated by improvements in access to education and information by men as well as women that enable them to make informed choices. In other words, there are positive synergies between different aspects of human development.

Eliminating the gender gap in human capabilities depends on these kinds of factors. However, it also depends on the

*Poverty
eradication
is ... as much
a question of
values as of
resources and the
value attached to
gender equality is
central to its
achievement.*

value attached to girls and women in the family, which in turn reflects their value in the wider society. This is only partly a question of economic value. It is also bound up with social values. Improvements in maternal mortality, for example, will also depend on the kind of nourishment and care that women have received in the course of their lives. Poverty eradication is thus as much a question of values as of resources and the value attached to gender equality is central to its achievement.

Human development outcomes at a regional level were discussed in Chapter 4. This chapter focuses at a lower level of analysis and considers in particular the relationship between household poverty and various forms of gender inequality.

Gender Inequality and Human Development: The Equity Rationale

One way of exploring gender equality in relation to human development is by looking at outcomes: the extent to which women and men, boys and girls achieve equivalent levels of well-being. This 'equity rationale' sees the issue as a manifestation of social injustice. It suggests that improving women's access to resources is one route through which the MDGs on human development – including those relating in gender inequalities – can be achieved.

Gender inequality and basic well-being

The form and severity of gender inequalities in basic needs are not uniform across the world. Nor are they related in a systematic way to the regional distribution of poverty. Instead, they seem to be connected to regional variations in women's economic activity, itself a reflection of differences in kinship and gender relations. The most extreme forms of gender inequality – those whose life-threatening consequences for women and girls are evident in excess rates of female mortality – are found in regions of extreme patriarchy, where women's economic options are most limited.

A more systematic relationship between poverty and gender inequality in human development outcomes might be expected to exist *within* regions, where the effects of regional differences in kinship patterns are less likely to apply. Indeed, an analysis of data on the 'gender gap' in school enrolment among 6–14-year-olds from 41 developing countries showed that, in 21 of the countries, the gap was larger among the poorest 20 per cent of households than among the 20 per cent of richest households. In some cases it was considerably larger. However, in none of the countries were gender inequalities in schooling greater among richer rather than poorer households.

A somewhat different set of findings was reported in relation to gender inequalities in under-five mortality. A study using data from 32 developing countries found in two-thirds of them that female advantage in under-five mortality was smaller, or male advantage larger, among the poor than the rich. In other words, the tendency to favour boys was greater among poor households than rich ones. On the other hand, there were a small number of low-income countries in which female mortality rates exceeded male rates among rich, but not among poor, households.

While the latter finding may be considered exceptional, it provides household-level support for the lack of a consistent relationship noted earlier between gender inequality in life expectancy and levels of national income below a certain level of per capita GNP. This suggests that gender inequality in certain basic outcomes is not always due to poverty, or at least not only to poverty, particularly in some poorer countries.

Gender inequality and child survival: the evidence from South Asia

Extreme forms of gender inequality of a life threatening kind have a long history in South Asia. Overall, women have had a lower life expectancy than men, unlike most other parts of the world. Analysis of age-specific mortality rates suggested that girls and women died in larger numbers than boys and men until the age of 35. Declining rates of maternal mortality, however, have meant that excess levels of female mortality are now largely found among the under-fives.

There is considerable variation in the distribution of this excess female mortality within the region. For example, using juvenile sex ratios (JSRs) from 1961/71, one study noted that

[G]ender inequality in certain basic outcomes is not always due to poverty, or at least not only to poverty, particularly in some poorer countries.

149

[In India the] intersection between region, social status and gender discrimination persists and continues to confound any straightforward relationship between gender inequality and poverty ...

it was largely concentrated in Pakistan and the north-west plains of India. The Himalayan zones of India and Nepal, the eastern and southern states of India and Bangladesh reported more balanced JSRs. Other analysis suggests that gender inequalities in life expectancy in India also reflected socio-economic differentials associated with caste, giving rise to a 'perverse' positive relationship between property and inequality.

This intersection between region, social status and gender discrimination persists and continues to confound any straight-forward relationship between gender inequality and poverty in the country. Research in 2000 confirmed that highly mascu-line sex ratios were concentrated in the north-west, with more favourable ratios in the northern and south-eastern states. The pattern for the scheduled castes was similarly differentiated by region, with evidence of gender discrimination greater in the north. By contrast, ratios for the scheduled tribes, the poorest social groups in the country, were the most balanced. Micro-level studies from within the different sub-regions confirm this 'perverse' pattern.

In terms of nutrition, studies from rural Punjab in northern India generally reported that gender disparities in nutrition among children were greater among landowning than landless households. Excess levels of female mortality there also tended to be much greater for higher order female births. The fact that first-born daughters were more likely to survive suggested that parents used the 'lethal neglect' of daughters to achieve their preferred number and gender composition of children. Moreover, while *absolute* levels of mortality were lower among the propertied classes, excess levels of female mortality were higher. In addition, it was also higher among educated mothers.

Studies from southern and central India, on the other hand, reported little evidence of gender disparity among the better off or the poor. Within these more egalitarian kinship regimes, the relationship between gender inequality and poverty takes the more conventional inverse relationship. For instance, unexpect-edly heavy rainfall in rural India, which increased income, was likely to improve girls' survival chances relative to boys in the first two years, thereby closing the gender gap in mortality. In rural south India, parents gave more weight to health-related outcomes for boys than girls during the lean season.

In rural Bangladesh, one study found that the literacy of

Box 6.1 The 'Prosperity' or 'Sanskritisation' Effect

The northern states of India with the highest per capita incomes in 1981 reported some of the lowest sex ratios (around 870 women to 1,000 men). This can be compared to 1,032 in Kerala and 977 in Tamil Nadu, both southern states with lower per capita incomes. Nationally, sex ratios have declined further from 933 women per 1,000 men in 1981 to 927 in 1991, despite the fact of declining poverty. In addition, 'masculine' sex ratios have begun to spread to the lower castes as well as to the southern states. This increase in gender inequality reflects what has been called a 'prosperity' or 'sanskritisation' effect. Across India, upward mobility and increased prosperity have led to the emulation of the practices of the northern propertied castes who have traditionally reported the most severe forms of gender discrimination. The seclusion of women, resistance to widow remarriage, increased kin and village exogamy and a rise in the practice and value of dowry – all traditionally associated with the propertied castes of the north – are spreading throughout the country as the poorest groups imitate those better off.

[In India] the seclusion of women, resistance to widow remarriage ... all traditionally associated with the propertied castes of the north – are spreading throughout the country as the poorest groups imitate those better off.

mothers had a positive effect on the nutritional status of boys. Another, using data from the mid-1970s, found that boys benefited more than girls from an improvement in household resources, although this did raise the nutritional status of all children. Discrimination against girl children appeared to be one aspect of household responses to economic crisis, so that excess female mortality in the under-five age group increased during the 1974 famine.

It is generally believed in the field of development studies that economic growth and increasing prosperity are likely to lead to a decline in gender discrimination, at least at the level of basic survival. Also, life expectancy and child survival do improve with growth. However, the 'perverse' relationship between poverty and gender discrimination shown in some of these studies gives room for pause. And more recent evidence

In countries characterised by extreme patriarchy ... there is troubling evidence that parents have achieved the reduction in the 'quantity' of children through a strategy of sex-selective investments in child 'quality'.

from South Asia provides further confirmation that gender discrimination does not necessarily disappear with economic growth or poverty reduction (*see box 6.1*).

Gender inequality and the quantity-quality trade-off

Demographic transition leading to lower levels of fertility has now occurred in many parts of the developing world and is ongoing in others. Family size in East and South-East Asia has halved. This transition is also underway in other parts of Asia as well as in Latin America. The least evidence of demographic change at the regional level is in sub-Saharan Africa.

Economists suggest that one of the factors behind demographic transitions is the 'quantity-quality' trade off: the reduction in numbers of children as more resources are invested in each child. Studies from South-East Asia suggest that fertility decline has been accompanied by increased investment in the education of girls as well as boys. This has led to a closing of the gender gap in education – and its elimination at primary level – in countries such as the Philippines, Thailand and Vietnam. In Latin America and the Caribbean too, there is little evidence of discrimination against girls.

In countries characterised by extreme patriarchy, on the other hand, there is troubling evidence that parents have achieved the reduction in the 'quantity' of children through a strategy of sex-selective investments in child 'quality'. In some parts of India, this has taken the form of sex-selective investments in children's education. Even more alarming, however, is evidence that fertility decline there has been accompanied by sex-selective investment in child survival. The relative chances of survival among female children has gone down so that the worsening of the JSR has been more marked than the sex ratio at all ages. Discrimination against girl children allows parents to simultaneously reduce their fertility rates and achieve the desired sex composition of children. These practices are now in evidence in the southern states of India, particularly in Tamil Nadu, where fertility decline has been most rapid. Even Kerala, long held up as a model of gender egalitarianism, appears to be achieving further fertility decline through a widening of gender disparities in child survival – though it continues to have higher levels of absolute welfare for girls and boys than the rest of the country.

Gender-discriminatory practices have also extended to the pre-natal stage so as to influence the sex composition of *births* as well as of surviving children. Amniocentesis and ultrasound screening technologies are increasingly used to detect the sex of the foetus and then the females are aborted. This is shown by a marked shift in sex ratios at birth in north and north-west India and urban areas of central India and supported by various smaller scale studies and reports.

These practices are not confined to South Asia, although they have been more extensively researched there. The Republic of Korea, along with China, has the highest male to female birth ratios in the world: around 113.6 males per 100 females in 1988. Because measures to identify the sex of a child, followed by sex-selective abortion, tend to be resorted to after the first birth, birth ratios become more male dominated for higher order births. Between 1985 and 1987, the sex ratio was more than 130 males to 100 females for third births and the estimate in 1988 was 199 for fourth births. However, it is probably in China – with its a rigidly enforced one-child policy and deeply-entrenched preference for sons – that the most devastating consequences on the survival and well-being of girl children have occurred (*see Box 6.2*).

East Asian economies all experienced very high rates of economic growth and remarkable declines in poverty in the 1980s. Indeed, they were the basis for the labour-intensive growth strategies advanced in the 1990 *World Development Report* (WDR). These findings are a reminder that neither economic growth nor rising rates of female labour force participation necessarily eradicate gender inequality. Sex selective investments in the human capabilities of children cannot be explained in this case in terms of differential employment opportunities. Instead the reason can be found in the social values and practices that reflect the patriarchal ordering of social relations. The state could potentially take action to undermine these values and practices but this has not occurred. From gender inequalities in citizenship rights entrenched in the constitutions of Bangladesh, India and Pakistan – all three of which recognise religious law in the arena of personal life – to China's one child policy and its tragic consequences, the state has been a force for greater inequality.

From gender inequalities in citizenship rights entrenched in the constitutions of Bangladesh, India and Pakistan ... to China's one child policy and its tragic consequences, the state has been a force for greater inequality.

> **Box 6.2 Gender Discrimination and Sex Ratios in China**
>
> It is evident in China that the 'lethal neglect' of infant girls is a factor in achieving desired sex composition of children. The 'normal' sex ratio among infant deaths is around 130 boys to 100 girls. The substantially lower rates here, particularly in rural areas, of around 114 during the 1980s suggest substantial neglect of infant girls. The Chinese estimates are comparable to Pakistan (118) and Tunisia (115), both characterised by extreme forms of patriarchy, but much lower than Malaysia and the Philippines (128) in South-East Asia. Moreover, there is also evidence of pre-natal discrimination in China. Studies show that the sex ratio of births went from around 105 boys per 100 girls for all birth order combined in the 1970s (before the introduction of the one child policy) to around 114 in the 1980s to even higher levels of 153 in 1993. Sex ratios of reported births increased between 1988 and 1993 from 133 for the first birth to 172 for the second to 1,100 for the third.

Gender inequalities, work burdens and nutrition

Elsewhere in the world, gender discrimination rarely takes the systematically life-threatening form that it takes in regions of extreme patriarchy. Moreover, it is generally related to poverty and tends to be greater among poor households and communities. Studies from South-East Asia, for example, reveal weak evidence of gender bias in well-being in the household. A study in Indonesia found little evidence of discrimination against girls in choice of health treatment and standardised child weights, but mild malnourishment among girls and higher birth-order children. Data from some of the poorer rural provinces in the Philippines found mild gender discrimination in favour of husbands, who received more of their protein requirements compared to wives and children. Among children, boys and lower birth orders were relatively favoured. Evidence from Vietnam does not show significant gender inequalities in basic nutrition and health care. Early analysis of nutritional data from 94 Latin American villages, however, indicated that girls aged 0–4 were 87 per cent of their expected weight/age measurements while boys were 90 per cent.

Studies from sub-Saharan Africa show high levels of infant and child mortality but little evidence of differences suggesting gender bias. A report from the Subcommittee on Nutrition of the UN Administrative Committee on Coordination (ACC/SCN) estimated that around 20 per cent of African women were under-nourished, compared to 60 per cent in South Asia. However, there is evidence of rising excess female mortality in recent years. Demographic and Health Surveys (DHSs) from the early 1990s report excess death rates among girls in the 0–5 age group in 9 out of 14 countries, while UN estimates suggest a decline in the ratio of women to men in most regions of Africa except the south. Inequalities in health care, rather than nutritional bias, probably explain this deterioration. In addition, there are high levels of maternal mortality (*see Box 6.3*).

Sub-Saharan Africa accounts for 20 per cent of the world's births but 40 per cent of its maternal deaths. These high levels of maternal mortality partly reflect the overall poverty of the region but also the lack of basic services.

Box 6.3 Levels of Maternal Mortality

While estimates of maternal mortality need to be treated with caution because of the absence of accurate data, a report by the World Health Organization (WHO) gives some idea of the magnitude of the problem in sub-Saharan Africa, particularly in West Africa. Figures of 1,750–2,900 per 100,000 births are reported for Mali and 500–1500 for Ghana. In contrast, in Asia they vary between 600 for Bangladesh and 900 for Papua New Guinea on the high side, and around 10–50 for China and 9–42 for the Republic of Korea. Sub-Saharan Africa accounts for 20 per cent of the world's births but 40 per cent of its maternal deaths. These high levels of maternal mortality partly reflect the overall poverty of the region but also the lack of basic services. West Africa performed more poorly in translating its per capita GNP into human development outcomes than other regions with similar levels of per capita GNP.

However, along with overall levels of poverty, high rates of maternal mortality in this region also show the effects on women's well-being of their survival strategies at the lower end

The intersection of women's long working hours in production and reproduction combined with their high rates of fertility takes its toll on their physical well-being. This is compounded by the risks of childbirth.

of the income scale. The value given to labour in otherwise resource-poor agrarian economies, which lack well-developed markets and basic health services, has resulted in high levels of both fertility and child mortality that are mutually reinforcing. The intersection of women's long working hours in production and reproduction combined with their high rates of fertility takes its toll on their physical well-being. This is compounded by the risks of childbirth.

While women work longer hours than men in most parts of the world, as noted in the previous chapter, it was in sub-Saharan Africa that the concept of women's 'time poverty' first emerged and where it continues to have the greatest resonance. For example, women's excessive workload was identified by both women and men in one poverty assessment based in Guinea as a major factor in their disadvantage.

Long working hours in energy-intensive forms of work also have implications for women's nutritional status. The most common nutritional deficiencies among females are iron-deficiency anaemia and protein-energy malnutrition. Variations in the severity of female nutritional deprivation draw attention to: (a) life cycle factors; (b) the poverty of their households; and (c) aspects of their wider environment. It is at its most severe among women in the reproductive age group, often reducing energy among mothers for any activities beyond those essential for basic survival. It also has a regional dimension. Along with high percentages of low birth weight infants (a reflection of mother's nutritional status) and high rates of maternal mortality, nutritional anaemia is also much higher among women from West Africa than the rest of the continent.

Women's nutritional status also has a seasonal dimension, reflecting fluctuations in their workloads during the agricultural cycle. The period of greatest nutritional stress for rural women is the 'lean months' of the pre-harvest period when household stocks and energy intake are low but the energy demands of agricultural work tend to be highest. Heavy work during pregnancy can lead to premature labour and, without increased caloric intake, to low birth weight babies.

Finally, and not surprisingly, women's nutritional deficiency has a poverty dimension. The main cause is household food insecurity due to unreliable food availability and very low incomes. The interaction between female nutritional deprivation and the heavy demands on their labour leads to high rates of miscarriage. In fact, 'reasonably adequate' birth weights reported in sub-Saharan Africa may reflect the fact that the most malnourished foetuses, infants and mothers simply do not survive.

Micro-level studies confirm not only that women from lower income households tend to be at a greater nutritional disadvantage than those in better off households but also that they often pay part of the price of household attempts to cope with crisis. A study from Côte d'Ivoire found no significant difference between the body mass index (BMI) of males and females but noted that women's nutritional status was more likely than men's to be affected by fluctuations in household income and per capita expenditure. In Zimbabwe, the drought of the early 1990s was found to have significantly decreased women's BMI but not men's. In situations of severe shortage in Cameroon, women coped by going hungry for the whole day while men were more likely to migrate.

It would appear, therefore, that while households' coping strategies in times of economic hardship and crises generally include cutting back on food consumption, women bear the brunt of this strategy far more than men. The link between poverty and female ill-being is also supported by evidence from the Gambia that an increase in overall household income – the result of increased productivity of rice production due to improved technology – led to improvement in the nutritional status of women and children and a reduction in seasonal fluctuations of women's weight.

Gender inequality and hazardous livelihoods

Another strategy adopted by households, particularly in times of crisis, is to resort to exploitative or hazardous forms of livelihoods. This is likely to have adverse effects on the well-being and also self-worth of members. For both men and women, there are certain forms of work that are more physically exhausting, worse for their health or more degrading. For example, rickshaw-pulling in South Asia, an extremely energy-consuming and almost entirely male occupation, is associated with tuberculosis (TB). Since these forms of work are avoided by those who can afford it, involvement in them is often an indicator of poverty.

[W]hile households' coping strategies in times of economic hardship and crises generally include cutting back on food consumption, women bear the brunt of this strategy ...

Prostitutes in Mumbai,
India
INTERNATIONAL LABOUR ORGANIZATION

Prostitution is one response to crisis more frequently adopted by women and girls than men and boys. In parts of South-East Asia, where tourism is a major source of foreign exchange, 'export-orientation' has been associated with the rise of a female-dominated 'hospitality industry' in which sex work plays an important role. Remittances from daughters who have entered prostitution represent the sole source of income for many poor rural households in the region.

While prostitution has traditionally been associated with a variety of sexually transmitted infections (STIs), the spread of AIDS has introduced a potentially fatal risk to what has always been a hazardous form of livelihood. Moreover, it is not only those who supply sexual services who are at risk but also those who 'demand' and, through them, the wider population. While this demand is not necessarily confined to any particular section of the population, it does appear to be higher in certain areas and among certain occupational groups (*see box* 6.4).

Box 6.4 Men Most at Risk of HIV/AIDS

Along with sex workers and 'single women', the Poverty Reduction Strategy Paper (PRSP) in Burkina Faso identified truckers and the military as most at risk of HIV/AIDS infection. In India, surveys also suggest that truck drivers are one of the largest causes of transmission of the virus. One survey in Calcutta found that over 5 per cent of truck drivers had HIV. More than 90 per cent visited at least one prostitute a week, they had an average of 200 sexual encounters a year and 68 per cent had never used a condom. They appeared to be the main channels through which HIV migrated from urban to rural areas as new transportation networks connect outlying areas with cities. Men more likely to visit sex workers are non-skilled and low-skilled workers in manufacturing industries located in urban areas; workers in various types of transportation industries such as rickshaw drivers, taxi drivers and bus drivers; construction workers; and traders and customers in periodic markets in both urban and rural areas.

While AIDS clearly poses risks for all sections of the population, it also has certain gender-specific aspects.

The highest rates of HIV/AIDS are currently found in sub-Saharan Africa, which accounts for 79 per cent of people living with the disease and 81 per cent of deaths associated with the epidemic, massively outweighing its share of the global population (10%). However, AIDS is spreading rapidly in other parts of the world, particularly in Asia.

While AIDS clearly poses risks for all sections of the population, it also has certain gender-specific aspects. As in the case with most STIs, women are at greater biological risk than men of contracting the HIV virus from each sexual intercourse. Forced sex increases this risk because micro-lesions make it easier for the virus to enter the bloodstream. Social beliefs that younger women are either free of or able to 'cure' AIDS has made them a particularly vulnerable group in Africa. Women under 25 represent the fastest growing group with AIDS in the region, accounting for nearly 30 per cent of all female cases. In Burkina Faso, where 7 per cent of the population is affected by the epidemic, the incidence among girls aged 19–24 is four or five times higher than boys of the same age. It has been found

Whenever sex is part of an economic exchange, women's ability to protect themselves from STIs is limited.

that circumcision provides men with some degree of protection from STIs and HIV, which partly explains the low incidence in West Africa.

In addition, however, the spread of AIDS is related to wider gender inequalities in income, wealth and economic opportunity. In contrast to, for example, South Asia where sex is viewed as either acceptable (marriage) or unacceptable (prostitution), there is a continuum of possible sexual relationships between these two extremes in other regions of the world. Women may exchange sex for money, goods or services as part of their survival strategy, and on a transient or permanent basis. Studies from Zimbabwe and South Africa have pointed out that the decision by women to sell sex is usually in response to economic need. Poverty, along with peer pressure, leads young schoolgirls to get involved in sexual relationships with fellow students and teachers in schools and 'sugar daddies' outside. They need money for basic necessities such as uniforms, books, fees and bus fare as well as to participate in the social life of the school. Whenever sex is part of an economic exchange, women's ability to protect themselves from STIs is limited.

Gender Inequality and Family Well-being: The Instrumental Rationale

As well as an end goal of development, gender equality can also be seen as a route to achieving other human development goals. There are a number of links between women's well-being, agency and resources, on the one hand, and a variety of demographic and welfare outcomes on the other. Some of these links work through biological synergies. One example noted above is that between a mother's nutritional status and the birth weight of her baby. Gender discrimination in access to food and health care explains why South Asia has the highest rates of low birth weight babies in the world. Nutritionally deprived women are likely to give birth to low-weight babies whose chances of survival are severely limited. While these links are biological, they reflect social processes. Moreover, there are other synergies where the social causalities are even clearer. They provide a rationale for investing in gender equality on the grounds of what might be called 'welfare instrumentalism'.

Gender, resources and children's well-being: the social connections

Some of these links work through improvements in women's education and many relate to demographic outcomes. One of the most widely documented findings, and one that appears to hold true across much of the world, is an inverse relationship between mother's schooling and child mortality, particularly in lower-income countries (*see box 6.5*).

[D]ata from 25 developing countries suggest that ... 1–3 years of maternal schooling reduce child mortality by 15 per cent ...

Box 6.5 Mothers' Schooling and Child Mortality

DHS data from 25 developing countries suggest that, other things being equal, 1–3 years of maternal schooling reduce child mortality by 15 per cent while an equivalent level of paternal schooling achieves a 6 per cent reduction. Despite some of the highest rates of infant mortality in the world, the relationship also applies in Africa. Analysis of 1975–1985 data for 13 African countries showed that a 10 per cent increase in female literacy rates reduced child mortality by 10 per cent but that changes in male literacy has little influence. In addition, there is broad-based evidence of a link between women's education and fertility rates. Again, the relationship is stronger than with father's education. While the effect is generally evident at primary school levels, it comes into operation somewhat later at secondary levels of education in sub-Saharan Africa.

A variety of explanations have been put forward for these findings. Education:

(a) delays women's age of marriage and hence age of l___ ___th;

(b) eases their access to contraception and to health services as well as their ability to use both more effectively; and

(c) improves their treatment by health providers.

There is considerable empirical evidence for this interpretation. In Kenya, for example, women were able to understand the instructions for administering oral rehydration salts after four or more years of schooling. Education in Nigeria was seen

A study in Côte d'Ivoire reported that raising women's share of household income reduced household expenditure on alcohol and cigarettes but increased spending on food.

to increase women's capacity to deal with the outside world, including the world of health service providers. In rural areas, uneducated women preferred not to deliver in hospitals because of the treatment they received at the hands of nurses, a treatment not meted out to more educated women.

Several studies show that mothers' education consistently affects the chances that:

* women will attend antenatal clinics;

* births will be attended by trained medical personnel;

* complete immunisation of children will take place; and

* sick children will receive timely and effective medical care.

This effect is particularly strong in poorer areas where proper health services are not available. In such cases, education puts women at an advantage in accessing available services.

Gender, resources and family welfare: preferences and priorities

In addition, there is evidence to suggest that women may use resources at their disposal differently to men. Brazilian data, for example, indicated that unearned income in the hands of mothers had a far greater effect on family health than income in the hands of fathers. For child survival, the effect was 20 times larger. The effect of maternal education was also larger than that of paternal education. Women were slightly more likely to use unearned income in favour of daughters while men were slightly more likely to favour sons.

A study in Côte d'Ivoire reported that raising women's share of household income reduced household expenditure on alcohol and cigarettes but increased spending on food. An increase in male share of income increased expenditure on alcohol and cigarettes but also on clothing for children and adults. In Rwanda, holding income constant, members of female-headed households consumed 377 more calories per adult equivalent per day than male-headed households. This difference was greatest among lower income households. In the Gambia, the share of cereal production under women's control added 322 more calories per adult equivalent per day to house-

Woman carrying her infant while selling pineapples in Côte d'Ivoire

INTERNATIONAL LABOUR ORGANIZATION

hold energy consumption. In Kenya and Malawi, moderate to severe levels of malnutrition were much lower among children in female-headed households, whether *de jure* or *de facto*, than children in male-headed households. In fact, children in *de facto* female-headed households received a higher proportion of total household calories than did children from other household groups.

Similar 'welfare' effects in relation to children are reported for the rural Philippines, where male household heads were found to be favoured in nutritional allocation. Increased wages for husbands and fathers had a positive effect on share of calories allocated to themselves and their spouses but a negative effect on children's share. However, an increase in the wages of wives and mothers had a significant positive impact on their own and their children's relative share of household calories and a negative effect on husbands' share.

The evidence of a link between women's access to resources

*[In South Asia]
female literacy
was associated
with lower levels
of under-five
mortality while
female literacy
together with
labour force
participation
reduced mortality
rates of female
children and led
to a closing of
the gender gap.*

or capacity to exercise agency and family welfare in South Asia has varied over time, location and level of analysis. However, an analysis that controlled for differences in 'gender regimes' across the subcontinent showed that variations in child mortality could be explained by variations in female literacy and labour force participation. Female literacy was associated with lower levels of under-five mortality while female literacy together with labour force participation reduced mortality rates of female children and led to a closing of the gender gap.

Box 6.6 Gender, Resources and Family Welfare in Bangladesh

In urban Bangladesh, an increase in the percentage of women working in manufacturing employment has been accompanied by a decline in the number of child labourers per urban household. The desire to educate children or younger siblings was a widely cited reason why women entered the factories. Evidence from rural areas suggests that access to micro-credit has also led to improvements in educational levels, particularly of girls. Detailed analysis of 1995 data from two districts found that:

* while the education of both mother and father increased the likelihood of children going to school, the effect of mother's schooling was statistically higher;

* only the mother's education reduced the likelihood of children working; and

* women's access to loans significantly increased the likelihood of children going to school while men's access to loans had no such effect. In fact, a 10 per cent increase in female credit increased the probability of a child going to school by 10–11 per cent and decreased the probability of full time work among children by 10%.

On the other hand, in those regions in India that practise extreme forms of gender discrimination, women are likely to share the values of the wider community. Here female education is not necessarily associated with a benevolent effect. For example, a study in rural Punjab reported that female education increased the likelihood of excess female mortality among daughters.

While evidence on education from India is complicated by the interactions between class, caste and gender, that from neighbouring Muslim countries appears less ambiguous. Studies from Bangladesh and Pakistan suggest that the educational levels of both parents have played an important role in increasing the likelihood of children's education. However, women's education levels were far more important than that of their spouse. A separate study using household data from Pakistan also found that mother's education was more powerfully associated than that of fathers with the likelihood of children going to school, but also of *girls* going to school. In Bangladesh, growing employment opportunities for women appears to be translating into higher levels of children's education – as well as on reducing the gender gap in education (*see box 6.6*).

Altruism or interests? Explaining the 'welfare' effect

Attempts to explain these findings have varied between those who emphasise gender-differentiated *preferences* and those who suggest they might reflect gender differentiated *interests*. The former tend to emphasise socialisation processes by which women acquire a more 'connected' sense of self and pursue more altruistic forms of behaviour while men define themselves in more 'separative' terms and display more self-interested forms of behaviour. This interpretation is supported by findings from a wide range of contexts that men are likely to retain a greater percentage of their income for personal use while women tend to spend a greater percentage of their income on collective welfare.

On the other hand, it has also been pointed out that women's fortunes are more closely bound up with the fortune of their families and children (particularly their sons in South Asia). Women tend to live longer in most parts of the world and will be reliant on their children for support in old age. Older men are also far more able to marry younger wives, particularly in polygamous marriages. The ideology of maternal altruism may thus merely disguise self-interested forms of behaviour (investments in family as a form of 'social capital')

[M]en are likely to retain a greater percentage of their income for personal use while women tend to spend a greater percentage of their income on collective welfare.

[P]atterns of behaviour at the micro-level, including improvements in women's access to education and employment, translate into discernible trends at the macro-level.

or distract attention from non-altruistic forms of discrimination against daughters.

Alternatively, of course, both explanations might be true. Gender differences in upbringing and socialisation play a role in shaping values and preferences and also experiences. The close physical bonding that occurs between mothers and children in the first years of the child's life and the very direct care and emotional support that mothers provide are all likely to make their bond with their children a special one. And women's domestic responsibilities means that they are more likely to hear a child crying from hunger than men who work away from the household. At the same time, inequalities in access to independent resources mean that women have a greater stake in nurturing their family networks and thus discriminating in ways that are likely to secure their status in the family. As those directly responsible for the care and welfare of infants, excess forms of female mortality must at least partly reflect women's agency. The finding from some places that educated mothers meant higher levels of excess female mortality among daughters, particularly those born later, suggests that education can increase women's effective agency in lethal, as well as benevolent, ways.

Nevertheless, these findings help show how patterns of behaviour at the micro-level, including improvements in women's access to education and employment, translate into discernible trends at the macro-level. These trends include demographic transition and the formation of human capital and human capabilities. They provide some of the micro-foundations for the macroeconomic models discussed in Chapter 1 that sought to explore the implications for the social distribution of income on the human capital dimensions of economic growth.

Conclusion

These various findings underscore the fact that the connection between women's productive and reproductive work is critical for their families (particularly their children) and for themselves. This is partly historical and entrenched in the deep structures of their societies. In regions where women have been denied an economically visible and socially acknowledged role in production, and have been confined to an economically devalued and socially invisible role in the domestic arena and reproductive work, they and their daughters have had shorter life expectancies, poorer health status and more circumscribed life choices than both men and boys in their own cultures and women and girls elsewhere. Such patterns persist into the present.

The issue of poverty is also crucial. Poorer women are far more likely than women from better off households to experience conflicting demands on their time from these two sets of responsibilities. Their attempts to balance them can lead to a variety of adverse outcomes, including:

* longer working hours than men in their families;

* greater fatigue and nutritional deprivation; and

* withdrawal of children, especially daughters, from school in order to relieve their mothers from domestic chores.

On the other hand, the positive synergies that have been identified between different aspects of human development can be built on. This means addressing gender inequality in access to resources, including time, within the household and various welfare failures, including gender inequalities in welfare distribution and the inter-generational transmission of poverty.

In regions where women have been denied an economically visible and socially acknowledged role in production ... they and their daughters have had shorter life expectancies ... than both men and boys in their own cultures and women and girls elsewhere.

7. Gender Equality and Women's Empowerment

Introduction

'Gender equality and women's empowerment' is the third of the Millennium Development Goals (MDGs) (*see Table 1.1*). It is therefore explicitly valued as an end in itself and not just as an instrument for achieving other goals. The indicators to monitor progress in achieving this goal are:

* closing the gender gap in education at all levels;

* increasing women's share of wage employment in the non-agricultural sector; and

* increasing the proportion of seats held by women in national parliaments.

Just as there is no explicit mention of gender in the MDG relating to poverty reduction, so there is no explicit mention of poverty in the goal relating to gender equality and women's empowerment. There is, of course, a poverty sub-text to the first two indicators noted above. Increasing the number of women in national parliaments, on the other hand, has no proven link to poverty reduction, although it is critical for the promotion of gender equality in its wider sense. To some extent, therefore, the reduction of poverty and the promotion of gender equality are independent goals. However, in line with the rest of the book, this chapter will focus on the goal of women's empowerment in the context of poverty reduction.

Poverty manifests itself as material deprivation, but its causes can be found in the power relations that govern how valued resources – material and symbolic – are distributed in a society. These relations position poor men, women and children as subordinate to, and dependent on, those with privileged access to these resources. Along with material deprivation, therefore, the poor lack power. The empowerment of poor women must clearly be part of an agenda that addresses the

Poverty manifests itself as material deprivation, but its causes can be found in the power relations that govern how valued resources ... are distributed in a society.

empowerment of the poor in general. At the same time, however, poor women are generally subordinate to poor men. The reduction of poverty thus has to take account of gender inequalities among the poor, including inequalities of power.

The discussion in this chapter is organised around the three 'resources' suggested by the indicators for achieving the goal of gender equality and women's empowerment: education, employment and political participation. Each of these resources has the potential to bring about positive changes in women's lives. In each case, however, the social relationships that govern access to the resource in question will determine the extent to which this potential is realised.

Conceptualising Empowerment: Agency, Resources and Achievement

It is important to clarify how 'empowerment' is being used here. One way of thinking about power is in terms of the *ability to make choices*. Using the concept of 'Human Poverty' to describe the Human Development Index (HDI), UNDP noted that this "does not focus on what people do or do not have, but on what they can or cannot do". The HDI is thus "not a measure of well-being. Nor is it a measure of happiness. Instead, it is a measure of empowerment" (*see Chapter 4*). The opposite of empowerment is disempowerment. To be disempowered implies to be denied choice, while empowerment refers to the processes by which those who have been denied the ability to make choices acquire such an ability. In other words, *empowerment entails a process of change*. People who exercise a great deal of choice in their lives may be very powerful, but they are not empowered because they were never disempowered in the first place.

However, for there to be a real choice:

(a) There must be alternatives, the ability to choose something different. Poverty and disempowerment thus go hand in hand because an inability to meet one's basic needs – and the resulting dependence on powerful others to do so – rules out the capacity for meaningful choice. This absence of choice is likely to affect women and men differently because gender-related inequalities often intensify the effects of poverty.

(b) Alternatives must not only exist, they must also be *seen* to exist. Power relations are most effective when they not perceived as such. Gender often operates through the unquestioned acceptance of power. Thus women who, for example, internalise their lesser claim on household resources or accept violence at the hands of their husbands do so because to behave otherwise is considered outside the realm of possibility. These forms of behaviour could be said to reflect 'choice' but are really based on the absence of choice.

Not all choices are equally relevant to the definition of power. Some have greater significance than others in terms of their consequences for people's lives. Strategic life choices include where to live, whether and who to marry, whether to have children, how many children to have, who has custody over children and freedom of movement and association. These help frame other choices that may be important for the quality of one's life but do not constitute its defining parameters.

The concept of empowerment can be explored through three closely inter-related dimensions: agency, resources and achievements. Agency is how choice is put into effect and hence is central to the processes of empowerment, resources are the medium through which agency is exercised and achievements refer to the outcomes of agency. Each will be considered in turn and also their inter-relationship in the context of empowerment.

The concept of empowerment can be explored through three closely inter-related dimensions: agency, resources and achievements.

Agency

Agency encompasses both observable action in the exercise of choice – decision-making, protest, bargaining and negotiation – as well as the meaning, motivation and purpose that individuals bring to their actions, their sense of agency. This in turn is critically bound up with how they are seen by those around them and by their society. Agency has both positive and negative connotations.

● Its positive sense – the 'power to' – refers to people's ability to make and act on their own life-choices, even in the face of others' opposition.

● Its negative sense – the 'power over' – refers to the capacity of some actors to override the agency of others through, for

Agency in relation to empowerment implies not only actively exercising choice, but also doing this in ways that challenge power relations.

example, the exercise of authority or the use of violence and other forms of coercion.

However, as noted above, power is at its most effective when it denies choice, and hence agency, without appearing to do so. Institutional bias can constrain people's ability to make strategic life choices by ruling out the possibility of certain choices. Cultural or ideological norms may deny either that inequalities of power exist or that such inequalities are unjust. Subordinate groups are likely to accept, and even collude with, their lot in society if the alternative either does not appear possible or else carries heavy personal and social costs.

Agency in relation to empowerment implies not only actively exercising choice, but also doing this in ways that challenge power relations. Because of the significance of beliefs and values in legitimating inequality, the process of empowerment often begins from within. It involves changes in how people see themselves (their sense of self-worth) and their capacity for action.

Resources

Agency, however, is not exercised in the abstract but through the mobilisation of resources. Resources are the medium of power. They are distributed through the various institutions and relationships in a society. As was discussed in Chapter 3, institutions are rarely egalitarian. Certain actors have a privileged position over others concerning how institutional rules, norms and conventions are interpreted as well as how they are put into effect. Heads of households, chiefs of tribes, directors of firms, managers of organisations and elites within a community all have decision-making authority in particular institutions by virtue of their position. The way resources are distributed thus depends on the ability to define priorities and enforce claims.

The terms on which people gain access to resources are as important in processes of empowerment as the resources themselves. Thus the reason why access to paid work might improve women's agency within the family is that it provides them with an independent source of income and hence a stronger 'fallback' position from which to bargain. The terms of access to paid work also matter. The greater its public visibility, the value of its returns and its independence from familial structures of authority, the stronger its effects on women's fall-back position.

Achievements

Resources and agency make up people's capabilities, their potential for living the lives they want. Their achievements refer to the extent to which this potential is realised or fails to be realised, i.e. the outcomes of their efforts. In relation to empowerment, achievements have to be looked at in terms of both the agency exercised and their consequences. For example, taking up waged work would be regarded by the MDGs as evidence of progress in women's empowerment. However, it is far more likely to actually be evidence of this if work was taken up in response to a new opportunity or in search of greater self-reliance than if it represented the 'distress sale' of labour. It is also far more likely to be empowering if it contributes to women's sense of independence rather than simply allowing them to survive from day to day.

Restaurant employee in South Africa
INTERNATIONAL LABOUR ORGANIZATION

[T]ransformative forms of agency and ... achievements ... suggest a greater ability on the part of poor women to question, analyse and act on the structures of patriarchal constraint in their lives.

The inter-relationship between agency, resources and achievements

There is a distinction, therefore, between 'passive' forms of agency, action taken when there is little choice, and 'active' agency, which reflects more purposeful behaviour. Access to resources can very often improve women's active agency. However, there is an important distinction to be made between greater 'effectiveness' of agency and agency that is 'transformative'. The former relates to women's greater efficiency in carrying out their given roles and responsibilities while the latter relates to their ability to question, reinterpret and perhaps change these roles and responsibilities. For example, the reduction of overall child mortality associated with female literacy in India noted in the previous chapter can be interpreted as the product of 'effective' agency on the part of women. However, the reduction of gender disparities in under-five mortality rates associated with higher levels of female literacy and paid activity has transformative implications. It shows an exercise of agency that acts against the grain of patriarchal values. The main focus in this chapter will be on transformative forms of agency and on those achievements that suggest a greater ability on the part of poor women to question, analyse and act on the structures of patriarchal constraint in their lives. This involves looking at a range of different questions:

* How do women perceive themselves and how are they perceived by intimate as well as distant others in society?

* How do they treat themselves and how are they treated by others?

* Are they able to make key decisions about matters relating to themselves (their own well-being) and to their children, particularly their daughters?

* What kind of say do they have in other aspects of decision-making within the family?

* Do they have any influence in matters relating to the community and society in which they live and is this influence decisive or merely symbolic?

It also involves looking at the relationships between individual and structural change. Individual empowerment is an important starting point for processes of social transformation, but unless it leads to some form of structural change it will do little to undermine the systemic reproduction of inequality. Equally, changing the law on property may represent an important attempt by the state to challenge systemic forms of inequality, but unless women feel able to claim their rights it will remain a symbolic gain.

The three dimensions that make up the concept of empowerment can be seen as the pathways through which the processes of empowerment occur. Changes in any one dimension can lead to changes in others. What is achieved through the exercise of agency in one period becomes the expanded resource base from which further actions and achievements can be undertaken in the next. These processes of change may occur over the life course of an individual or group but also across generations as mothers seek to give their daughters the chances that they themselves never had. The reverse is also true. Inequalities in immediate benefits feed into unequal abilities of individuals or groups to take advantage of future benefits and thus sustain present inequalities into the future.

These processes of change may occur ... across generations as mothers seek to give their daughters the chances that they themselves never had.

Access to Education and Women's Empowerment

There is considerable evidence for the claim that access to education helps to empower women. However, there are also studies that suggest that the potential of education to transform can be overstated. There are lessons to be learnt from both sets of findings.

Positive effects of education

The positive findings suggest that education brings about change in a number of different ways. Firstly, it has certain effects at the level of individual cognition and behaviour. These are relevant to all marginalised groups in society because they promote agency as 'the power to'. Secondly, it improves access to knowledge, information and new ideas as well as the ability to use these effectively. These changes apply to young

In Nigeria, for example, less-educated women were as likely as educated ones to have their children immunised; educated women were more likely than uneducated ones to know about family planning; but only secondary-schooled women revealed an in-depth understanding of disease and prevention.

men as well as young women, but the former are more likely to also be exposed to new ideas and possibilities through their wider contacts with the world outside family and local community. The way education opens up new ideas may underlie the positive association between women's education and family welfare noted in the previous chapter.

Education appears to improve women's ability to process and utilise new information, although more rapidly for certain issues than others. In Nigeria, for example, less-educated women were as likely as educated ones to have their children immunised; educated women were more likely than uneducated ones to know about family planning; but only secondary-schooled women revealed an in-depth understanding of disease and prevention.

Education increases the likelihood that women will look after their own, as well as family, well-being. A study in rural Zimbabwe found that among the factors that increased the likelihood of women using contraception and accessing ante-natal care – both of which reduce maternal mortality – were education and paid work. Women with low levels of education were less likely to visit ante-natal facilities. In rural Nigeria, 96 per cent of women with secondary and higher education, 53 per cent of those with primary education and 47 per cent of those little or no education had sought post-natal care in the two years prior to the study.

There are also other effects associated with education that may have an impact on power relationships within and outside the household. It may lead to a greater role for women in decision-making and a greater willingness on their part to question male dominance in the home and community. In Sierra Leone and Zimbabwe, educated women were found to have more leverage in bargaining with their families and husbands and a greater say in spending household income than uneducated women. Education in rural Bangladesh was strongly linked to women's control over their own earnings as well as those of their husbands, even after controlling for age, marriage patterns and husbands' characteristics. A study in India found that better educated women scored higher than less educated women on a composite index measuring their access to and control over resources, as well as their role in economic decision-making.

Educated women also appear less likely to suffer from domestic violence. A study in India noted that educated women were better able to deal with violent husbands. A similar finding was documented in rural Bangladesh.

Limits to education as a route to empowerment

While this evidence is undoubtedly persuasive, other studies suggest that the value given to education and how it is utilised may be influenced by the wider context in which it is provided. In societies that are characterised by extreme forms of gender inequality, women's access to education is more likely to be curtailed by various forms of restrictions on their mobility and by their limited role in the wider economy. The effects of education are also more limited. Where women's role in society is defined purely in reproductive terms, education is seen as equipping girls to be better wives and mothers or increasing their chances of getting a suitable husband. Although these are legitimate aspirations, given the realities of the society, they do little to equip girls and women to question the world around them and the subordinate status assigned to them.

This is evident in a study that compared women's role in decision-making in the family, their ability to move in the public domain, their control over economic resources and the incidence of domestic violence in Tamil Nadu in the south of India and Uttar Pradesh in the north. Not only did women in Tamil Nadu do better on these indicators of women's agency than those in Uttar Pradesh but what determined their agency varied considerably. In Tamil Nadu, both female employment and, even more strongly, female education were associated with women's exercise of agency. In Uttar Pradesh, however, it was the extent to which women conformed to patriarchal norms – the size of their dowries and the likelihood that they had borne sons – that gave women a greater role in household decision-making and greater freedom from domestic violence. In addition, while female employment had significant and positive implications for most of the empowerment indicators, education was not significant.

These findings make sense only in relation to their context. Women in Tamil Nadu are less constrained by patriarchal norms and many more of them work, hence the weaker effect

Educated women ... appear less likely to suffer from domestic violence. A study in India noted that educated women were better able to deal with violent husbands.

of employment. In Uttar Pradesh, conformity to patriarchal norms increased women's status within the family. While participation in waged employment here is likely to be a response to poverty, it may signal a greater assertiveness on the part of women as well as giving them some earnings of their own. Indeed, a recent study found that higher wages for women in both northern and southern India consistently improved their mobility and decision-making authority, while male wages decreased them. Education in Uttar Pradesh, on the other hand, is a sign of prosperity rather than poverty and more likely to characterise women from better-off households. In this part of northern India, this is the social strata that is likely to be most restrictive in relation to women. Education may thus increase women's effectiveness in the traditional roles assigned to them but is unlikely to override, and may indeed reinforce, restrictive interpretations of these roles (*see box 7.1*).

Box 7.1 The Socialising Function of Education

A study of social change in an agriculturally progressive village in Maharashtra, India, between 1975 and 1987 found that improvements in the standard of living had led to a decline in female wage employment and greater leisure, particularly for better-off women. However, it had also led to a reduction in their mobility in the public domain and in their control over economic resources. There had been an increase in education, with a much larger increase among women aged 15–26 than their husbands. This, however, had reinforced gender roles and traditional values concerning womanhood. It enabled girls to attract a 'better' husband and boys to ask for a higher dowry. Mobility had a greater effect on women's attitudes than education.

A second set of qualifications concerning education as a route to women's empowerment relates to its delivery, particularly in the formal educational system. The content of education can often mirror and legitimate wider social inequalities, denigrating physical labour (largely the preserve of the poor) and domestic activities (largely the preserve of women). There is gender stereotyping in the curriculum, particularly in text-books, where girls tend to be portrayed as passive, modest, and shy while boys are seen as assertive, brave and ambitious. This reinforces traditional gender roles in society and is a barrier to the kind of futures that girls are able to imagine for themselves. In addition, policy-makers have tended to see the benefits of educating girls and women as connected with improving family health and welfare, rather than with either economic opportunities or social transformation. Thus the design of edu-cation has often reinforced the biases of many parents that the purpose of schooling is to prepare girls for their domestic roles. Quite often, different subject choices may be made available to girls and boys (maths and science for boys; home economics for girls). This form of education leaves girls with few options in terms of earning their living, except in poorly-paid, casualised forms of work on the margins of the labour market, and limits the potential of education to transform their life chances.

Social inequalities are also reproduced through interactions within the school system. In India, for example, not only do the children of the poor and scheduled caste households go to different, and differently resourced, schools, but also different groups of children are treated differently even within the same school. Dalit children are sometimes made to sit separately from others, are verbally abused, used for running menial errands and more often physically punished. There is also evidence of widespread gender bias, with teachers showing more attention to boys and having a lower opinion of girls' abilities. The absence, or minority presence, of female teachers is a problem in many areas. Reinforcing the male dominance of public services, it can act as a barrier to girls' access to and completion of schooling.

Teachers in Africa also have different attitudes towards male and female students (a boy needs a career whereas a girl needs a husband). They tend to be dismissive and discouraging towards girls and give more classroom time to boys, who are usually more demanding. Even when girls are encouraged to pursue a career, they are expected to opt for the 'caring' pro-fessions, in other words, teaching and nursing. Moreover, the 'hidden curriculum' of school practice reinforces messages about girls' inferior status on a daily basis and provides them

The curriculum ... reinforces traditional gender roles in society and is a barrier to the kind of futures that girls are able to imagine for themselves.

Girls in Kenya consistently drop out of school earlier and obtain lower test scores than boys. Teachers' attitudes were found to be the primary obstacle to girls' learning. They described girls as stupid and lazy and tolerated their being bullied by boys.

with negative learning experience, thus creating a culture of low self-esteem and low aspirations (*see box 7.2*).

Box 7.2 Problems Faced by Girls in Schools in Kenya and Zimbabwe

Girls in Kenya consistently drop out of school earlier and obtain lower test scores than boys. Teachers' attitudes were found to be the primary obstacle to girls' learning. They described girls as stupid and lazy and tolerated their being bullied by boys. Both male and female teachers who expressed a preference for teaching one sex or the other preferred boys. They more often allocated menial chores to girls and teaching tasks to boys. Even in schools where girls performed nearly as well in exams, teachers awarded twice as many prizes to boys. The teachers thus created a context in which the girls performed badly.

In Zimbabwe, older male students forced their attentions on young female students, demeaning and humiliating them if they were turned down. In addition, male teachers abused their positions of trust and authority to openly pursue female students and attempt to lure them into sexual relationships through offers of money and gifts. This reflected the subordinate position of girls and women in general, but poverty also made girls particularly vulnerable. Many reported that their families were unable to provide them with enough money to pay for school fees, bus fares, lunches and books.

Less attention has been paid to alternatives to formal schools as sites of education, including non-formal educational provision, vocational training and adult literacy programmes. However, there is evidence that, with a few exceptions, they tend to reproduce many of the problems of the formal system.

These limitations to education as a route to empowerment do not negate the earlier, more positive findings. However, they suggest the need for caution in assuming that effects will be uniform across all contexts. They also point to the various aspects of educational provision that militate against not only its empowerment potential but also its ability to attract and retain women and girls, particularly those from poor backgrounds. Moreover, the design of educational curricula, whether within the formal schooling system or in later vocational training, has not yet taken account of the fact that many more women around the world play a critical role in earning household livelihoods, and increasing numbers of them head their own households.

There is persuasive evidence that access to paid work can increase women's agency in critical ways.

Access to Paid Work and Women's Empowerment

There is persuasive evidence that access to paid work can increase women's agency in critical ways. In fact, even paid work carried out in the home can sometimes shift the balance of power in the family. For example, a study of Bangladeshi women working in home-based piecework in Britain noted that, with rising male unemployment, many had become primary breadwinners, slightly altering the balance of power between the genders. Similarly, a detailed study of women engaged in industrial homework in Mexico City noted that, particularly in households where women's economic contribution was critical to household survival, women had been able to negotiate a greater degree of respect.

Studies of micro-credit in rural Bangladesh, where women have traditionally been excluded from the cash economy, found that women's access to credit led to a number of changes in women's own perceptions of themselves and their role in household decision-making. It also led to a long-term reduction in domestic violence as well as an increase in women's assets. Such effects were, however, stronger when these loans were used to initiate or expand women's own income-generating activities, despite the fact that these continued to be largely home-based.

However, the strongest effects of paid work in destabilising power relations, both within and outside the family, relates to women's access to wage employment.

Waged work in the agricultural sector

As noted in Chapter 3, the rise of non-traditional agricultural exports (NTAEs) in a number of African and Latin American

Evidence of changes in women's life chances as a result of entry into waged work is even more marked when the focus is on the non-agricultural sector.

countries led to a rise in wage employment for women in medium and large-scale production units. The income they earn has brought about economic improvements for themselves and their families. A number of studies also suggest that women exercise a considerable say in how this money is spent. A study in Ecuador found that more than 80 per cent of women in the flower industry managed their own wages. Among female employees in the Kenyan vegetable industry, single women managed and controlled their own wages while married women often managed their incomes jointly with husbands.

There is also significant evidence from the vegetable industries of Guatemala and the Dominican Republic and the flower industry of Mexico that women's participation in wage employment has led to greater independence in household decision-making. In some cases, as among women working in the fresh vegetable industry in the Dominican Republic, it has allowed them to escape abusive marriages. Women working in the flower industry in Colombia reported widening their social networks in ways that would otherwise have proved difficult in rural areas. Workers in the fresh vegetable industry in Kenya not only reported greater economic independence but also new opportunities for meeting with women from other parts of the country.

Waged work in the non-agricultural sector

Evidence of changes in women's life chances as a result of entry into waged work is even more marked when the focus is on the non-agricultural sector. This is partly because such employment is generally associated with migration by women out of rural areas and away from the patriarchal controls of kinship and community. Women workers in the garment industry in Bangladesh expressed their satisfaction at having a 'proper' job and regular wages compared to the casualised and poorly paid forms of employment that had previously been their only options. Many had used their new-found earning power to renegotiate their relations within marriage, others to leave abusive marriages. Women who had previously not been able to help out their ageing parents once they got married now insisted on their right to do so. Yet others used their earnings to postpone early marriage and to challenge the practice of dowry. Among the other advantages mentioned in relation to garment work were:

* access to new social networks on the factory floor;

* the greater voice enjoyed in household decision-making;

* the respect received from other family members, including their husbands;

* an enhanced sense of self-worth and self reliance; and

* greater personal freedom and autonomy.

Similarly positive evaluations are reported in a number of other studies. As in Bangladesh, women in Turkey had previously been permitted to work outside the home only if it was necessary for family survival. In a study of the clothing industry, however, many of those interviewed no longer saw their work as subordinate to their familial roles, to be abandoned when they got married or had children. Rather they saw it as a more permanent way of life. The overwhelming majority had made their own decision to enter factory work, giving as their reasons their desire to make use of their skills and to be outside the home. Forty per cent of the workers, mainly young single women, indicated their preference to work a considerable distance from home in order to escape the control exercised by their family and neighbours. They wanted to work somewhere where they could move about freely during their lunch breaks and take the opportunity to meet their friends, including their boyfriends.

In Honduras, women working in *maquiladoras* earned higher wages than workers elsewhere and reported improvements in household relationships and help in domestic work from male members. They were more likely to have voted in the last election and more likely to feel that they carried some weight with the government. These trends became stronger over time. This may explain why, although most workers wanted to see improvements (especially in their wages), 96 per cent reported that they were very (49%) or somewhat (47%) satisfied with their jobs. Similarly, married women workers in export-oriented manufacturing units in a number of Caribbean

[In Turkey] forty per cent of the workers, mainly young single women, indicated their preference to work a considerable distance from home in order to escape the control exercised by their family and neighbours.

Despite their increased labour input into paid work, women ... either continue to bear the main burden of domestic work, or share it with other female members of the household, often their daughters.

countries reported improvements in household relations as a result of their greater economic contributions, with greater sharing of decision-making with male partners.

On the other hand, all of these studies also highlight the exploitative conditions of work in industries that promote flexible labour practices in order to compete internationally. Export-oriented manufacturing is associated with extremely long hours of work during busy seasons, often combined with lay-offs in the slack season, and poor conditions. There are also health hazards. Maquila workers in Honduras, for example, were more likely to report a health problem in the previous month than those who had been working elsewhere and they had less leisure.

Moreover, studies do not always report positive findings concerning women's capacity to have greater control over their lives. Many women who leave rural areas to take up jobs in towns in order to make new friends and build a life for themselves do not have time to take up such opportunities. The division of labour in domestic chores and childcare is rarely renegotiated between the genders. Despite their increased labour input into paid work, women (particularly married women) either continue to bear the main burden of domestic work, or share it with other female members of the household, often their daughters. By and large, gender inequalities in work burdens appear to be intensified.

In addition, despite the visibility of export-oriented waged employment in agriculture and industry, the vast majority of women in low-income countries continue to work in the informal economy in various forms of economic activities that may or may not be affected by global markets but that are characterised by far worse conditions. Within this informal economy, poorer women are concentrated in the most casualised forms of waged labour and low-value own-account enterprise. It is difficult to see how earnings generated by prostitution, domestic service or daily labour on construction sites – which is where the poorest women are likely to be found – will do much to undermine women's subordinate status at home or at work.

Voice, Participation and Women's Empowerment

Women in national parliaments

The last of the indicators for monitoring progress on gender equality and women's empowerment relates to the number of seats held by women in national parliaments. It moves the focus of empowerment into the arena of politics and into the struggle for representation. The right to representation is clearly central to civil and political rights. Gender equality implies 50 per cent representation by women. Such an achievement could, with certain qualifications, represent the most ambitious of the three forms of change singled out to measure progress on women's empowerment and have the most potential for transformation. Furthermore, again with certain qualifications, it could potentially address many of the constraints that limit the life chances of poor women.

However, because these qualifications relate to the same constraints that have prevented women from all social class and groups from having a 'strategic presence' in national parliaments, it is also the form of social change least likely to be achieved in the near future. A review of the relevant statistics suggests that, regardless of political system, the percentage of women in national parliaments around the world is extremely low, averaging 13.8 per cent in 2000 (*see Table 7.1*). This is an extraordinary under-representation of women in the highest structures of governance in their countries. Various forms of bias in the institutions of civil society and the political sphere – along with conscious discrimination – operate to exclude women, including women from privileged elites.

The structure of the political sphere makes a difference to how many women are fielded as candidates and how many win. This includes the extent to which political parties:

- are institutionalised;

- have clear rules about candidate selection;

- identify policy concerns; and

- operate in a political culture that is conducive to the promotion of women's involvement in politics (e.g. the strength or weakness of patriarchal ideology, the existence of pluralist forms of organisation and the degree of religious opposition to gender reforms).

[T]he percentage of women in national parliaments around the world is extremely low, averaging 13.8 per cent in 2000.

A woman carries dried bricks to a construction site in Madagascar.
UN/DPI

Table 7.1: Women in Public Life

	% parliamentary seats in single or lower chamber occupied by women			% women in decision-making positions in government			
				Ministerial level		Sub-ministerial level	
	1987	1995	1999	1994	1998	1994	1998
MIDDLE EAST/ NORTH AFRICA							
Morocco	0	1	1	0	0	0	8
Egypt	4	2	2	4	6	0	4
Algeria	2	7	3	4	0	8	10
Kuwait	0	0	0	0	0	0	7
Oman				0	0	2	4
Saudi Arabia				0	0	0	0
UAE	0	0	0	0	0	0	0
Yemen, Rep. of		1	1	0	0	0	0
SOUTH ASIA							
India	8	8	8	3		7	
Bangladesh	9	11	9	8	5	2	0
Pakistan	9	2	2	4	7	1	1
Nepal	6		6	0	3	0	0
Sri Lanka		5	5	3	13	6	5
EAST ASIA							
Taiwan							
Rep. of Korea	3	2	4	4		0	
Dem. People's Rep. of Korea	21	20	20	0		2	
China	21	21	22	6		4	
Japan	1	3	5	6	0	8	3
SOUTH EAST ASIA							
Thailand	3	6	6	0	4	2	7
Malaysia	5	8	8	7	16	0	13
Indonesia	12	12		6	3	1	1
Lao PDR		9	21	0	0	5	0
Vietnam	18	18	26	5	0	0	5
Philippines	9	9	12	8	10	11	19
Cambodia	21	6	8	0		7	
WEST AFRICA							
Ghana		8	9	11	9	12	9
Cameroon	14	12	6	3	6	5	6
Burkina Faso		4	8	7	10	14	10
Côte d' Ivoire	6	5	8	8	3	0	3
Mali	4	2	12	10	21	0	0
Gambia	8		2	0	29	7	17
Senegal	11	12	12	7	7	0	15
Nigeria				3	6	11	4

Table 7.1: Women in Public Life (continued)

| | % parliamentary seats in single or lower chamber occupied by women | | | % women in decision-making positions in government | | | |
| | | | | Ministerial level | | Sub-ministerial level | |
	1987	1995	1999	1994	1998	1994	1998
EAST AFRICA							
Tanzania		11	16	13	13	4	11
Kenya	2	3	4	0	0	4	9
Uganda		17	18	10	13	7	13
SOUTHERN AFRICA							
Zimbabwe	11	15	14	3	12	25	6
Zambia	3	7	9	5	3	9	12
Mozambique	16	25	25	4	0	9	15
Malawi	10	6	8	9	4	9	4
CARIBBEAN							
Jamaica	12	12	13	5	12	17	22
Barbados	4	11		0	27	16	20
Trinidad and Tobago	17	19	11	19	14	13	19
Guyana	37	20	18	12	15	25	22
LATIN AMERICA							
Brazil	5	7	6	5	4	11	13
Mexico	11	14	17	5	5	5	7
Argentina	5	22	28	0	8	3	9
Chile		8	11	13	13	0	8
Peru	6	10	11	6	10	11	23
OTHER COMMONWEALTH							
UK	6	10	18	9	24	7	19
Australia	6	10	22	13	14	23	17
New Zealand	14	21	29	8	8	17	31
Canada	10	18	21	14		20	

Source: *The World's Women 2000*, UN Statistics Division

Electoral systems are also important. The ones more likely to bring women into political office are those:

* where more than one person can represent a constituency;

* that have multiple parties competing for votes; and

* that practise proportional representation (PR) in party lists.

Mozambique has 30 per cent female parliamentarians while South Africa has 29 per cent. Bangladesh, Burkina Faso, India, Tanzania and Uganda have all reserved seats for women in national or local government.

Those less likely to do so are majoritarian systems that create the incentive to field a single candidate per constituency and appeal to the majority rather than accommodating diversity. A review of 53 legislatures in 1999 found that national assemblies in PR systems had nearly 24 per cent of women compared to 11 per cent in majoritarian systems. In almost every case where women exceed 15 per cent of elected representative bodies, this has been the result of special measures that advantage female over male candidates: Mozambique has 30 per cent female parliamentarians while South Africa has 29 per cent. Bangladesh, Burkina Faso, India, Tanzania and Uganda have all reserved seats for women in national or local government.

The way that quotas are applied makes a difference to whether the presence of women is 'token' or a legitimate form of representation. Where, as in Bangladesh, women's seats were filled by the party in power, they simply became an additional vote bank for the ruling regime. In South Africa, on the other hand, there have been attempts by the women's movement to encourage members from within their ranks to enter politics. A woman MP there was active in initiating the process of examining national budgets from a gender perspective and the Women's Budget Initiative (WBI), established in 1995, brought together women parliamentarians and NGOs (*see Chapter 8*).

At the same time, it should be noted that, at present, the women who enter national parliaments tend not to be drawn from the ranks of the poor in any part of the world, nor is there any guarantee that they will be more responsive to the needs and priorities of poor women than many men in parliament.

Women in local government

It is possible that greater participation and influence in local government structures may be a more relevant goal for poor women than increasing women's seats in national parliaments. These, after all, make the decisions that most directly affect the lives of the poor. In recognition of this, a number of states in India, where there is now 33 per cent reservation of seats for women in local government, have added further inducements to local communities to encourage women's participation. Madhya Pradesh and Kerala, for example, require that one third of participants in the regular open village meetings be female before there is considered to be a quorum. Kerala also earmarks 10 per cent of development funds received by local councils from the state to be used for 'women's development' and managed by representatives of female groups of the village assembly.

Box 7.3 Gender Priorities and Preferences in Village Councils in West Bengal

A study comparing budgetary allocations in village councils in West Bengal found that councils led by women were more likely to invest in public goods that had practical relevance to the needs of rural women (water, fuel and roads) while male-led councils were more likely to invest in education. These effects were consistent with gender differences in expressed policy priorities. However, women's main preoccupations were also important issues for men. If both male and female expressed preferences were combined, drinking water and roads were the most important issues. While villages with female leadership were more likely to be visited by health workers, male leaders invested more in informal education centres and expressed greater concern about teacher absenteeism.

The other important finding was that other women were more likely to participate in local councils when they were led by a woman, more likely to ask a question and significantly more likely to have made a request or complaint in the past six months. Moreover, the fact that women in the reserved seats came from poorer backgrounds and smaller villages than men suggests that such efforts at the local level can help to change the gender and class/caste composition of key policy-making bodies.

[G]reater participation and influence in local government structures may be a more relevant goal for poor women than increasing women's seats in national parliaments.

Clearly, all these measures, including the reservation policy itself, are open to abuse. There has been much discussion in India about the possibility that women are merely proxies for husbands or powerful men within their family or caste, that

Collective action is central to social transformation.

only supporters of parties in power attend village meetings or that women are being harassed to spend funds in ways that do not benefit poorer women. While these are valid concerns, they may also alter over time as women become more experienced in the political arena. Studies in West Bengal, for example, showed that many of the elected women were gaining self-confidence. They questioned the priorities of panchayat development programmes, emphasised issues affecting women such as fuel and water and had begun to build broad alliances among themselves (*see box 7.3*).

Agency and Collective Action: Building Citizenship from the Grassroots

There is clearly room for further public policy to help realise more fully the potential that these changes – in the social, economic and political arenas – have for transforming the structures of patriarchal constraint in women's lives. It is also clear that there are likely to be powerful forces, some within the policy domain itself, that will militate against this happening. However, not all forms of public action need to be undertaken by the state or international development agencies. Indeed, it is likely that the political pressure needed to ensure these actions from above will have to come 'from below'. It will come from various forms of agency exercised by, and on behalf of, marginalised groups seeking to claim their rights in various different arenas.

Collective action is central to social transformation. The kinds of change signalled by the MDGs help increase women's agency, even if it is on the individual level of challenging power structures within the family or the immediate community. However, while this may be an important precondition for larger processes of transformation, it is the collective struggles of subordinated groups that drive these processes. The bottom up pressures for greater gender equity in the political sphere will therefore come from new forms of associations that bring women into the public domain to collectively challenge patriarchal power across a wide range of institutions.

There is, of course, nothing inherent in associations to make them promoters of gender equity goals, whether they are women's organisations or not. Many may be specifically set up to protect an elitist status quo or to promote a welfarist agenda for women. Equally, however, others can help to expand the space available for democratic activity. These groups may not necessarily operate in the political sphere, but all forms of struggle against the arbitrary exercise of power by those in a position of authority (managers, landlords, party bosses) contribute to the struggle to expand democratic space. Having a say in the way one is ruled is part of the process by which recognised procedures for participation and accountability are established. Struggles to improve the public provision of social services and make them more responsive to the needs of the poor may also be counted as a part of the process of building and strengthening citizenship identity. Thus, it is not only formally constituted political organisations that are relevant to the practice of citizenship, but all forms of organisation and interest-groups that build the conditions to enable citizens to act as citizens.

Examples of collective action and social mobilisation that have given a voice to women, as well as men, from poorer sections of the population can be found in many contexts and take many forms. In India, the formation of self-help groups of women by such organisations as the Centre for Youth and Social Development (CYSD) in Orissa have not only helped to create new affiliations for poor women where there was no 'chosen' group they could belong to, but have also begun to build their political participation. Women who are members of self-help groups have the social support to run for, and be elected to, different tiers of the Panchayat system. These new associations have helped to build the inner competencies that women need to participate in the democratic life of their community.

In Bangladesh, Nijera Kori has been organising groups of landless women and men for the past two decades around key livelihood issues such as land and wages. It has increasingly begun to turn its attention to making demands on the state for greater accountability to the poor. Its members seek to get potential candidates to explain their stance on poverty or else run for elections themselves. Most of the protests and struggles initiated by Nijera Kori members are not segregated by gender. Women are involved in 'male' issues such as resistance to

Examples of collective action and social mobilisation that have given a voice to women, as well as men, from poorer sections of the population can be found in many contexts and take many forms.

[SEWA] in India has moved from organising women in the informal economy through a combination of trade union and co-operative principles to seeking to put pressure on the state government for greater responsiveness to the needs of poor women.

powerful land-grabbers while men are active in 'women's' issues, such as rape and other forms of assault on women.

The Self-Employed Women's Association (SEWA) in India has moved from organising women in the informal economy through a combination of trade union and co-operative principles to seeking to put pressure on the state government for greater responsiveness to the needs of poor women. More recently, it has been lobbying to make the International Labour Organization (ILO) less a voice for organised, predominantly male workers and more representative of the world's informal workers. It has linked up with informal workers' organisations and researchers from other parts of the world as a global network, Women in Informal Employment Globalizing and Organizing (WIEGO), to promote this set of interests.

In Trinidad and Tobago, the National Union of Domestic Employees (NUDE) has struggled since the mid-1970s to be recognised under the country's Industrial Relations Act. This allows unions and workers to represent their grievances to an Industrial Court and hold employers accountable for state employment practices. Because domestic workers are governed by the Masters and Servants Act (put in place by the British to regulate relations between employers and domestic workers after the abolition of slavery), they do not enjoy the same guarantees as other workers. NUDE has drawn on various international agreements signed by the government as well as linking up with the Wages for Housework Campaign to reinforce its demands.

In Mexico, Indian women participated in the Zapatista movement to change the oppressive situation of their community. They also presented through their leaders a revolutionary 'programme of demands' that sought to challenge the status given to them in their family, community and society at large. This demanded, among other things, the rights to choose their husbands, go to meetings, continue studying beyond the basic level and be elected to their community's decision-making bodies. Research into the reactions of a cross section of Mexican women revealed the desire for an alternative political culture to the authoritarian, male-dominated model that had dominated so far. The Zapatista movement was seen as offering one such alternative.

In West Bengal, an initiative to raise awareness about AIDS among sex workers was not only successful in its own terms but also led to the setting up of an independent collective (the Durbar Women's Co-ordination Committee) to campaign for the respect, recognition and rights that sex workers had been denied. A key strategy in the campaign was to define sex work as like any other form of work and hence entitled to the same rights as other self-employed groups. The campaign included demands for a change in the law that made sex workers vulnerable to police harassment, setting up a savings-and-credit co-operative, coming out in solidarity with 'minority' groups that they saw as similarly marginalised and various cultural initiatives through which they sought to exercise the right to free, open and public self-expression.

Conclusion

The discussion in this chapter makes a different set of links between production and reproduction to those in the previous chapter. It looks at how access to a variety of resources – social, economic and political – impacts on women's agency in re-negotiating their roles in production as well as reproduction in ways that have implications for the larger renegotiation of the patriarchal order. The findings discussed in this chapter have important implications for how gender relations are theorised in the context of social change.

Gender relations, like all social relations, are multi-stranded: they embody ideas, values and identities; they allocate labour between different tasks, activities and domains; they determine the distribution of resources; and they assign authority, agency and decision-making power. This means that gender inequalities are multidimensional and cannot be reduced simply to the question of material or ideological constraint. It also suggests that these relationships are not always internally cohesive. They may contain contradictions and imbalances, particularly when there have been changes in the wider socio-economic environment. Consequently, a shift in one aspect of social relations is likely to initiate a series of adjustments with unpredictable consequences.

While some of these changes are likely to leave the power

[A]ccess to a variety of resources – social, economic and political – impacts on women's agency in renegotiating their roles in production as well as reproduction in ways that have implications for the larger renegotiation of the patriarchal order.

aspects of social relations unaltered, others may have intended or unintended results that open up the possibility of transformation. For example, women's entry into paid work has had very different kinds of effects, depending on the context and nature of the work. In some cases, it has led to an increase in women's workloads to the extent of extreme levels of exhaustion and burn-out. In other cases, it has led to some re-allocation of the domestic division of labour, either to other women or children within the home or, more rarely, to men. It may also lead to adverse changes in the division of responsibilities for the family as men withdraw their contributions to household needs, leaving women to shoulder an ever-increasing share of the burden.

However, access to paid work has also brought about changes in gender relations in other ways. It has:

* altered perceptions, such as the value given to women by others within the household or community (social respect) or their own sense of self-worth (self respect);

* increased the resources at women's disposal and given them a greater say in household decision-making;

* allowed women to make various strategic life choices, such as postponing the age of marriage and investing in children's survival chances and education (often closing gender gaps in these areas);

* enabled women to leave abusive husbands or re-negotiate the terms of their marriage; and

* provided young women with the ability to think about their own destinies rather than having their future decided for them by dominant family members.

While individual forms of empowerment are critical, and may be a starting point for more lasting social change, this chapter has also stressed the importance of collective action to promote gender equality. This is an important route through which changes at the micro-level can be institutionalised at the social level. While these collective actions do not necessarily take place in the formal political arena, they are political in that they seek to challenge patriarchal power in their societies. They may not achieve their chosen goals, but what is transformative about them is that they challenge 'given' models of gender relations and open up the possibility of looking for alternatives. They also demonstrate the fluidity of campaigns and movements around gender equality as they shift their focus from individual to social issues or from national to global campaigns. These forms of collective action will ultimately help to transform the target of expanding women's share of seats in parliament into a genuinely empowering form of social change.

> *[C]ollective action will ultimately help to transform the target of expanding women's share of seats in parliament into a genuinely empowering form of social change.*

8. Institutionalising Gender Equity Goals in the Policy Process

Introduction

This book has focused on gender equality, both as a Millennium Development Goal (MDG) in its own right, but also as a route to the more effective achievement of the other MDGs. Poverty reduction, in particular, occupies a central place in current development efforts and pro-poor growth has been identified as the key route through which it can be achieved. In this final chapter, various arguments put forward in the book are considered for their policy implications. One concern of the discussion has been with the relationship between gender equality and pro-poor growth. This chapter considers the extent to which the evidence implies a trade-off between the two or a synergy. Next, since current efforts to make poverty concerns central to national development policies are often organised around Poverty Reduction Strategy Papers (PRSPs), it offers a gender audit of these papers. It also reviews the role of gender-responsive budget (GRB) analysis. Finally, it looks at the role that the institutionalisation of gender competencies in the policy process and an active constituency for gender equity interests could play in ensuring that gender equality as a goal in itself and as a route to the achievement of pro-poor growth remain at the forefront of efforts to achieve the MDGs.

Gender Equality and Economic Growth: Synergy or Trade-off?

Two contrasting conclusions have been drawn about the relationship between gender equality and economic growth:

(a) It is one of synergy – the promotion of gender equality leads to economic growth and this in turn will have a positive effect on gender equality (as suggested by Dollar and Gatti).

[W]omen are much more likely than men to use their income to address the basic needs of family members, particularly children.

(b) There is a trade-off – higher levels of gender equality lead to lower levels of growth (as suggested by Seguino).

It is important to remember that the positive synergy between gender equality in secondary educational attainment and per capita income reported by Dollar and Gatti did not kick in until a certain overall level of education had been reached. Below that level, the relationship was not significant. The authors suggested that this was because places where secondary education was not widespread also tended to be poor, agrarian economies where economic returns to education were likely to be restricted to a small formal sector.

While this explanation is plausible in relation to secondary education, the evidence discussed in this book suggests that other forms of gender inequality might have a more direct bearing on economic growth in these cases. It has highlighted the barriers faced by women, particularly those from poor households, in achieving decent returns to their labour. These include:

* gender inequalities in basic human capabilities (e.g. nutrition, health and skills), giving rise to gender inequalities in the productivity of labour;

* gender inequalities in access to non-labour resources (e.g. land, equipment, finance and infrastructural support), leading to gender inequalities in capacity to generate a surplus;

* gender inequalities in control over the disposition of own labour, giving rise to various forms of allocational inefficiencies; and

* gender inequalities in returns to different forms of human capital and capabilities, reflecting gender discrimination in access to market opportunities.

This suggests that one reason why Dollar and Gatti did not find evidence of a positive relationship between gender equality and economic growth in poor agrarian economies relates to their choice of variable in measuring gender equality. Measures relevant to economic growth are likely to vary by levels of development, the structure of the economy and the kinds of livelihood strategies available to the general population. They are also likely to vary between poor and less poor groups. In relation to human capital and capabilities, for example:

* investments in improving basic health and nutritional standards are critical to those who rely mainly on their physical labour power to earn their livelihoods, mainly the poor in poor agrarian economies;

* investments in primary education and basic skills are important for diversification into better-paid opportunities as economies become structurally differentiated; and

* investments in secondary and higher education becomes increasingly important to take advantage of new opportunities, requiring more formal qualifications, that emerge as economies shift to knowledge-based production.

Measures of gender equality appropriate to the context of poor countries might have yielded evidence of a synergy. How can this support for the 'synergy' hypothesis be reconciled with Seguino's conclusion that there is a trade-off between the two? One important reason is that Seguino's measure of equality is wages, which measures market returns to the labour effort, whereas the synergy relationship relates to resources likely to directly improve labour productivity. Gender disparities in wages will only reflect differences in productivity in perfectly competitive markets. In the highly segmented labour markets that operate in the real world, gender disparities in wages may be a better measure of disparities in bargaining power than in productivity. The greater the gender disparity in wages, the more likely it is that women have historically been excluded from mainstream employment opportunities. When countries shifted from import-substituting industrialisation to the export of labour-intensive goods, their competitive advantage shifted from a protected and better-paid male workforce to an unprotected and less well paid female one. Consequently, it is precisely those countries that practised the greatest exclusion of female labour in an earlier period that have grown most rapidly with the shift to export competition. In relation to wages, then, there *does* appear to be a trade-off between gender equality and economic growth.

When countries shifted from import-substituting industrialisation to the export of labour-intensive goods, their competitive advantage shifted from a protected and better-paid male workforce to an unprotected and less well paid female one.

A number of countries at the higher end of the per capita income scale enjoy high rates of both economic growth and human development ('positive synergy') and others at the lower end of the income scale report low rates of both factors ('negative synergy').

Gender equality and pro-poor growth: synergy or trade-off?

This conclusion, however, has to be qualified in a number of ways. If the focus is pro-poor growth rather than economic growth *per se*, the trade-off is less stark. This can be illustrated by looking at variations in the relationship between economic growth and human development achievements in different countries. In general, there is a synergy between them. Economic growth permits investment in human capabilities while investment in human capabilities in turn feeds into economic growth. There is thus a 'standard' relationship between the two. A number of countries at the higher end of the per capita income scale enjoy high rates of both economic growth and human development ('positive synergy') and others at the lower end of the income scale report low rates of both factors ('negative synergy').

However, there are also countries that deviate from the 'standard' relationship:

(a) Some deviate in a positive way, achieving far higher rates of human development than predicted by their per capita income levels. These used state policy early on in their development process to invest in the basic human capabilities of their population rather than waiting to achieve 'take-off' into economic growth.

(b) Others deviate in a negative way, with human development achievements that fall significantly short of the expected levels. These countries prioritised economic growth in the early phase of their development. Some (e.g. Brazil) did little to ensure that this growth subsequently improved the living standards of the poor. Others used the fruits of growth to expand human capabilities (a 'growth-mediated' approach. They were then able to reap the benefits of the 'virtuous' cycle between the two at a later stage of their development.

Many of the countries that report higher rates of economic growth as well as higher gender disparities in wages in Seguino's study are in East Asia. The Republic of Korea, Singapore and Taiwan all adopted a 'growth-mediated' approach to development. The state intervened actively to shape the growth trajectory. It suspended free trade union activity and repressed workers' rights, but its involvement in income redistribution and welfare programmes was small by international standards (although it did invest in basic education). It also drew on cultural norms about female docility and secondary worker status to reinforce patriarchal controls over female labour and ensure a compliant work force. While there has been a rise in overall real wages, the female to male wage ratio in both manufacturing and services in the Republic of Korea remains among the lowest of the countries covered by UN data (around 45 per cent in 1997).

The story on gender equality from countries that initially prioritised human development is somewhat different. Costa Rica, for example, had lower gender disparities in wages than the Republic of Korea (around 70%) as well as lower levels of growth. However, the apparent trade-off between equality and growth in the former has to be viewed in the context of its human development achievements. There was a state-mediated expansion of human capabilities, including social protection and public health care, and a number of supportive measures were instituted for women in their capacity as mothers as well as workers. Thus while it may have grown more slowly than the Republic of Korea, Costa Rica's growth rates imposed lower costs on its poorer and more disadvantaged sections.

The trade-off between gender equality and economic growth thus looks less stark if it is recast in terms of gender equality and pro-poor growth. It is even less stark when looked at in the long-run. The 'support-mediated' expansion of human capabilities in the early phase of development appears to be more likely to lead directly to a virtuous cycle in the long run than strategies that prioritise economic growth. Investment in female education appears to play a critical role here. A study using data from a sample of 35–76 developing countries (depending on availability of data) over three periods of time (1960s, 1970s and 1980–1993), found that about a third of the countries that had prioritised human development in earlier decades were able to move over time onto the virtuous cycle between human development and economic growth. However, *the overwhelming majority of countries that had prioritised economic growth reverted to 'vicious cycle' category over time.* Very few countries managed to go directly from vicious to

The trade-off between gender equality and economic growth looks less stark if it is recast in terms of gender equality and pro-poor growth. It is even less stark when looked at in the long-run.

[W]hile women face more opportunities for work, their working conditions have not improved to an equivalent extent.

virtuous, but some succeeded in moving to a focus on human development, from which it was possible to move into the virtuous category. The analysis concluded that it was not possible to move directly into the virtuous cycle via an emphasis on economic growth.

The effects of economic growth on gender equality

Along with the positive effect of gender equality on economic growth, Dollar and Gatti also suggest the converse: that economic growth has positive effects on gender equality. Again, this only happens above a certain level of per capita income and is more marked for some regions and religious groups than others. For countries below this level, the effect of economic growth appears less clear-cut. Once again, the absence of a positive relationship between economic growth and gender equality at lower levels of national income might reflect the measures of gender equality selected in the analysis. For example, cross-country analysis suggests that economic growth through participation in global trade may be gradually closing the gender gap in wages, particularly in the traded sector of national economies, a measure not included in the Dollar and Gatti study.

However, there are also a number of reasons why the effects of economic growth on gender equality may be weak below a level of national income. First of all, countries attempting to grow in the present era face a far more competitive global economy than countries that grew in an earlier period. Global competition has weakened the bargaining power of workers *vis-à-vis* employers. The international mobility of capital means that businesses can threaten to relocate if workers resist exploitative working conditions. While genuine trade unionism, as opposed to state-controlled trade unions, was associated with a closing of the gender gap in wages in an earlier era, today's trade unions are increasingly helpless to confront globally mobile capital with demands for better working conditions. Moreover, in many parts of the world, they have not proved particularly responsive to the needs of women workers. Thus, while women face more opportunities for work, their working conditions have not improved to an equivalent extent.

A second reason why economic growth has not succeeded in eradicating gender inequality to the expected extent across the world relates to differences in regional patriarchy. The evidence cited in earlier chapters suggests that improvements in women's access to paid work – one result of economic growth – has increased their bargaining power in the household, helping to reduce gender disparities in food, health care and education. Maternal mortality has declined in much of the world and women's life expectancies relative to those of men have improved. However, in regions of extreme patriarchy, economic growth has failed to address some forms of discrimination and seems to have made others worse. An example is the highly imbalanced sex ratios in the fast-growing economies of East Asia. At the same time, however, the gender gap in education has been closing in these countries. It is thus possible for countries to show progress in certain aspects of gender equality while failing to tackle discrimination in the most basic areas of human rights: the right to survival, nutrition and health care.

[I]n regions of extreme patriarchy, economic growth has failed to address some forms of discrimination and seems to have made others worse. An example is the highly imbalanced sex ratios in the fast-growing economies of East Asia.

Box 8.1 Women's Key Role in Achieving Developmental Goals in Bangladesh

In Bangladesh, women have been at the forefront of three major 'revolutions' of the past three decades. In a country where population growth rates had been identified as the country's 'number one development problem', women spearheaded one of the most rapid declines in fertility rates the world has ever seen. Women have also led the 'micro-credit' revolution, proving to the world that the poor are indeed 'bankable'. And finally women make up the overwhelming majority of workers in the country's newly emergent export-garment industry, earning the bulk of its foreign exchange and contributing to recent declines in national poverty.

Achieving gender equality, in other words, is as much as a question of social values, political commitment and public action as it is of the availability of resources. While economic growth may lead to improved legislation on gender equality, it

Women's interests and agency ... are one of the most powerful means available to policy-makers to achieve a variety of developmental goals.

is not likely to change patterns of inequality in a society without dedicated public action to counter deep-seated prejudice. For macroeconomic strategies to reduce poverty and address gender inequality, they must be based on an understanding of the various synergies and trade-offs as well as the deep-rooted prejudices that operate in different contexts rather than on 'one size fits all' formulae. Women's interests and agency, if analysed correctly, are one of the most powerful means available to policy-makers to achieve a variety of developmental goals (*see box 8.1*).

Poverty Reduction Strategy Papers: A Gender Audit

There is now an explicit commitment to both poverty reduction and gender equality by various national and international development actors – and much greater understanding of the links between the two. This suggests that the development community is well placed to 'mainstream' gender and poverty concerns in all aspects of policy. Poverty Reduction Strategy Papers (PRSPs), which have rapidly become an integral component of aid co-operation in a wide range of countries, provide an opportunity to explore the extent to which this commitment has become part of the policy process.

The content and process of PRSPs

PRSPs consist of a number of core components:

* an analysis of the poverty situation in the country;

* a strategy for poverty reduction, based on this analysis;

* the commitment of budgetary resources to implement the strategy;

* a monitoring framework to assess the achievement of strategic goals; and

* consultations at every stage with primary and secondary stakeholders to ensure broad-based national ownership of the strategies.

Each of these is critical to ensuring that the strategy is relevant to the poverty situation in the country and that efforts to address it will be effective. The analysis sets the boundaries within which priorities are identified and policy formulated. This gives rise to the strategies (the identification of key sectors for action and the nature of the actions to be taken), the resources to be made available and a system to monitor progress. If the gender dimensions of the poverty situation are not picked up in the analysis, they will either be absent from its translation into policy or else brought in as an afterthought. On the other hand, they may be part of the analysis but not followed through in the subsequent stages.

However, apart from the 'content' aspect of the PRSPs, there is also a 'process' aspect. This holds out considerable promise that these pitfalls will be avoided. Both governments and donors have committed themselves to building and strengthening participatory approaches to poverty assessments and to wide-ranging stakeholder consultations. These should enable researchers, practitioners and activists with knowledge of the relevant empirical linkages to ensure that these are incorporated and acted on. The consultative process also provides a valuable opportunity for different interest groups, including those representing marginalised constituencies, to learn about the nuts and bolts of policy-making in their countries. This will strengthen citizenship as active practice rather than as formal status.

The picture emerging out of the first round of PRSPs is not very encouraging in relation to gender ... If gender issues are not brought up at the diagnostic stage, it is very unlikely that they will appear in the 'action' or 'monitoring' stages.

Gender issues in the PRSPs

The picture emerging out of the first round of PRSPs is not very encouraging in relation to gender. A review by the World Bank's Gender Division of 15 Interim PRSPs (I-PRSPs) and three PRSPs completed by early 2001 found that less than half discussed gender issues in any detail in their diagnosis of poverty. Even fewer integrated gender analysis into their strategy, resource allocation and monitoring and evaluation sections. Gender issues were, predictably, better integrated into the 'health, nutrition and population' sectors (the reproductive sector) and to some extent in education (a quasi-social sector). Elsewhere, if mentioned at all, it was "often a passing reference or a vague intention". If gender issues are not brought up at the diagnostic stage, it is very unlikely that they will appear in the 'action' or 'monitoring' stages.

Limited integration of gender issues: the PRSP from Burkina Faso

The PRSP from Burkina Faso exemplifies some of these problems. In terms of poverty, the analysis here suggests that low levels of productivity in farm and off-farm activities, together with fragmented and imperfect markets for goods and services, are critical causes of rural poverty. In terms of gender, the analysis refers to:

* disparities in school attendance between girls and boys;

* women's high rates of fertility and maternal mortality;

* high levels of HIV sero-prevalence among certain sections of the population (including truckers, military personnel, prostitutes and single women, especially very young single women); and

* a decline in the proportion of women delivering in a health facility.

A special section entitled 'Women and Poverty' suggests that unequal educational opportunities have held back women's employment in the modern sector. It also draws attention to their poor health status and the limited availability of health care, lower literacy and limited access to credit and participation in national political life and decision-making. However, there is no indication of how these inequalities fit into the overall poverty analysis.

This unevenness is reproduced in the strategy section. There is a broad statement that strong growth in the rural development sector would help reduce poverty and increase the income of small farmers and rural women, but no discussion on whether rural women would benefit automatically from economic growth or would need specific measures to ensure that benefits occurred. Explicit references to women and girls are confined to sections on education and health, particularly in the context of AIDS. The strategy here includes actions targeted at specific groups, and the fact that there are specific budget line items for these activities suggest they may be implemented.

Much of the language of the paper is gender-neutral, using terms such as small farmers, traders, poorer segments, service users, vulnerable groups and rural producers. However, very little thought seems to have been given to whether these categories include women as well as men and, if so, whether the policies and measures in question might need to take account of possible gender differences in constraints and opportunities. For example, there is no attention to how the design of transport, infrastructure and water provision might be relevant to the relationship between gender and growth. There is no clear indication of what the 'socio-cultural' constraints that are said to limit women's livelihood options consist of or how they can be addressed. And while the promotion of export-oriented industry is identified as a route to future growth, little thought appears to have been given to skills training for the women who are likely to be a major source of its labour. In addition, while AIDS is clearly a key development problem in the country, addressing this through a focus on prostitution without tackling the underlying poverty that leads women into this work is likely to have limited results. Finally, the absence of gender concerns in strategies to promote good governance suggests either that the steps outlined in the paper are considered sufficient to involve women along with men in the democratisation of the society or, the more plausible explanation, that this is not considered a priority. Given these omissions, the repeated assertions about the relevance of gender to the achievement of economic growth or poverty reduction take on the status of a meaningless mantra.

[In the PRSP from Burkina Faso] there is no attention to how the design of transport, infrastructure and water provision might be relevant to the relationship between gender and growth.

Making the links between gender and poverty: PRSPs from Vietnam and the Gambia

One example of papers that have tried to tailor their analysis and strategies to local links between gender and poverty, rather than grafting on token statements, is the Vietnam PRSP. Poverty is seen to be largely rural in the country and higher in some regions than others. Among its causes, the report singles out high dependency ratios, lack of employment opportunities, female-headship, lack of education and capital, vulnerability to seasonal difficulties, land-poverty, inability to diversify out of a single crop, remoteness and lack of market access. The challenge for the government is seen to be the creation of employment opportunities, access to basic social services and greater security of livelihoods.

Sorting fish in Vietnam
INTERNATIONAL LABOUR ORGANIZATION

The analysis of the links between gender, poverty and pro-poor growth is thus largely confined to the recognition that poor and hungry households have high dependency ratios and are either headed by women or are reliant on their earnings to make ends meet. However, it does at least recognise the relevance of gender issues to both production and reproduction in the formulation of its strategy. The poor, especially those in rural areas, 'with priority given to women', are mentioned in relation to the goal of improving access to credit. This – refreshingly – is not equated with micro-credit. Strategies to improve training, extension services and skills development in relation to business, agriculture, forestry and fisheries also stress "the poor, especially women". Women and children are singled out in the context of strategies creating favourable conditions for the poor to access education, health and social services. The policy matrix outlined in the appendix includes the promotion of gender equity and the enhancement of women at all levels of leadership as part of the policies and measures planned to ensure equitable participation in economic growth.

The Gambia I-PRSP is another example that attempts to consider women's productive and reproductive responsibilities in tandem. It notes that the gender division of labour can act as a constraint on women's access to public services. It identifies the primary activities of rural women, the overwhelming majority of whom are subsistence farmers, and points out that they have less access to the forms of mechanisation that have improved men's agricultural productivity. It notes that women in general work longer hours than men fulfilling traditional household tasks as well as farming. The lack of basic services in rural areas, such as a reliable water supply, dependable health centres, transport and stores, are seen to add considerably to women's workloads. Proposals that comes out of this analysis are the promotion of labour-saving devices to help women in their farming, post-harvesting and domestic duties, and activities to create employment and income generation for women.

If little attention is paid to women's role in the productive economy in the PRSPs, there is even less to gender inequalities in voice, power and influence.

Gender inequalities in voice, power and influence in the PRSPs

If little attention is paid to women's role in the productive economy in the PRSPs, there is even less to gender inequalities in voice, power and influence. Issues such as domestic violence, political education, legal literacy and promotion of women's participation in local government to ensure to its responsiveness to their needs are apparently not considered relevant to poverty reduction strategies by most countries.

There are a number of exceptions. For example, the Nicaragua I-PRSP is one of the few to address gender-based violence directly. It notes the likelihood that the highest incidence is among poor urban women and among the least educated. Although the most common risks that poor women face are prostitution and sexual and physical abuse, the poorest communities usually lack the formal structures to protect them. The actions proposed include activities to prevent and penalise family violence and assist victims. In addition, a national action plan will be developed on the topic of domestic violence. This is expected to lead to draft legislation.

The Rwanda I-PRSP is one of the few to include legal issues related to gender. Specifically, it discusses the recent revision

The Tanzania PRSP provides the most thorough discussion of inclusive consultations ... villagers were grouped according to religion and gender, with women accounting for 22 per cent of participants.

of the matrimonial code, which now offers couples a choice of property regimes, including ownership of assets in common. In addition, it proposes a new labour code and land legislation that would remove restrictions on women's ability to work and own property.

The Tanzania PRSP provides the most thorough discussion of inclusive consultations. To ensure active participation, villagers were grouped according to religion and gender, with women accounting for 22 per cent of participants. The PRSP states that one-sixth of the focus groups identified gender discrimination as an obstacle to poverty reduction, especially in regard to customary ownership of property, wage employment and decision-making at the national and household levels. It also noted concerns about male alcoholism raised by female focus groups.

These are scattered example, however, rather than part of a systematic consideration of gender issues in the analysis of poverty or in strategies for poverty reduction. As the Bank review notes, most documents simply contain pro forma references and vague intentions (e.g. to increase girls' access to education). While actual actions taken have not yet been assessed, the review comments that the low level of attention to gender in the diagnosis suggests that the proposed actions are unlikely to address poverty reduction optimally or most efficiently. Furthermore, the fact that gender issues are least visible in the monitoring sections of the papers suggests that progress towards gender equity goals is considered irrelevant to the achievement of poverty reduction and will not be tracked over time in monitoring efforts.

Some lessons from the PRSP experience

A review of the PRSP papers produced so far thus makes for depressing reading but also provides some important insights.

PRSPs are heavily influence by World Bank/IMF approaches

While much of the discussion in the preceding section draws from a 'gender audit' of the PRSPs produced by the Gender Division of the World Bank, the biases and omissions described faithfully reproduce those of the Bank's own poverty assessment in the 1990s (*see Chapter 4*). In fact, the treatment of gender in the PRSPs is entirely consistent with the practices – as opposed to the rhetoric – of the World Bank and other multilateral development banks (MDBs). Evaluations of MDB investments show that, aside from those in girls' education, reproductive health and micro-finance, they rarely pay any attention to gender disparities.

The overlap in the analysis contained in PRSP and World Bank poverty assessments is not confined to gender, nor is it coincidence. While the PRSPs have been presented as independently produced and 'nationally-owned', questions have been raised as to the extent to which this is indeed the case. There is concern that countries are reluctant to consider approaches other than those advocated by the Bank and the International Monetary Fund (IMF) because they know the limits to the kinds of policies that the international financial institutions are prepared to accept. As a result, there is heavy reliance on external technical advice to assist governments in preparing the appropriate analysis. This tends to displace local experts and weaken capacity. It also means that PRSPs from very different countries use similar vocabulary, form and content and come to similar conclusions.

External factors constrain national policy efforts

In addition, the range of options available in the PRSPs is influenced by factors that cannot easily be addressed by national policy efforts, but that limit the capacity of poor countries to grow out of poverty.

The most important of these relate to the global rules of trade. The current trade regime remains one of the most powerful factors curtailing the capacity of poor countries to take advantage of the promise of globalisation. Despite rich countries' rhetoric about commitment to free trade, global markets are regulated by a confusing plethora of bilateral and multilateral trading agreements, tariff and non-tariff barriers, global labour standards and corporation-specific codes of conduct. The upshot is that when developing countries export to rich country markets, they face tariff barriers four times higher than those encountered by rich countries. These barriers cost them $100bn a year, twice as much as they receive in international aid.

When rich countries lock poor people out of their markets,

[T]here is heavy reliance on external technical advice to assist governments in preparing the appropriate analysis. This tends to displace local experts and weaken capacity. It also means that PRSPs from very different countries use similar vocabulary, form and content and come to similar conclusions.

The current trade regime remains one of the most powerful factors curtailing the capacity of poor countries to grow out of poverty.

they close the door to one of the most important escape routes from poverty. The last of the MDGs dealing with global development partnerships commits the international community to providing duty- and quota-free access to the exports of the least developed countries. While steps have been taken in the right direction by a number of Commonwealth countries (Australia and Canada) and by the European Union, much more could be done to promote market access for the exports of the world's poorer countries.

Orthodox thinking constrains national policy efforts

A further factor constraining the capacity of policy-makers to develop effective poverty reduction strategies is the powerful biases that exist in orthodox economic thinking, including the 'deflationary' bias, the 'marketisation' or 'commodification' bias and the 'male breadwinner' bias.

1. *The 'deflationary bias'*, which characterises orthodox economic thinking, has entrenched itself in the world view of the World Bank and IMF. 'Sound' economic policies are associated with price stability and avoidance of high inflation, elimination of financial deficits, privatisation and the creation of a climate favourable to foreign investment. Any deviation from this constitutes 'profligacy' on the part of governments. A concern with ' sound' economic policy constitutes one of the leading chapters in the handbook developed by the Bank to guide developing countries in preparing PRSPs and is reproduced in the overwhelming majority of them. The dominant policy discourse presents this as the 'common-sense' of economics, but the soundness of macroeconomic policy has to be judged from the point of view of social justice, not simply of economic growth. A concern for price stability and avoidance of high inflation does not rule out the expansion of public provision of health care, education and social security. Similarly, a concern for deficit reduction does not justify user fees for public services, irrespective of the effects of such fees on the well-being and freedom of the entire population, and especially the poor. There may well be a trade-off between the reduction of budget deficits and achievement of longer term or pro-poor, gender-equitable growth.

2. *The 'marketisation' bias* reflects the widespread failure of policy-makers to give value to any form of activity that does not command a price in the market place. There is clearly a gender subtext to this since it renders invisible the unpaid work, both productive and reproductive, that is primarily the responsibility of women – particularly women from poor households in the world's poor countries. The marketisation of public services places many of them out of the reach of such households, intensifying workloads for women who have to combine increased responsibility for social reproduction with extensive hours of work in productive activity.

3. *The 'male breadwinner' bias*, which has been looked at in some detail in earlier chapters, is seen when policy-makers design measures, including those to promote and protect livelihoods, on the assumption that it is the male household head whose earnings provide for the cash needs of a set of dependent family members (women, children, the sick, disabled and elderly). This has led to the exclusion of women from a range of economic entitlements, including those intended to provide a safety net in times of crisis, despite the fact that they play a key role in household livelihoods and coping strategies.

The case has to be made to growth-minded policy-makers that not all forms of public expenditure that promote human capital and human capabilities can be justified in terms of short-term economic gains.

These biases, taken together, lead to policies that seek to promote economic growth through market forces and individual efforts without any recognition of inequalities of access to market opportunities. Such policies are unlikely to promote the pro-poor, gender-equitable forms of growth that the MDGs demand from the international community. The case has to be made to growth-minded policy-makers that not all forms of public expenditure that promote human capital and human capabilities can be justified in terms of short-term economic gains. Some may feed into economic growth in the longer run, but others may be necessary on other equally valid grounds such as poverty reduction and social justice.

New opportunities for gender advocacy
Since such claims go against the grain of received wisdom in orthodox circles, it is clear that – along with compiling the evidence to back them up – collective action needs to be taken by women's advocacy groups and their allies to mobilise around them. The PRSPs, with their emphasis on consultation,

[T]he critical role that an active constituency can play in championing gender equity in the PRSP process is one key lesson from the process so far.

participation and national ownership, would seem to offer a unique opportunity to do this. However, it is evident from accounts of actual processes in different countries that the rushed timetables attached to many have prevented full participation by civil society, even where this was intended.

Nevertheless, agreement on the principle of consultation is a critical step in the right direction. It opens up possibilities for participation by a wider range of stakeholders than in the past. PRSPs are available on the World Bank's website for public scrutiny and cross-country learning. Lessons from experience can be disseminated and utilised strategically to ensure an improved voice in the future. Indeed, the critical role that an active constituency can play in championing gender equity in the PRSP process is one key lesson from the process so far (*see box 8.2*).

Box 8.2 The Role Played by Active Mobilisation in Rwanda and Kenya

The I-PRSP in Rwanda contained scattered references to gender issues, typical add-on paragraphs and ad hoc references but demonstrated very little attempt to mainstream gender concerns. This was partly because the short time period in which it was produced allowed for only a single round of consultations with the Ministry of Gender, Women and Development. However, the close relationship between the Ministry and women's organisations in the country gave strength to women's voices in the decision to undertake a more gendered analysis in the PRSP itself. A workshop was conducted to bring in representatives from a broad range of governmental and non-governmental sectors, an inter-agency PRSP committee was set up to ensure oversee the work and a consultant with gender expertise was brought in to work with the Ministry in preparing the PRSP. Another example is the experience of the Collaborative Centre for Gender and Development in Kenya in the lead up to development of the budgetary framework that had been outlined in the PRSP. It kept a clear 'women's agenda' parallel to the so-called 'common agenda' to prevent it from getting lost or submerged. This paid off in increased budget allocations to women and gender issues in the final paper.

The chapter on gender in the World Bank's handbook on preparing PRSPs underlines the importance of preventing gender issues from being lumped together with a range of issues, leading to a loss of focus. It notes that, while there is a need for explicit attention to gender issues at all stages of the PRSP process, it is particularly crucial to ensure that it is integrated into poverty analysis. Otherwise the scope for mainstreaming gender in the resulting strategies will be limited. One way that this can be achieved is through the development of a national Poverty Reduction Strategy Gender Action Plan. This would ensure that key gender gaps, problems and shortfalls identified by the poverty analysis are reviewed, their causalities analysed and assessments carried out of various policies, programmes and projects that could address them. Some of the more pressing gender-specific constraints and shortfalls could then be integrated into the main body of the PRSP in a strategic way.

[I]t is particularly crucial to ensure that [gender] is integrated into poverty analysis. Otherwise the scope for mainstreaming gender in the resulting strategies will be limited.

> **Box 8.3 Using the PRSP to Improve on National Polices**
>
> Financial sector reform in Uganda has introduced a number of new statutes to rectify weaknesses in previous banking acts and to bring the legal framework for Ugandan banks up to international standards. While the Ugandan Chapter of the Council for the Economic Empowerment of Women in Africa considers such prudential controls to be necessary, it also suggests that they take no account of gender differences in access to credit. The new legislation has imposed difficulties on micro-financial institutions (MFIs), often the only source of credit for the majority of women, poor as well as not-so-poor, in the country. Capital adequacy standards have created barriers to entry by non-governmental organisations that may wish to grow into alternative formal credit institutions or banks. The risk weighting formula for bank assets penalises institutions with assets in the forms of advances and discourages bank investment in microfinance lendings. A PRSP could highlight these issues in ways that have an impact on the shape of financial legislation.

[W]omen's time constraints could be addressed in a variety of ways, including the (subsidised) distribution of labour-saving technology and improved access to credit.

It is also important to bear in mind that the PRSP is one component of larger national policies in which public action is located. If gender issues are totally subsumed within a poverty agenda, there is a danger that gender inequalities in the wider sense of the word will remain intact in the institutions of society. On the other hand, if there is participation and ownership of the PRSP process, it can be used to move gender beyond the given national framework of priority topics or sectors. Especially in a context of very limited gender policies, a PRSP with potential for greater participation may help to improve on national policies (*see box 8.2*).

Sectoral strategies for poverty reduction

There is further scope for participatory processes when priorities and strategies are being translated into sectoral policies and programmes. This is important to ensure that the analysis captures key opportunities and constraints within, and across, the different sectors. Insights into interlinkages at the sectoral (or 'meso') level can be provided by combining: (a) micro-level analysis of livelihood strategies, with its stress on the range of ways poor people meet their needs and secure their future; and (b) macro-level analysis of broad-based growth that recognises the importance of human, social, financial, natural and physical capital.

Poverty reduction strategies that considered gender-related synergies, both within and across sectors, would be more effective. For example, time constraints were identified earlier as an important limitation to the productivity of women's farming efforts in Africa. Poor productivity in farming and poor returns to off-farm enterprise reduce the incomes available to women and their ability to hire in labour and purchase other agricultural inputs. Instead, it is men who are most able to use their incomes from farming to diversify into off-farm enterprise, the profits from which can be ploughed back into improving farm productivity. Clearly men may choose to share their profits with female family members. Where they do not, however, women's time constraints could be addressed in variety of ways, including the (subsidised) distribution of labour-saving technology and improved access to credit.

Alternatively, women would benefit along with men from

various kinds of infrastructural support that reduced demands on their labour. One example would be improving the supply of clean water and sanitation. Recent estimates suggest that an African woman spends an hour a day on average (up to 100 minutes in rural areas) collecting water, and walks a distance of over one kilometre in rural areas to fetch it. Lack of clean potable water and safe sanitation increases the likelihood of disease and illness and hence imposes additional demands on her time. When women spend long hours caring for sick members of the family due to cut-backs in health services, this reduces the time they could put into farming – another connection between agriculture and health. The existence of synergies across sectors is illustrated by an evaluation of public works programmes in Bangladesh (*see box 8.4*).

Without explicit gender analysis ... the synergies and trade-offs between and within sectors that are relevant for reducing gender inequalities are unlikely to be appreciated.

> **Box 8.4 Gender-related Synergies at the Sectoral Level**
>
> A public works programmes in Bangladesh designed to increase all-weather use of feeder roads was found not only to provide employment for destitute women but also to facilitate other achievements that are relevant to the MDGs. Household incomes rose because of more roadside business, the improvement in the marketing of agricultural goods and the generation of waged employment in non-agricultural activities (because of the increased mobility of labourers). In addition, the evaluation also found increased access to schooling, to NGO programmes and to various government services, particularly by women and girls.

Without explicit gender analysis, however, the synergies and trade-offs between and within sectors that are relevant for reducing gender inequalities are unlikely to be appreciated. Gender-disaggregated data are clearly crucial to such an appreciation but needs to be guided by, and grounded in, gender-aware poverty analysis. This analysis needs to look beyond immediate causes and effects to the underlying structural inequalities that gave rise to them as well as to their longer term effects. The distinction between gender-specific, gender-intensified and gender-imposed shortfalls and constraints can provide a

[W]hile the poor and disadvantaged enjoy less access to health care services generally, women may be at a greater disadvantage because their well-being is culturally discounted within the family, because men make the key decisions about health consultations and expenditure or because women's mobility in the public domain is restricted.

useful set of guidelines for translating analysis into goals and action, separating those intended to address women or men directly and those intended to address the relationships between them. The health and education sectors provide examples of this.

Health

Unequal health outcomes may reflect the fact that health services are imbalanced. Certain health needs are likely to be gender-specific, and are often linked to reproduction in the case of women. Maternal mortality is one key example and has been included in the MDGs. Another is access to contraceptives, failure in which penalises women more than men. Others stem from the kinds of jobs that men or women do. For example, men develop certain types of ill-health due to their responsibility in some cultures as the main providers. For women, particular categories of health hazards have been documented for work on labour-intensive assembly lines, for example, or prostitution. In addition, certain health needs may be shared by women and men but take on a gender dimension as a result of greater inequalities in access and provision. Thus while the poor and disadvantaged enjoy less access to health care services generally, women may be at a greater disadvantage because their well-being is culturally discounted within the family, because men make the key decisions about health consultations and expenditure or because women's mobility in the public domain is restricted. Women may also suffer from imposed disadvantages in access if their constraints are not taken into account, if the behaviour of providers discriminates against them or if the gender of providers is a constraint.

Education

Gendered needs and interests in education also reflect inequalities in access and provision. For example, a study of sector-wide approaches to education policy in Uganda found that, despite a strong commitment to closing the gender gap in education at the level of national policy, practical measures were based on a very partial gender analysis. In particular, gender concerns were largely confined to equality of access rather than equality of outcomes. In terms of the latter, the educational plan noted the need to screen textbooks according to various quality and equity criteria, including gender-related ones. It had incorporated an information, education and communication component, intended to reach parents and communities directly. There was also recognition of the need to encourage girls to take non-traditional subjects and to train women teachers to improve access in the post-primary levels. However, there was no analysis of the underlying causes of gender inequalities in access to, and benefits from, educational provision. This would have looked at, for example:

* the implications for long school day for poorer children, particularly girls, with higher work loads;

* how outreach efforts could be used to promote greater awareness of gender within the community; and

* the extent to which issues of sexual harassment within schools, by teachers as well as male pupils, had been addressed by the teacher development management systems.

Moreover, achievements at the level of 'access' are unlikely to be sustained without greater attention to gender at higher levels of management and to building capacity within the sector.

In terms of both health and education, the evidence cited in this book suggests that women's empowerment may lead to the kinds of outcomes promoted by the MDGs. Poorer women who are empowered are more likely:

* to seek out contraception and maternal health services;

* to ensure the survival and health of their children and other family members;

* to promote the education of their children;

* to reduce gender discrimination against daughters in health and education and seek a better life for them than they may have had themselves; and

* to negotiate successfully for 'safe sexual practices' both within and outside marriage so as to reduce the risks of HIV-AIDS.

In terms of both health and education, the evidence cited in this book suggests that women's empowerment may lead to the kinds of outcomes promoted by the MDGs.

Looking at the budget of the PRSP shows whether gender commitments in analysis and strategy are backed by appropriate financial resources.

Gender-responsive Budget (GRB) Analysis

The critical importance of ensuring that gender issues are addressed in all parts of the PRSP and at all stages of the process was noted earlier. Clearly the resources made available to put the strategy into effect, and their implications for the poor (poor women in particular), will play an important role in both its effectiveness and gender sensitivity. Looking at the budget of the PRSP shows whether gender commitments in analysis and strategy are backed by appropriate financial resources. In fact, the gender-responsiveness of budgets has been coming under increasing scrutiny in a number of countries, independently of the PRSP process. Budget analysis can play a number of different roles, depending on how it is conducted:

● It can promote greater transparency of policy processes, helping to demystify what has been seen as a secretive and closed aspect of official decision-making.

● It is a way to match policy intent with resource allocation and see whether policy commitments to gender issues by the government are rhetoric or reality.

● It can strengthen accountability by making it more likely that officials and citizens will try to find out what is actually done with public money.

Gender-responsive budget (GRB) analysis has been conducted at a variety of different levels: national, local, sectoral and even programmatic. It has sometimes been led by government, has sometimes been carried out in collaboration with it and sometimes been independent of it. While different approaches have been associated with different results, the importance of the political climate for such analysis to have any influence on the design of policy is very clear from different country experiences. In Australia, South Africa and the UK, for example, GRB analysis gained a place in the government through the coming to power of progressive political parties, suggesting that it was seen as associated with particular political platforms rather than as an essential aspect of development strategy.

For a number of Commonwealth countries, the fact that the Commonwealth Secretariat was mandated by its member states to promote gender equality throughout the association has made it politically possible for Ministers Responsible for Women's Affairs to work with the Secretariat to experiment with GRB at the government level. For the Secretariat itself, the task of 'en-gendering' government budgets provided a strategic entry point for making macroeconomic policies more gender aware. Since budget analysis involves all government ministries and departments, it provides a practical opportunity for officials across sectors to integrate gender into their areas of work. And finally, given the central role of the finance and planning in budget management and general policy decision-making, GRB initiatives could introduce gender issues into the heart of government operations and financial management.

The experience to date has yielded a variety of approaches and instruments for carrying out GRBs. The gender implications of decisions about overall levels of deficit or surplus can be explored by, for example, examining their likely feedbacks in terms of unpaid time or estimating the economic costs of various actions that might affect women and men differently (such as wage restraint in the public sector). Computable general equilibrium (CGE) models may be useful for making such estimates and can also be used to anticipate likely future scenarios and hence permit forward planning (see box 2.6). An alternative approach might be through soliciting the views of women and men in relation to proposed policy measures (see box 8.5). Beneficiary assessment exercises in developing countries have mainly been carried out in relation to specific programmes, but there is no reason why they cannot be 'up-streamed' to the assessment of policy measures.

The focus of most GRBs has been on the expenditure side, partly because direct impacts in terms of meeting needs and promoting opportunities were easier to assess. A three-way break-down of the government expenditures of different departments has been suggested:

1. expenditures specifically targeted at women (e.g. income generating projects for women);

2. expenditures intended to promote gender equality in the public sector (e.g. training of women managers or provision of childcare); and

For the Commonwealth Secretariat itself, the task of 'en-gendering' government budgets provided a strategic entry point for making macroeconomic policies more gender aware. Since budget analysis involves all government ministries and departments, it provides a practical opportunity for officials across sectors to integrate gender into their areas of work.

3. the gender impacts of mainstream budget expenditure (e.g. how will the educational budget promote gender equality within society, aside from special schemes for women or girls? Who uses health care facilities? Who receives agricultural support?)

> **Box 8.5 Inviting Public Comment on Proposed Policy Measures**
>
> A study carried out by the Women's International League for Peace and Freedom (WILPF) invited women to comment on their government's budget allocations. WILPF initiated a Women's Budget Project in the US in 1996 at a time when there was a great deal of public discussion about the national debt 'crisis' and the need to cut government expenditure in order to reduce the public deficit. Noting that very few women benefited from military spending, given their severe under-representation in the armed forces and military contractor jobs, the project estimated the costs of various defence-related programmes and compared them with the costs of a number of welfare-related programmes. Women were asked to choose how they would like to see public money spent. The project estimated how the savings from possible cuts in military expenditure could be used to finance services that would benefit women.

An important instrument for answering some of these questions is public expenditure incidence analysis or benefit incidence analysis. This calculates the unit cost (per person) of providing a particular service and the pattern of utilisation by women and men, girls and boys (*see box 8.6*). Other tools recommended for budget analysis include gender-aware policy appraisal of various policies and programmes (that could highlight the extent to which they would help to increase or reduce gender inequalities) and the production of GRB statements, summarising the main findings and drawing out the implications of different patterns of revenue and expenditure.

> **Box 8.6** The Value of Benefit Incidence Analysis in Assessing Government Budgets
>
> A study in Ghana using benefit incidence analysis noted that government spending on education and health was partly offset by cost recovery that lowered the subsidy element in these services. In terms of utilisation, it found that girls received 45 per cent of subsidies at the primary level of education although their gross enrolment ratio was 67 per cent. This gender bias was more marked among poor households. Because the poor were less likely to go for treatment when they were ill, richer households were found to use both public and private health services to a greater extent. However, women were found to gain more of the public subsidy than men in health, partly because of the existence of gender-specific services targeted to their needs.

Experiences with GRBs in different countries have made important contributions to the understanding of gender-differentiated impacts of various budgetary decisions.

National experiences of GRBs

Experiences with GRBs in different countries have made important contributions to the understanding of gender-differentiated impacts of various budgetary decisions. For example, 'the woman's budget' in Australia was first introduced in the Federal budget in 1984, making it one of the earliest. The initiative played an educational role in sensitising government departments to the implications of their policies for women and helped to reduce 'gender-blindness'. The initiative was able to persuade the Department of Industry, Technology and Commerce, one of the 'economic' departments, of the disproportionate impact of macroeconomic reforms on women. Far more had been spent by government to cushion the effects of adjustment on male-dominated industries (e.g. motor vehicles) than on those that employed high percentages of women (e.g. clothing, textiles and footwear). A special retraining allowance was announced for married women clothing workers who would have otherwise have been ineligible on the grounds of their spouses' income.

After Australia, South Africa was one of the first countries to set up a Women's Budget Initiative (WBI). It was started as

After Australia, South Africa was one of the first countries to set up a Women's Budget Initiative (WBI). It was started as a collaborative venture between women parliamentarians committed to gender equity issues and two policy-oriented research NGOs.

a collaborative venture between women parliamentarians committed to gender equity issues and two policy-oriented research NGOs. It focused primarily on issues that affected the most disadvantaged: those who, in addition to being female, were black, rural and poor. For example, research in the country had shown that the considerable public expenditure associated with land reform was unlikely to directly benefit women, primarily because of legal restrictions on women's right to own land and to conclude contracts. The Department of Land Affairs has now begun to integrate gender analysis into its monitoring and evaluation and provide training to its staff. The WBI has also taken up an issue that affects women across class, race and other divides: violence against women. Three aspects of government financing of initiatives to combat violence against women have been investigated and the research turned over to the parliamentary committee on the Improvement of the Quality of Life and Status of Women. This committee focuses on violence against women, poverty and HIV/AIDS as the most serious problems facing women in the country.

Gender budget analysis in Sri Lanka by the Department of National Planning found that downsizing the public sector did not have the expected disproportionate impact on women. Rather, the closure of semi-government institutions had a greater effect on male employment while women benefited from the expansion of professional occupations at both national and provincial levels. It also found that, although access and utilisation of social services were relatively equal, women were under-represented in economic services provided by the government in agriculture and industry. As the report pointed out, it was important that such services reached women if women's improved education was to have an effect on productivity and incomes.

Policy options highlighted by GRB analysis

GRB analysis has highlighted a number of different policy options. These include:

* reprioritisation rather than new initiatives, e.g. away from the tertiary level of education towards adult basic education

and training and pre-school initiatives (in South Africa these received only 1 per cent of the education budget but would have directly benefited poor women and children);

* ensuring better distribution of given expenditure, e.g. giving public works programmes features likely to be conducive to the participation of poor women as well as poor men;

* 'trimming the fat', i.e. cutting salary extravagances and perks enjoyed by senior civil servants, the majority of whom are usually men, and using the resources released to improve terms and conditions of work among those responsible for service delivery (whose levels of motivation are critical to performance); and

* focusing on the desirability of the size of military expenditures.

Gender is not viewed as a 'core competence' of policy-making bodies, either in the international development community or at national and local levels.

Mainstreaming Gender in Policy-making Institutions

Despite a much greater level of overall awareness on gender issues, and despite the solid body of research and analysis that now exists, policy and programmes continue to show very limited and compartmentalised concerns with gender equity. This was evident in the analysis of the PRSPs conducted so far. Among the various factors put forward to explain this, two in particular tend to feature most frequently:

1. Gender is not viewed as a 'core competence' of policy-making bodies, either in the international development community or at national and local levels. There is thus a lack of gender expertise in these bodies. Where such expertise exists, it tends to be found in either: (a) the sectors traditionally associated with gender and women's issues; or (b) the programmes that directly address women's concerns or gender equality efforts.

2. Limited consultation takes place with primary stakeholders. While having poor people participate directly in such consultations may take longer to achieve, the consultations have also failed to include, or have included in a very token way, organisations that work with the poor as well as those that work for gender equity goals. The ones consulted also

Even in some of the higher income countries, such as Australia, Canada and New Zealand – where women's machineries have enjoyed cross-party support and hence survived conservative governments – the shift away from state responsibility for social justice to market-based solutions in the 1990s has limited the achievements of women's machineries to ensuring 'least worst outcomes'.

tended to be those who already had a relationship with governments and donors.

The need to institutionalise gender equity in the organisations responsible for making policy at national and international level has long been recognised. Progress on this has been uneven to date in both sets of organisations and in richer as well as poorer countries. Among the various barriers that have been identified are:

* a lack of the elusive political will;

* the under-funding of the units and ministries given responsibility for mainstreaming efforts;

* the marginalisation and frequently shifting location of units within bureaucratic structures;

* the institutionalisation of patriarchal interests in the norms, rules and practices of organisations; and

* a deep-seated resistance by different divisions to taking on cross-cutting issues, such as gender, that would encroach on their budgetary allocations.

Even in some of the higher income countries, such as Australia, Canada and New Zealand – where women's machineries have enjoyed cross-party support and hence survived conservative governments – the shift away from state responsibility for social justice to market-based solutions in the 1990s has limited the achievements of women's machineries to ensuring 'least worst outcomes'.

The Gender Management System (GMS)

Some of the lessons from these experiences are addressed in the Gender Management System (GMS) developed by the Commonwealth Secretariat. The GMS is a set of concepts and methodologies intended to build a comprehensive network of structures, mechanisms and processes for ensuring that a gender perspective is brought to bear on development policies, plans, programmes and projects. It suggests that central to the success of 'gender mainstreaming' within government is the creation and implementation of a Gender Action Plan that:

* provides a comprehensive analysis of gender inequalities in a given society together with an analysis of their causes and effects;

* proposes a set of strategic interventions needed to address them, with attention to prioritising on the basis of likely synergies, complementarities and trade-offs;

* costs the implications of these interventions; and

* institutes a monitoring framework to track progress and promote accountability.

In addition, the success of gender mainstreaming also requires reviews of national development plans and the PRSPs as well as of the regular policy, planning and implementation cycles of different ministries.

However, in order for this to occur mechanisms need to be developed with the capacity, commitment and political backing to champion change across different institutions. While the GMS is mainly concerned with the development of national machineries for achieving this outcome, some of the lessons can be extended to other kinds of organisations as well. As the Secretariat points out, the GMS is intended to bring about fundamental and lasting change in society as a whole, but it starts with organisational change in government since it is the state that is responsible in principle for representing the interests of all its citizens. The institutional arrangements to bring this about are key:

* a lead agency that takes responsibility for spearheading change, most likely the national women's machinery;

* a management team that brings together representatives of different departments as well as members of civil society to co-ordinate the implementation strategy;

* a network of gender focal points, responsible for promoting gender concerns within their departments and liaising with other departments;

* an inter-ministerial steering committee to oversee the links between different ministries;

* a Parliamentary Gender Caucus made up of parliament-arians who are committed to gender equality goals and seek to lobby for them in the formal political arena; and

* civil society interactions with this machinery to ensure a two-way flow of information and influence between government and the wider society.

Organisational change requires a number of levers to ensure that it occurs. Three are identified in the context of the GMS:

1. *The awareness lever:* addressing the formal and informal norms, rules, attitudes and behaviour that institutionalise inequalities within an organisation. Gender training has been the conventional route to achieve greater awareness on this front. However, unless such training becomes a core aspect of organisational development, rather than made up of one-off, discretionary events, it will fall short of its objec-tives. The awareness lever should be utilised to identify blockages to gender equity on a collective basis in the organisation.

2. *The communications lever:* the timely flow of information and analysis across the system in order that all policies and programmes are designed from a gender perspective. This requires investment in building up gender expertise across an organisation so that it becomes an aspect of different sec-tors rather than the property of a stand-alone group of gen-der specialists who are required to address all the govern-ment's concerns.

3. *The incentives lever:* there has been a move towards performance-based appraisal within government as a part of overall public sector reform. Staff are increasingly assessed on their success in achieving the goals of government and of their departments. Gender mainstreaming requires that all performance appraisal systems incorporate incentives and penalties in relation to the achievement of gender equity goals.

Some of the wider factors that would increase the likelihood of this machinery achieving its goal include a legislative structure that promotes women's rights as human rights, a political environment that encourages an increase of women in decision-making positions and the support of international agencies such as the Secretariat itself. A supportive relationship with civil society is critical since it is pressure from civil society in democratic societies that gives legitimacy to gender equity goals within government as well as the political clout needed to follow them through.

Mobilising Around Gender Equity Goals: Building Active Citizenship

As well as a lack of gender expertise in policy-making bodies, the second factor put forward to explain why policy and programmes continue to demonstrate very limited concerns with gender equity was a lack of consultation with primary stakeholders. This would be most effectively addressed through building up active and organised constituencies at the grassroots level to exercise pressure for gender equality goals and to hold governments, donors and international agencies accountable for their action or inaction.

The previous chapter offered several examples of bottom-up mobilisation around gender equity goals that, despite different aims and strategies, all challenged the grain of class and patriarchy in a particular situation. While an earlier generation of women's organisations focused on consciousness-raising and self-reliance, and generally had an adversarial stance towards the state, there is increasing evidence in recent decades of organisational efforts that seek to engage with current policy processes in order to influence them. Part of this engagement has required developing civil society expertise in areas of general policy, as well as in analysis of the gender dimensions of policy.

For example, not all gender budget initiatives are bureaucratically-led. The WBI in South Africa, for instance, can be largely seen as made up of civil society representatives (women parliamentarians and NGOs). It provides an example of how increasing the numbers of women in parliament can have a direct influence on pro-poor policies. Along with lobbying the state, the WBI has pursued a policy of active dissemination, producing materials written in a simple style and in a number

[T]here is increasing evidence in recent decades of organisational efforts that seek to engage with current policy processes in order to influence them.

of different local languages. Another example of engagement by grassroots women with the policy structures of their country comes from Uganda (*see box 8.7*).

Box 8.7 Consultations with Grassroots Women in Uganda

In 1990, the national women's machinery in Uganda launched an unprecedented process of consultation with women all over the country to solicit their views on the country's constitution for submission to the constitutional commission. This was possibly the first time in history that the female citizens of a country were so closely involved in framing their constitution. Using simplified training manuals, it consulted with women from all walks of life to develop a series of recommendations that faithfully reported on women's views, registering agreements as well as conflicting opinions. The heightened politicisation of women on constitutional issues led to 30 women contesting seats in the constituent assembly elections in 1994. It has also had a lasting effect on the Ministry Responsible for Women's Affairs, giving it greater orientation to the concerns of its rural constituency than is the case in many countries.

In Bangladesh, a number of NGOs working with women's or pro-poverty issues (Nari Pokhho, Nijera Kori, Proshika) have set out to monitor government service delivery at the local level. While this has alerted local providers to the need for accountability, their ability to respond has been thwarted by the lack of decentralisation to local government (so that decisions for tackling structural problems remain the responsibility of the centre). However, making this analysis clear gives strength to wider demands for democratic decentralisation.

In Mexico, the Grupo de Educación Popular con Mujeres, which works to promote the economic capabilities of women in poor communities, adopted a participatory learning process involving continuous reflection and feedback. Over time, community women involved with the group have moved beyond the early concern with skills training and income-

A family harvesting
potatoes in Bolivia
INTERNATIONAL LABOUR ORGANIZATION

generation to activities aimed at policy change. Having successfully lobbied for an office for women's issues in one of the state governments, they have been working with the state legislature to develop a two-year plan to address their gender concerns.

Elsewhere, UNIFEM has played an important role in bringing together civil society actors to promote GRB analysis. In the Andean region, the methodologies that emerged out of these efforts are building a public culture of understanding around national and municipal development plans and budgets. In Bolivia, for example, while civil society groups are expected to participate in budget formation as part of decentralisation reform, women's groups had not been involved in budget implementation and monitoring. The initiative there has focused on spending plans associated with its PRSP. It seeks to empower women and women's organisations to influence budget decisions and do advocacy work with different levels of government by building their technical budget expertise.

The one overarching lesson for policy-makers that emerges out of the analysis in this book is the central role that women's agency can play in achieving many of the MDGs.

Conclusion

The road to gender equality is not a linear one. For each victory reported by gender advocates and grassroots activists across the world there are many setbacks. While patriarchal oppressions are still very much in evidence, however, looking back on three decades of research, advocacy and activism in the field of development suggests that there has been important progress on a number of fronts. It is important to acknowledge these if the movement for equality is to be remain vigorous and hopeful. For example:

* there has been a closing of gender gaps in survival chances, in health and in education;

* women now play a far more visible role in the economies of their countries, and if these jobs do not have the levels of protection that male workers enjoyed in a previous era, they have still helped to challenge the myth of the male breadwinner and lessened women's economic dependency; and

* women are more aware of their rights, not only among the educated middle circles that enjoy some degree of access to the corridors of power, but also increasingly in poorer communities.

The one overarching lesson for policy-makers that emerges out of the analysis in this book is the central role that women's agency can play in achieving many of the MDGs. Enhancing women's access to various resources and ensuring that greater social value is given to their contributions lies within the domain of policy-makers and its pay-offs are likely to be enormous.

More progress needs to be made on bringing men in as allies, but giving up privileges of any kind has always been difficult – particularly if this is bound up with a core sense of identity and does not appear to hold out any immediate gains. Nevertheless, here too many more men are speaking out, moved by humanitarian concerns, by efficiency considerations or simply out of solidarity with an oppressed group.

It has become evident that while authoritarian regimes may be effective in addressing welfare aspects of gender equality, democratic space is far more conducive to the self-organisation of oppressed groups and the pursuit of rights than charity. There is evidence of growing concern by gender equity activists to engage more directly with the policy processes. The new stress on participation that is being attached to current policy efforts can thus be seized as an opportunity, however cynical the motivations might be that have given rise to them. Yet engagement at the national level can bring only limited gains in a world that is characterised by increasing global inter-dependence and where actions taken in one country have ramifications for others. The major challenges for gender advocates and activists in the twenty-first century will be to form alliances with others who seek a more equitable inter-national order and to make sure that gender equity interests remain at the forefront of the struggle.

The major challenges for gender advocates and activists in the twenty-first century will be to form alliances with others who seek a more equitable inter-national order and to make sure that gender equity interests remain at the forefront of the struggle.

Select Bibliography

Adams, J. 'Female Wage Labor in Rural Zimbabwe'. *World Development* 19(2/3) (1991): 163–177.

Agnihotri, S. *Sex Ratio Patterns in the Indian Population: A Fresh Exploration.* New Delhi: Sage Publications, 2000.

Amis, P. 'Indian Urban Poverty: Labour markets, gender and shocks'. *Journal of International Development* 6(5) (1994): 635–42.

Baden, S. 'Gender Issues in Agricultural Liberalization'. *Bridge briefings on development and gender, Report 41*. Brighton: Institute of Development Studies, 1998.

——— and Wach, H. 'Gender, HIV/AIDS Transmission and Impacts: A review of issues and evidence'. *Bridge briefings on development and gender, Report 47*. Brighton: Institute of Development Studies, 1998.

Bardhan, K. 'Women's Work, Welfare and Status: Forces of tradition and change in India'. *Economic and Political Weekly XX* (50 and 51) (1985).

Benería, L. and Roldán, M. *The Crossroads of Class and Gender: Industrial Homework Subcontracting, and Household Dynamics in Mexico City.* Chicago: University of Chicago Press, 1987.

——— and Feldman, S. (eds) *Unequal Burden: Economic Crisis, Persistent Poverty, and Women's Work.* Oxford: Westview Press, 1992.

Bennett, L. 'Women, Poverty and Productivity in India'. World Bank EDI seminar paper 43. Washington, DC: World Bank, 1992.

Booth, D., Holland, J., Lanjouw, P. and Herbert, A. 'Participation and Combined Methods in African Poverty Assessment: Renewing the agenda'. Report commissioned by DfID for the Working Group on Poverty and Social Policy, Special Programme of Assistance for Africa, 1998.

Boserup, E. *Woman's Role in Economic Development.* New York: St. Martin's Press, 1970.

Bruce, J. and Dwyer, D. *A Home Divided: Women and Income in the Third World.* Stanford, CA: Stanford University Press, 1988.

Budlender, D. 'The Political Economy of Women's Budgets in the South'. *World Development* 28 (7) (2000): 1365–1378.

——— , Elson, D., Hewitt, G. and Mukhopadhyay, T. *Gender Budgets Make Cents.* London: Commonwealth Secretariat, 2002.

——— and Hewitt, G. *Gender Budgets Make More Cents.* London: Commonwealth Secretariat, 2002.

Buvinic, M. and Gupta, G. R. 'Female-Headed Households and Female-Maintained Families: Are they worth targeting to reduce poverty in developing countries?' *Economic Development and Cultural Change* 49(2) (1997): 259–93.

Chambers, R. 'Participatory Rural Appraisal (PRA): Analysis of experience'. *World Development* 22(9) (1994): 1253–68.

Chant, S. *Women-Headed Households: Diversity and Dynamics in the Developing World.* New York: St Martin's Press, 1997.

—— and Craske, N. *Gender in Latin America.* London: Latin American Bureau, 2002.

Commonwealth Secretariat. *Engendering Adjustment for the 1990s: Report of a Commonwealth Expert Group on Women and Structural Adjustment.* London: Commonwealth Secretariat, 1989.

—— *Gender Management System Handbook.* London: Commonwealth Secretariat, 1999.

Davin, D. 'The Impact of Export-Oriented Manufacturing on Chinese Women Workers'. UNRISD Project on Globalization, Export Oriented Employment for Women and Social Policy. Geneva: UNRISD, 2001.

Davison, J. and Strickland, R. 'Promoting Women's Capabilities and Human Rights'. Washington, DC: International Centre for Research on Women and Centre for Development and Population Activities, 2000.

DAWN. *Markers on the Way: The DAWN Debates on Alternative Development.* DAWN's Platform for the UN Fourth World Conference on Women, Beijing, 1995.

Demery, L. and Walton, M. 'Are the Poverty and Social Goals for the 21st Century Attainable?' *IDS Bulletin* 30(2) (1999).

Development and Change. Special issue on gender and poverty, 30(3) (1999).

Dijkstra, G. and Hanmer, L.C. 'Measuring Socio-Economic Gender Inequality: Toward an alternative to the UNDP Gender-Related Development Index'. *Feminist Economist* 6(2) (2000): 41–76.

Dolan, C. S. with Sorby, K. *Gender and Employment in High Value Agriculture Industries.* Washington, DC: World Bank, forthcoming.

Dollar, D. and Gatti, R. 'Gender Inequity, Income, and Growth: Are good times good for women?' Background paper for *Engendering Development.* Washington, DC: World Bank, 1999. Available online at www.worldbank.org/gender/prr/dg.pdf

Doyle, L. *What Makes Women Sick? Gender and the Political Economy of Health.* London: Macmillan, 1995.

Dreze, J. and Sen, A. *Hunger and Public Action*. Oxford: Clarendon Press, 1989.

—— *India, Economic Development and Social Opportunity*. Oxford: Oxford University Press, 1995.

Dwyer, D. and Bruce, J, (eds) *A Home Divided: Women and Income in the Third World*. Stanford: Stanford University Press, 1988.

Dyson, T. and More, M. 'On Kinship Structure, Female Autonomy and Demographic Behaviour in India'. *Population and Development* (March 1983): 35–60.

Elson, D. *Male Bias in the Development Process*. Manchester: Manchester University Press, 1991.

Eviota, E. *The Political Economy of Gender: Women and the Sexual Division of Labour in the Philippines*. London: Zed Books, 1992.

Feminist Economics. Special issue on gender and globalisation, 6(3) (2000).

Figueroa, M. 'Making Sense of the Male Experience: The case of academic underachievement in the English-speaking Caribbean'. *IDS Bulletin* 31(2) (2000): 68–74.

Fontana, M. 'Modelling the Effects of Trade on Women: A closer look at Bangladesh'. *IDS Working Paper* 139. Brighton: Institute of Development Studies, 2001.

—— and Wood, A. 'Modelling the Effects of Trade on Women, at Work and at Home'. *World Development* 28 (7) (2000): 1173–1190.

Gadwin, C. (ed.) *Structural Adjustment and African Women Farmers*. Florida: University of Florida Press, 1991.

Garbus, L. 'Gender, Poverty and Reproductive Health in Sub-Saharan Africa: Consolidating the linkages to enhance poverty reduction strategies'. *Background Paper for the 1998 SPA Report on Poverty in Africa*. Washington, DC: World Bank, 1998.

Ghosh, J. 'Globalization, Export-Oriented Employment for Women and Social Policy: A case study of India'. Draft prepared for the UNRISD project on Globalization, Export-Oriented Employment for Women and Social Policy. Geneva: UNRISD, 2001.

Goetz, A-M. 'The Politics of Integrating Gender to State Development Processes'. *UNRISD Occasional Paper No 2*. Geneva: UNRISD, 1995.

—— 'Women's Political Effectiveness: A conceptual framework'. In *No Short-Cuts to Power: African Women in Politics and Policy Making*. London: Zed Books, forthcoming.

Greenhalgh, S. 'Sexual Stratification: The other side of growth with equity in East Asia'. *Population and Development Review* 11(2) (1985).

Haddad, L., Hoddinott, J. and Alderman, H. *Intrahousehold Resource Allocation in Developing Countries*. Baltimore: Johns Hopkins University, 1997.

Hanmer, I., Pyatt, H. and White, H. *Poverty in Sub-Saharan Africa: What Can we Learn about the World Bank's Poverty Assessments?* The Hague: Institute of Social Studies Advisory Services, 1997.

Hashemi, S. M., Schuler, S. R. and Riley, A.P. 'Rural Credit Programs and Women's Empowerment in Bangladesh'. *World Development* 24(4) (1996): 635–653.

Hill, K. and Upchurch, D. M. 'Gender Differences in Child Health: Evidence from the Demographic and Health Surveys'. *Population and Development Review* 5(6) (1995): 127–51.

Hirshman, C. and Guest, P. ' The Emerging Demographic Transitions of South-East Asia'. *Population and Development Review* 16(1) (1990): 121–152.

Howes, C. and Singh, A. 'Long-Term Trends in the World Economy: The gender dimension'. *World Development* 23(11) (1995): 1895–1912.

IDS Bulletin. Tactics and Trade-offs: Revisiting the Links Between Gender and Poverty. Special issue, 28(3) (1997).

Jacka, T. 'The Public/Private Dichotomy and the Gender Division of Labour'. In A. Watson (ed.) *Economic Reform and Social Change in China*. London: Routledge, 1992.

Jejeebhoy, S. *Women's Education, Autonomy, and Reproductive Behaviour: Experience from Developing Countries*. Oxford: Clarendon Press, 1995.

Joekes, S. and Weston, A. *Women and the New Trade Agenda*. New York: UNIFEM, 1994.

Kabeer, N. *Reversed Realities: Gender Hierarchies in Development Thought*. London and New York: Verso Press; New Delhi: Kali Press for Women, 1994.

—— 'Gender, Demographic Transition and the Economics of Family Size: Population policy for a human-centred development'. *UNRISD Occasional Paper 7*. Geneva: UNRISD, 1996.

—— and Subramanian, R. (eds) *Institutions, Relations and Outcomes: A Framework and Case Studies for Gender-aware Planning*. New Delhi: Raj Press, 1999.

—— *The Power to Choose: Bangladeshi Women and Labour Market Decisions in London and Dhaka*. London: Verso, 2000.

—— 'Resources, Agency, Achievements: Reflections on the measurement of women's empowerment'. *SIDA Studies 3*. Stockholm: Novum Grasfiska, 2001.

Kapadia, K. *Siva and Her Sisters: Gender, Caste, and Class in Rural South India*. New Delhi: Oxford University Press, 1996.

Kurth, A. (ed.) *Until the Cure: Caring for Women with HIV*. London: Yale University Press, 1993.

Leach, F., Machakanja, P. and Mandoga, J. 'Preliminary Investigation of the Abuse of Girls in Zimbabwean Junior Secondary Schools'. *Education Research Paper 39*. London: Department for International Development (DfID), 2000.

Lloyd, C. and Blanc, A. ' Children's Schooling in Sub-Saharan Africa: The role of fathers, mothers, and others'. *Population Council Research Division Working Paper* 78 (1995).

Lukes, S. *Power: A Radical View*. New York: Palgrave, 1974.

Marcoux, A. 'The Feminization of Poverty: Claims, facts, and data needs'. *Population and Development Review* 24(1) (1998): 131–9.

Pitt, M. and Khandker, S. R. 'The Impact of Group-based Credit Programs on Poor Households in Bangladesh: Does the gender of participants matter?' *Journal of Political Economy* 106 (1998): 958–96.

Massiah, J. *Women as Heads of Households in the Caribbean: Family Structure and Feminine Status*. Colchester: UNESCO, 1983.

Mehra, R. and Gammage, S. 'Trends, Countertrends, and Gaps in Women's Employment'. *World Development* 27(3) (1999): 533–550.

Mensch, B. S. and Lloyd, C. B. 'Gender Differences in the Schooling Experiences of Adolescents in Low-Income Countries: The case of Kenya'. *Policy Research Division Working Paper 95*. New York: Population Council, 1997.

Miller, B. D. 'Social Class, Gender and Intrahousehold Food Allocations to Children in South Asia'. *Social Science and Medicine* 44(11) (1997): 1685–1695.

—— *The Endangered Sex: Neglect of Female Children in Rural North India*. Ithaca, NY: Cornell University Press, 1981.

Momsen, J. and Townsend, J. (eds) *Geography of Gender in the Third World*. London: State University of New York Press, 1987.

Murthi, M., Guio, A. and Dreze, J. 'Mortality, Fertility and Gender Bias in India: A district level analysis'. *Population and Development Review* 21(4) (1995): 745–782.

Naples, N. and Desai, M. (eds) *Women's Activism and Globalization: Linking Local Struggles to Transnational Politics*. New York: Routledge, 2002.

Narayan, D., Chambers, R., Shah, M. and Petesch, P. *Voices of the Poor: Crying Out for Change*. Oxford: Oxford University Press, 2000.

Norton, A. and Elson, D. *What's Behind the Budget? Politics, Rights and Accountability in the Budget Process*. London: Overseas Development Institute, 2002.

Oxaal, Z. and Baden, S. 'Challenges to Women's Reproductive Health: Maternal mortality'. *Bridge Report 38*. Brighton: Institute of Development Studies, 1996.

Palmer, I. 'Gender and Population in the Adjustment of African Economies: Planning for change'. *Women, Work and Development* 19. Geneva: ILO, 1991.

Palriwala, R. *Changing Kinship, Family and Gender Relations in South Asia: Processes, Trends and Issues*. Leiden: Women and Autonomy Centre (Vena), Leiden University, 1994.

Presser, H. and Sen, G. (eds) *Women's Empowerment and Demographic Processes: Moving Beyond Cairo*. New York: Oxford University Press, 2000.

Quisumbing, A. 'Male-Female Differences in Agricultural Productivity: Methodological issues and empirical evidence'. *World Development* 24(10) (1996): 1579–95.

——, Lawrence, R. and Peña, H. 'Are Women Over-represented Among the Poor? An analysis of poverty in ten developing countries'. *IFPRI Discussion Paper 115* (2001).

Rajuladevi, A.K. 'How Poor are Women in Rural India?' *Asia-Pacific Journal of Rural Development* 2(1) (1992): 1–34.

Razavi, S. (ed.) *Shifting Burdens: Gender and Agrarian Change under Neoliberalism*. Bloomfield: Kumarian Press, 2002.

—— and Miller, C. 'Gender Mainstreaming: A study of efforts by the UNDP, the World Bank and the ILO to institutionalise gender issues'. *UNRISD Occasional Paper 4*. Geneva: UNRISD, 1995.

Rao, V. 'Wife Beating in Rural South India: A qualitative and econometric review'. *Social Science and Medicine* 44(8) (1997): 1169–1180.

Rowbotham, S. and Mitter, S. (eds) *Dignity and Daily Bread: New Forms of Economic Organizing among Poor Women in the Third World and the First*. London: Routledge, 1994.

Sathar, Z. and Kazi, S. *Women's Autonomy, Livelihood and Fertility: A Study of Rural Punjab*. Islamabad: Pakistan Institute of Development Economics, 1997.

Sawer, M. 'Femocrats and Ecorats: Women's policy machineries in Australia, Canada and New Zealand'. *UNRISD Occasional Paper 6*. Geneva: UNRISD, 1996.

Seguino, S. 'Gender Inequality and Economic Growth: A cross-country analysis'. *World Development* 28(7) (2000): 1211–1230.

Sen, A. *Collective Choice and Social Welfare*. San Francisco: Holden Day, 1970.

—— *Poverty and Famines: An Essay on Entitlement and Deprivation*. Oxford: Clarendon Press, 1981.

—— 'Gender and Co-operative Conflicts'. In I. Tinker (ed.) *Persistent Inequalities*. Oxford: Oxford University Press, 1990.

—— 'More than 100 million women are missing'. *The New York Review*, Dec. 20, 1990.

—— and Ghosh, J. 'Trends in Rural Employment and the Poverty-Employment Linkage'. *ILO–ARTEP Working Paper*. New Delhi: ILO, 1983.

Sen, G. *Gender Mainstreaming in Finance: A Reference Manual for Governments and Other Stakeholders*. London: Commonwealth Secretariat, 1999.

Sen, P. 'Enhancing Women's Choices in Responding to Domestic Violence in Calcutta: A comparison of employment and education'. *European Journal of Development Research* 11(2) (1999).

Sender, J. 'Women's Struggle to Escape Rural Poverty in South Africa'. *Journal of Agrarian Change* 2(1) (2002).

—— and Smith, S. *Poverty, Class and Gender in Rural Africa*. London: Routledge, 1990.

Sethuraman, S. V. 'Gender, Informality and Poverty: A global review: Gender bias in female informal employment and incomes in developing countries'. World Bank, Poverty Reduction and Economic Management, Washington, DC and WIEGO, Geneva, 1998.

Shaffer, P. 'Gender, Poverty and Deprivation: Evidence from the Republic of Guinea'. *World Development* 26(12) (1998): 2119–135.

Standing, G. 'Global Feminization Through Flexible Labor'. World Employment Programme, Geneva: ILO, 1989.

—— 'Global Feminization Through Flexible Labor: A theme revisited'. *World Development* 27(3) (1999): 583–602.

Subrahmanian, R. 'Gender and Education: A review of issues for social policy'. *Social Policy and Development Programme Paper 9*. Geneva: UNRISD, 2002.

Svedberg, P. 'Undernutrition in Sub-Saharan Africa: A critical assessment of the evidence'. *Wider Working Papers 15*. Helsinki: Wider Publications, 1987.

The Probe Team. *Public Report on Basic Education in India*. Oxford: Oxford University Press, 1998.

Tinker, I. (ed.) *Persistent Inequalities*. New York: Oxford University Press, 1990.

Todaro, R. and Rodrigues, R. (eds) *El Género en la Economía*. Santiago, Chile: Centro de Estudios de la Mujer and ISIS International, 2001.

Townsend J. H. and Momsen, J. *Geography of Gender in the Third World*. London: Hutchinson, 1987.

Tzannatos, Z. 'Women and Labor Market Changes in the Global Economy: Growth helps, inequalities hurt and public policy matters'. *World Development* 27(3) (1999): 551–569.

United Nations. *World Survey on the Role of Women in Development: Globalization, Gender and Work*. New York: UN Division for the Advancement of Women, 1999.

—— *United Nations Millennium Declaration Document A/RES/55/2*. New York: UN, 2000.

—— *Roadmap Towards the Implementation of the United Nations Millennium Declaration: Report of the Secretary-General*. Document A/56/326. New York: UN, 2001.

United Nations Development Programme (UNDP). *Human Development Report 1990*. New York: Oxford University Press, 1990.

—— *Human Development Report 1995*. New York: Oxford University Press, 1995.

—— *Human Development Report 2000*. New York: Oxford University Press, 2000.

White, R. O. and Whyte, P. *Rural Asian Women: Status and Environment*. Singapore: Institute of South Asian Studies, 1978.

Whitehead, A. 'Wives and Mothers: Female farmers in Africa'. *Population and Labour Policies Programme Working Paper 170*, World Employment Programme Research, 1990.

—— and Lockwood, M. 'Gender in the World Bank's Poverty Assessments: Six case studies from sub-Saharan Africa'. *UNRISD Discussion Paper 99*. Geneva: UNRISD, 1999.

Whitehead, A. and Kabeer, N. 'Living with Uncertainty: Gender livelihoods and pro-poor growth in rural sub-Saharan Africa'. *IDS Working Paper 134*. Brighton: Institute of Development Studies, 2001.

Wolf, D. L. *Factory Daughters: Gender, Household Dynamics and Rural Industrialization in Java*. Berkeley, CA: University of California Press, 1992.

World Bank. *World Development Report: Attacking Poverty*. Oxford: Oxford University Press, 2000.

—— *Engendering Development: Through Gender Equality in Rights, Resources and Voice*. Washington, DC: World Bank, 2001.

World Development. Special Issue on gender and the macro-economy, 23(11) (1995).

—— Special Issue, 28(7) (2000): 1347–1364.

Glossary

Aggregation: The combining of two or more kinds of economic entities into a single category. Data on international trade necessarily aggregate goods and services into manageable groups. For macroeconomic purposes, all goods and services are usually aggregated into just one.

Allocative inefficiencies: Inefficiencies arising because resources have not been allocated to their most productive use.

Budget: The budget is the annual announcement of the government's fiscal policy changes. It announces the tax changes proposed for the following tax year, and also how the government plans to spend that revenue.

Commodification (or marketisation): The extent to which a market value has been given to previously non-commercial goods and services.

De facto **female-headed households** are those where male family members are absent, usually because they have migrated in search of work.

De jure **female-headed households** are those where women have become heads as a result of divorce, widowhood or abandonment or as wives in polygamous marriages.

Demographic transition refers to the change from high birth and death rates to low birth and death rates. In developed countries this transition began in the eighteenth century and continues today. Less developed countries began the transition later and are still in its earlier stages.

Endogenous growth: Growth derived or originating internally within a system (in economics, usually a state).

Exogamy: The custom of marrying outside the tribe, family, clan or other social unit.

Exogenous growth: Growth derived or originating externally to a system.

Gender refers to those rules, norms, customs and practices by which biologically associated differences between the male and female of the human species are translated into socially constructed differences between men and women, boys and girls which give them unequal value, opportunities and life chances.

Gender-blindness means ignoring the different socially determined roles, responsibilities and capabilities of men and women. Gender-blind policies are based on information derived from men's activities and/or assume those affected by the policy have the same (male) needs and interests.

Gender-disaggregated data: This focuses on issues of particular relevance to women and men, girls and boys, and their different roles and positions in society. Statistics on household distance from water or fuel, for example, have different implications for women and men since it is usually the former who spend time collecting these necessities when they are not readily available.

Gender mainstreaming: "Mainstreaming a gender perspective is the process of assessing the implications for women and men of any planned action, including legislation, policies or programmes, in any area and at all levels. It is a strategy for making women's as well as men's concerns and experiences an integral dimension in the design, implementation, monitoring and evaluation of policies and programmes in all political, economic and societal spheres so that women and men benefit equally and inequality is not perpetuated. The ultimate goal is to achieve gender equality." (Agreed conclusions of the UN Economic and Social Council 1997/2).

Gender-neutral: Gender-neutral policies are not specifically aimed at either men or women and are assumed to affect both sexes equally. However, they may actually be gender-blind (see above).

Gender-responsive budget (GRB): GRBs (also called 'gender-sensitive budgets', 'gender budgets', 'women's budgets' and 'women's budget statements') aim to assess the impact of government budgets, mainly at national level, on different groups of men and women. They include analysis of gender-targeted allocations (e.g. special programmes targeting women); they disaggregate by gender the impact of mainstream expenditures across all sectors and services; and they review equal opportunities policies and allocations within government services.

Gross domestic product (GDP) measures output generated through production by labour and property that is physically located within the confines of a country in a given time period (usually a year).

Gross national product (GNP): The market value of all final goods and services produced for consumption in society during a given time period (usually a year) by nationals no matter where they are located.

Macroeconomics: The study of the behaviour of the overall economy, including inflation, unemployment and industrial production. It focuses on the level of income or output of the economy, including the level of employment, aggregate investment, total consumption and the money supply.

Matrilineal: Descent is traced and property inherited through the female line.

Microeconomics: The study of the behaviour of small economic units, such as individual consumers, households or companies. It focuses on the determination of the prices that induce these agents to act, including wages for labour and return rates of investment funds. These concerns cover issues of demand and supply, welfare and distribution.

Non-governmental organisations (NGOS): An NGO is any non-profit, voluntary citizens' group that is organised on a local, national, regional or international level. NGOs perform a variety of services and humanitarian functions, bring citizens' concerns to governments, monitor policies and encourage political participation at the community level. Some are organised around specific issues, such as human rights, the environment or health.

Patrilineal: Descent is traced and property inherited through the male line.

Patrilocal: Of or relating to residence with a husband's kin group or clan.

Poverty Reduction Strategy Papers (PRSPs) describe a country's macroeconomic, structural and social policies and programmes to promote growth and reduce poverty, as well as associated external financing needs.

Reproductive sector: The reproductive sector is concerned with caring for the present and future labour force, and the human population as a whole, including providing food, clothing and shelter in the household. Work in this sector is generally unpaid and usually excluded from national accounts. Reproductive labour is mainly performed by women, and takes up an extremely high proportion of their time.

Structural adjustment programmes (SAPs): SAPs are intended to restore a sustainable balance of payments, reduce inflation and create the conditions for sustainable growth in per capita income. Typical measures are spending cuts in the public sector and tight monetary policy. At least 75 developing countries undertook SAPs in the 1980s, with loans from the World Bank and IMF. It has been argued that these policies have a disproportionate effect on women because they fail to take into account women's roles in the reproductive sector, the gender division of labour and inequalities in household allocations.

System of National Accounts (SNA): This is a set of macroeconomic accounts, balance sheets and tables based on internationally agreed concepts, definitions, classifications and accounting rules. The 1993 revision of the SNA recommended that all production of goods in households for their own consumption be included in the measurement of economic activity. Unpaid household work, such as caring for children and the elderly, is still excluded.

Usufruct: The rights to farm a piece of land and profit from the produce but not to ownership.